THE UNFINISHED REVOLUTION

THE UNFINISHED REVOLUTION

*An Essay on the Sources
of Influence of
Marxism and Communism*

ADAM B. ULAM
Harvard University

RANDOM HOUSE · *New York*

PREFACE

This book is not a genealogy of political ideas. My main interest has been to find out what makes Marxism alive and relevant in certain societies, while elsewhere socialism and communism remain the creeds of insignificant sects or intellectual coteries.

It would take me much too long to list all the people to whom I am indebted in connection with this book. But I should certainly mention with gratitude Mr. Charles D. Lieber of Random House, Miss Mary Towle, my secretary, and Mr. Gabriel Grasberg, my assistant during one phase of this work.

It is perhaps appropriate in view of one of the main themes of the book, that this study of socialism should have been assisted by Guggenheim, Rockefeller, and Carnegie, the names being those of the foundations which have been very generous. The Russian Research Center at Harvard has provided me with leisure not usually available to a college teacher. I am grateful to its personnel and to my colleagues on its staff and particularly to its first director, Mr. Clyde Kluckhohn.

Eliot House
Cambridge, April 1960

CONTENTS

THE UNFINISHED REVOLUTION

THE PROBLEM

What Marxism is and is not is a question that has occupied and divided scholars and politicians for a long time. The difficulty is obvious. Here is a doctrine of enormous intricacy and subtlety addressed not to the intellectuals but to the masses; a philosophy of liberation and freedom that in our day has given fruit in two of the most despotic and bureaucratized states history has seen. The earliest Marxists assumed that their doctrine would triumph in fully industrialized and modernized society: by contrast, history has shown Marxism victorious and influential mainly in societies groping their way toward industrialization and modernity, and not in the cradle of the doctrine, the industrialized West. Such is a small sample of the paradoxes of Marxism, which may well convince the average American or Englishman that life is difficult enough and sufficiently complicated by the visible results of the doctrine—Soviet Russia and China and their satellites—without the additional trouble of comprehending the intricate system of thought that is somehow behind it all. Furthermore, the doctrine is not only intricate but elusive. The mutual relationship of the elements of the triad Marxism-socialism-communism is far from simple. An academician may look condescendingly at the obtuseness of the people who do not understand how *Communist* Russia can proclaim itself to be a *socialist* state, yet no less an expert on the subject than

Molotov is censured by his Soviet colleagues, allegedly because of an incorrect definition of the relationship between the two terms. There is a suspicion among both statesmen and academicians in the West that "serious people," in this case the rulers of international Communism, cannot really be motivated by theories and analyses devised a century ago by two German thinkers. The ideology is relegated to the realm of propaganda; or, conversely, some of the leaders of Communism are dubbed fanatics, and every step in their policies is related to the blueprint of world conquest emerging from Marxism-Leninism.

The uncertainty about the nature of the challenge is accompanied in Western thought by uncertainty about the nature of policies designed to meet it. If the doctrine of Marx and Engels implants in its devotees an implacable resolve to destroy the capitalist world, then the premise of the ideological motivation of the Soviet system must lead the Western exponents of democracy to concentrate on concrete tasks of defense. If, on the other hand, the doctrine presents danger mainly from the propagandist point of view, isn't the right response to prevent its spread among the underprivileged parts of the globe through technical and economic assistance? To the newspaper reader, the challenge of Communism resolves itself into a blurred composite: a military review in the Red Square; a Communist agitator haranguing an Oriental crowd; Russia's laboratories, with their eager masses of engineers and mathematicians; and somehow behind it all two bearded German thinkers. The whole development of the Western, especially Anglo-American, world, during the past century has conditioned people's minds to envisage political and economic problems as being concrete, easily classifiable, easily "seizable." Here we are dealing with a complex of problems that seemingly elude our grasp. Both "reasonableness" and "firmness" fail to arrest the assertiveness of Soviet policies. Emancipation of the colonial peoples and economic help to the underdeveloped areas appear incapable in themselves of endowing the new states with democratic institutions or immunity to Communism. Problems of an international society undergoing an economic and ideological revolution seem to defy the social scientist's expertise, just as they defy the democratic citizen's common-sense analyses and the generosity—granted its qualifications and errors—that has characterized the policy of the leading democratic powers of the West.

It is at least instructive to take a closer look at the origins of the doctrine, which, whatever else it may be, deals with the phenomenon of the economic revolution that has transformed the world during the last century and a half. Knowledge of the origins and structure of Marxism may not help in the solution of an international crisis. But that knowledge is in itself a form of action (the notion Marxism inherited from ancient philosophy) is perhaps the least debatable Marxist tenet. The origins and the structure of the Marxist system explain much about the spread of Marxism and its offshoots like Communism, a spread that has often taken place in societies and circumstances quite different from those that Karl Marx and Friedrich Engels had assumed would welcome their system. If it appears presumptuous to add yet another to the long list of interpretations and explanations of Marxism, then it may be offered as a partial excuse that events since World War II have enabled us to see new dimensions and facets of the problem.

Karl Marx wrote in the midst of and about a revolution that was changing Western society and affecting all parts of the globe—with all its destructive effects on the old orders of Europe. We who have taken the industrial system for granted and assumed that we have seen all its political and social effects, we in the West, have all but lost the conception of the first spontaneous reactions to its arrival: the wonder at the power of technology and science, the bewilderment and resentment at the abrupt destruction of the old social and political institutions and beliefs, and the gropings for a system that would somehow explain it

all and put the whole world together again. We have tended
to consider reactions to industrialism not found in our own
society (or at least assumed not to be found there) as expressions
of primitivism, or of the exoticism of a given society, or of a
national or economic catastrophe. Even the Bolshevik revolution and its consequences have been usually taken (and this
is only to a degree less true of Western Marxists than of their
opponents) as something quite exceptional, a freak of history,
perhaps attributable to the peculiarities of the Russian national
character.

It is only since World War II that we have realized that we
are in the midst of a yet unfinished revolution. Its character is
more complex than commonplace Communist propaganda would
have it; and it also defies the usual Western editorializing, which
always sees in revolutionary stirrings the result of an inadequate
standard of living, or corruption and oppression by a particular
government. The conditions underlying the current revolution
are in many ways similar to those that disturbed and transformed
Western European society during the first half of the nineteenth
century. Under different conditions and in a different world
situation, we see parts of Asia, Africa, and Latin America entering
the initial or intermediate stages of the Industrial Revolution.
The birth pains of modern industrial society, which Marx often
mistook for the death throes of capitalism, are being enacted
before our eyes. We can see more clearly what Marxism was
about than could the generations for whom it was a movement
of protest against capitalism, an obsolete economic theory, or
a philosophical justification for an international Communist conspiracy. Also, in another dimension, within the context of a
highly industrialized society, both the insights and the limitations
of Marxism are more clearly perceptible now that a society
based on Marxist ideology is challenging the greatest nonsocialist
state for industrial and political supremacy.

In other words, we can begin to see Marxism not only as a set of theories and prophecies postulated by its author and his disciples, but as something that "exists in nature" as well. We need not agree with Marx's own appraisal of his theories: that he was discovering the laws of social development. Certainly his doctrine has been victorious under conditions quite unforeseen by him, and Marxism got hold of societies which the very "laws" of Marxism would have precluded from falling under its influence, while conditions and societies thought by him most appropriate for the realization of socialism have developed in a quite different direction. But a thinker may be supremely important and his thought of world significance not only because he formulates historical laws, but also because his thought reflects the essence of the mood of great historical periods. This has been the great significance of Marx. Philosopher, economist, a would-be politician and revolutionary, his ideas are still alive and important because they are attuned to the two greatest tendencies of the industrial age: the worship of science and mechanization and limitless faith in their power to transform mankind; and the very opposite—protest against the soullessness and destructiveness of the machine age. Every society reaching for industrialization and modernization has its "Marxist" period, when some of the ideas of Marx are relevant to its problems and are reflected in everyday sentiments of the masses of people, even though the name of Marx and his movement may be unknown to them. Hence the attraction for Marxism, and the quasi-Marxist character of social protest in many areas of the world—an attraction which would still exist, though perhaps in a different form, were Marxism not represented by one of the two greatest powers of the world. Hence also the stubborn character of the appeal of Marxism to the intellectual and scientist as well as the masses in a society undergoing industrialization. For Marxism comes to them not entirely as a new argument attempting to convince with facts and figures, but as something which co-ordinates and brings together their own ideas and sentiments.

Marxism, then, is not only the complex of theories bequeathed by Marx and Engels and developed, interpreted, and acted out in countless ways by countless theorists, parties, and movements. To use an analogy from physics: science has learned to produce in the laboratory elements found in nature. Imperfect as such comparisons must be, Marxism to a remarkable degree reproduces the social psychology of the period of transition from a pre-industrial to an industrial society. If this is correct, then it is not surprising that Marxian socialism found little response in late nineteenth-century England and a great deal in Russia at the turn of the century. The industrialized United States has experienced Marxism in the last generation only as an intellectual reaction to the Depression; but large parts of Latin America, drawn increasingly into modern economy and its concomitants, are experiencing social and political turbulence which, while not directed by Marxists and not necessarily inspired by socialism or communism, is Marxist in its mood if not in its postulates.

It is always dangerous as well as ungracious to condescend to great men's ideas because the passage of time has inevitably shown their incompleteness or partial errors. A college student is not a greater physicist than Newton because he knows the incompleteness or limitations of Newton's theories. The great body of literature that has grown up in the exposition of Marx's errors, the incompatibilities of his theories with historical facts, and his inconsistencies has served—only a little less than the incredible intellectual calisthenics of the defenders of the literal truth of every single postulate of his canon—to obscure the main meaning and importance of his doctrine. It is not proposed here to minimize the importance of critiques of the Marxist system or to consider them merely as emanations of their times.

But it is possible and sensible to look at Marxism not as an infallible canon or as a series of intellectual aberrations. Lenin, for all his dogmatism, used to quote fondly Goethe's saying about the grayness of the dogma and the greenness of the tree of life. In this case the grayness of the dogma often conceals the passion and movement of life. The surplus-labor theory may be "wrong" from the point of view of a non-Marxist economist, yet it implies the supreme value of human labor and individuality in the midst of societies where the worker views himself as an adjunct of the machine. The economic historian may patiently prove that under capitalism the fate of the worker has not grown worse, but this Marxist "error" still communicates to the worker in an *industrializing* society his loss of the stability and security he enjoyed in his previous status of peasant or craftsman.

This does not mean Marx was manufacturing social myths or dealing in symbolism. Again the context of his times enables us to understand how he came to believe with the intensity of a religious fanatic in many, to us, bizarre notions, just as the context of our own times shows how a simplified version of the same ideas can drive people into political action. In many respects, Marx culminates rather than transcends the ideas of his times and society. His economics are in the final flowering of the tradition of classical political economy. His philosophy and dialectic, those sources of exasperation to would-be Marxists in the pragmatic Anglo-Saxon countries, conclude the main Hegelian stream in German philosophy as well as subvert it. In Marx, socialism from sporadic sects and movements and from philosophers became an international movement and a definite body of thought. And even some of the postulates of liberalism, his main intellectual target, are, as we shall see, enshrined in his philosophy more rigorously and dogmatically than in the work of the most typical representatives of liberalism itself.

Marxism, then, as a *system of thought,* cannot be understood except through an understanding of the intellectual traditions that made up nineteenth-century thought. The source of the historical influence of Marxism can be understood only if we realize how *recurrent* the kind of social and intellectual situation of Western Europe in Marx's time has been in other parts of the world up to our own times.

It is not proposed here to establish a new form of determinism. The existence of Marxist situations in large parts of the world does not inevitably portend the victory of Communism there. It was a grouping of fortuitous events and forces that enabled Marxism to triumph in Russia. But it was *not* an accident that in 1917 Marxism in Lenin's version appealed to large segments of Russia's working class and intelligentsia. Similarly today: whether the Marxist situations all over the world become Communist preserves depends mostly on the relative strength and policies of the Western and the Soviet camps. But the outcome must be affected by the naturalness or inappropriateness of the setting for Communism in any given society. The study of the underdeveloped territories, and the attempt at their economic development by Western resources and skills, must take into realistic account the fact that at the crucial point of transition from a pre-industrial society to a modern, at least partly industrialized state, Marxism becomes in a sense the natural ideology of that society and the most alluring solution to its problems.

Another dimension of the contemporary problem of Marxism is equally important to practical politics. What of Marxism in the Soviet Union? If Marxism's alternative roles are the expression of protest against the pains and deprivations of industrialization and modernization and, simultaneously, the ideology under which this modernization and industrialization are accomplished, what are the prospects for Marxism in the largely industrialized Soviet state? Is the ideology still important to an analysis of the Soviet Union, or has it become a mere façade behind which practical people make practical decisions aimed at the maximization of their own power and that of the totalitarian state over which they rule?

To sum up: from a variety of vantage points a study of Marxism is a study not of disembodied ideas, but of crucial social and political ideas; not only of theories but also of human emotions which have shaped and continue to make the modern world.

THE ARGUMENT

MATERIALISM

It was over the grave of his friend and associate, in 1883, that Friedrich Engels said:

As Darwin discovered the law of evolution in organic nature, so Marx discovered the law of evolution in human history; the simple fact, previously hidden under ideological growths, that human beings must first of all eat, drink, shelter and clothe themselves, before they can turn their attention to politics, science, art and religion.

Engels was carried away by profound emotion; elsewhere in his address he was to ascribe to Marx important discoveries in mathematics. The father of modern socialism, though modesty was not a prominent trait of his, would not have claimed the discovery of historical materialism. The latter as an explanation of human behavior is as old as recorded thinking about society. Marx in his youth exposed the more naïve versions of materialism, culminating in Feuerbach's "Man is what he eats." Admirer of Hobbes, student of the Utilitarians, Marx could not have claimed to have discovered the general principle of materialism which indeed emanated from the intellectual atmosphere of his age.

If Marxism belongs in the great tradition of materialist thought, yet the character of Marx's materialism already displays one of those striking inconsistencies and ambiguities that are interspersed throughout his whole system. We are the products of our material environment, in the sense that our ideas, as well as our mode of existence, are determined by the type of economy within which we live, or more concretely by our status within it. Systems of politics, art, religion, etc., are eventually traced back to their economic roots. Nothing exists in the mind that cannot be traced back to the economic environment. The dominant mode of production determines the character of society; the relationship of an individual or class to the means of production decides his or its social consciousness and mode of behavior. Such is the gist of Marx's materialist argument. Who would quarrel with Marx if he had said that material factors are important—if before each "determined" he had inserted "largely" or even "mostly"? Marx's rigorous dogmatism has set his critics on a gleeful and rather easy hunt for exceptions, qualifications, and inconsistencies in each step of his materialist argument. Yet the fashion for generalizing in dogmatic terms about man's social behavior and history was prevalent in Marx's times. If one accepts Marxism as a historical phenomenon and does not seek to accept or reject it as gospel, there is no reason to get excited over Marx's materialistic dogmatism. It is in the spirit of his era.

The interesting inconsistency lies elsewhere. The first naïve question a student is likely to ask about Marxism points up the real problem: If we are determined by our environment, what chance is there for conscious human activity to change society? The passion of Marx and Engels for social justice and revolutionary activity, their propaganda and their literary activity seem to belie their teaching. Whatever unlovely personal characteristics one discovers in Marx himself, one cannot avoid the impression of a Prometheus-like person struggling against the world, attempting to expose the injustices and hypocrisies which, according to his theories, are the unavoidable features of contemporary society.

The above dilemma is that of many a philosopher and scientist who attempts to revolutionize or reform his world. And to the accusation of inconsistency there is the not entirely convincing answer that revolutionary activity, like scientific activity, does not deny the facts of nature, but seeks their understanding and control by men. But the ambiguity in Marx's determinism flows from his search for a *new* type of determinism and a *new* type of materialism. The beginnings of the search are perhaps to be found in an occurrence quite common in young intellectuals: fascination with somebody else's ideas and, at the same time, desire to appropriate them by improving upon them, by seizing them in a new way. Certainly this intent is visible in *Theses on Feuerbach,* the eleven exceedingly epigrammatic statements jotted down by young Marx in 1845. If they were read without bearing in mind Marx's future activity, they would be dismissed as incoherent exercises on the theme, "materialism is not enough," and as a fatuous attempt to grasp for something else. But in the context of Marx's future development they can be seen as not only a projection of ambition, or of the exasperation of a young and sensitive man with an academic approach to human problems and his disgust with both materialism and idealism as then defined. The theses set before him the problem of the search for an understanding of the material world that would contribute to and lead toward a liberation of mankind. The development of his own theories henceforth bore the imprint of an unresolved conflict between, first, submission to the spirit of the age with its materialism and search for laws governing social reality in economics, and second, a romantic's rebellion not only against society but against the current theories of social problems. Materialism is not enough. Idealism is irrelevant, and the contemporary theories of socialism are the works of quacks and moralists. It is a heartfelt cry that is heard at the end of the theses: "The philosophers have only *interpreted* the world in various ways; the point, however, is to *change* it": a direct challenge to Hegelian strictures of philosophy coming too late to teach the world what it should be. Knowledge as formulation of laws by a dispassionate observer versus knowledge as a form of action—these are two clashing concepts before young Marx.

The search for a new type of materialism can be seen in the whole Marxist system. The forces of history work through the changing forces of production and the changing civilizations that correspond to them. Progress toward freedom is man's continuing progress in mastering the forces of nature until full mastery is achieved under socialism. Marx's materialism is an intricate combination of eighteenth-century mechanistic materialism, common-sense liberal materialism, which saw men influenced by their "interest," and Hegelian dialectic. In his own mind and to his own satisfaction, Marx achieved the creation of a new materialism promised in another thesis on Feuerbach: "The standpoint of the new [materialism] is human society or socialized humanity." Thus both a new *interpretation* of the world *and* a way of *changing* it are promised by Marxist philosophy. Man is a slave of his environment not only in the way he lives but also in his ideas, until science enables him to break the shackles of his environment and by liberating his labor liberates his personality. Materialism is thus not only a sober realistic way of viewing human affairs, an antidote to religions, myths, and superstitions which have imprisoned the human mind. It is also the equivalent of the original sin that, until socialism is reached, keeps mankind imprisoned in the network of selfish economic interests and makes utopian the postulates of freedom, equality, and fraternity. It is vain to pray for a change in men's hearts, for we are all slaves of economic necessity until . . .

The scaffolding of Marx's argument discloses Marx the romantic revolutionary assailing his contemporary society for its preoccupation with money; Marx the materialist rejecting moralistic and idealistic solutions as fraudulent; and finally Marx the Hegelian reconciling the two conflicting principles by a march of history that, through an evolution of material forces, brings freedom for the first time within the grasp of mankind. It is a brilliant intellectual exercise, a brilliant synthesis performed by a mind chafing under the world's injustices and yet rejecting solutions ignoring the reality of human relations. But what can be the source of attraction in an argument so tortuous and involved, with its "negation of negations" and its "alienation"?

A preliminary answer must acknowledge how universal is the inner dialectic of Marx's argument. How often we are struck by the conflict between ideals and "things as they are." How enticing it is to resolve the conflict "realistically" by postulating a material progress, whether of individuals or societies, that will bring about the desired moral results. Behind its complicated structure, Marx's concept of materialism has all the power of a commonplace. And much more than that: within the fully developed system, Marxist economic determinism (which is the form his materialism takes) acts not to weaken but to strengthen the moral component of the revolutionary impulse. Superficially, no moral blame can, strictly speaking, be attached to the capitalist as capitalist: he acts in accordance with economic forces that determine his behavior. Yet in a sense his crime is all the greater. His function lies athwart the historic forces that ordain society to move beyond capitalism into socialism. Economic predetermination, like religious predetermination, does not absolve from but enhances moral judgment. Whatever a logician may think of the various steps in its argument, Marxist economic determinism will always retain its human appeal.

To a society encumbered by class, caste, and bureaucratic distinctions, materialism comes as a philosophy of liberation. This is difficult for us to realize, living as we do in a materialistic age and in a materialistic society. Yet in the middle forties of the last century in Germany, materialism burst forth as an iconoclastic creed, challenging the rationale of dynastic and class distinction. In a country attempting to shake off traditionalism and enter the modern industrial world, materialism, often announced with the naïve air of discovery, was the first component of a rationalistic revolution against the force of obsolete customs and distinctions. It "exposed" the immemorial customs, privileges, and philosophies of the status quo. That Marxism made its plea for social justice under the guise of materialism rather than in moral terms has always enhanced its appeal in tradition-bound societies. The "discovery" that Marx made has often been the first discovery made by a young man in a social system that denies him advancement or self-expression. A typical Marxist paradox: the most simplified version of Marxist materialism is often the most effective incentive to revolutionary idealism.

Marx's materialism is of course far from being simple. The tortuous arguments of economic determinism have led some, like Professor Schumpeter, to assert that "Marx's philosophy is no more materialistic than is Hegel's." [1] Yet its first appeal is the appeal of the simplicity of materialism: man is made by his environment and not by forces over which he has no control. One does not often pause to reflect that in taking this first step one may be exchanging a religious or psychological determinism for an economic one. The first step offers liberation from the irrationalities of one's society and culture, and also the challenge to remake them. The second step, the postulate of economic determinism, seemingly negates the first one: human control over the social environment is illusory, because it is subject to the rigid laws of economic phases. Nothing can soften the oppression of the serf under feudalism, or of the worker under capitalism, until each system, having fully developed its potentialities, is ready to pass on and be replaced by its successor—feudalism by capitalism and capitalism by socialism. To Marx himself, the contradiction was encompassed by revolutionary optimism and a historical illusion that the birth pains of capitalism in Western Europe were its death throes. A new way of interpreting the world was to demonstrate how to change it, not in the distant

---

[1] Joseph A. Schumpeter, *Capitalism, Socialism and Democracy*, New York, 1950, p. 11.

future but immediately. As his revolutionary optimism waned, the simple argument of his youth became an elaborate theoretical structure. Perhaps in their own old age Marx and Engels themselves forgot how convincing and how endowed with immediate revolutionary potentialities their original and primitive materialism had seemed to two young intellectuals in a Europe undergoing the most painful phase of economic transition.

In his general formulation of economic determinism Marx drew close to English liberalism and its materialist viewpoint. We shall attempt to show later how, in his fascination with and bitter critique of the English school of political economy and its ally liberalism, Marx managed to import into his creed some of the most rigorous and dogmatic characteristics of the liberal economic *Weltanschauung*. Here it is necessary to note certain general resemblances and differences between the two brands of materialism.

Like Marxism, early liberalism saw in materialism a doctrine of intellectual and political liberation. Rationalism and materialism became practically synonymous to the early liberals. A sober realization of the healthy earthiness and selfishness of human nature is a prerequisite to the study of society and history and a necessary antidote to the obsolete claims of tradition and supranatural religion to dominate human conduct. The world of liberalism, the world of a middle-class, intellectually inclined Englishman of the nineteenth century who read Hume and Bentham, was a world of concrete and tangible objects. This frame of mind did not tolerate myths, deities, or abstract principles as explanations of human behavior. Bentham ridiculed the Declaration of the Rights of Man as a rationale for political emancipation. Adam Smith looked to enlightened self-interest as the basis for prosperous, hence free, society. The institutions of the West have grown within the liberal tradition of the last century and a half. It is something of a shock, therefore, to realize how "Marxist" this tradition was in its original formulation of materialism. The dispassionate language of the early liberals (in comparison with Marx's) and their happy ignorance of Hegelian terminology may blind us to the rigid economic determinism which their writings exude. Indeed, reading Marx, one sometimes gets the impression that he spells out with excessive emphasis what the early liberals asserted almost nonchalantly, so great was their belief in the obviousness of their conclusions.

It goes without saying that there are considerable differences between the two philosophies. The liberals' materialism is unselfconscious. Unlike Marx's, it is unaccompanied by an inner revulsion at the *merely materialistic* basis of human action and hence by a search for a philosophy which *through materialism* will eventually free man from his complete dependence on his economic environment. There is no sense of original sin and therefore no elaborate theology of how to overcome it. The mood of liberalism and of the English political economy is optimistic. The reservations of Ricardo and the pessimism of Malthus find no general response in a generation impressed by the miraculous power of science and the prodigious growth of the productive powers of the economy. If individuals are allowed to carry out their own lives with a minimum of interference by the state or organized religion, if economic forces are permitted to work out their benevolent effects, mankind will emerge from its unhappy condition. Human progress is visible and concrete, not only as a long-run proposition, but as a day-to-day improvement in the assertion of human rationality over obsolete institutions and customs. One does not need, as one does in Marxism, cataclysmic clashes of historical forces to accomplish the liberation of mankind; this is being accomplished, step by step, by the improvement of material environment through science and education.

Such is the general spirit of early liberalism, concealing under its broad-minded view of progress a rigid materialist bias. The absorption of Marxism into the liberal outlook is accompanied by Marxism's dislike of liberal bourgeois society and its rejection of liberal conclusions. As young Marx, largely under the influence of Engels, turned to reading the English political economists and historians, his materialism, from being a mere philosophical postulate, a counterpoint of Hegel, grew into a vision of science, industrial labor, and industrial achievement civilizing and liberating men through the conditions of their lives and not through moral preachings or abstract ideas. The sense of Marxism is materialism not only as a materialist philosophy and as economic determinism, but also as admiration for the tangible fruit of materialism: the bourgeois industrial civilization.

ECONOMICS

The trouble with Marxism lies in its economics. Such at least has been the opinion of many would-be Marxists, especially in the English-speaking countries. The assertion of the class struggle and the postulate of socialism are clear and simple challenges to capitalism. Why spoil them by dragging in an involved economic argument and making it the crucial part of the equally unnecessary Hegelian apparatus of history with its dubious "inevitabilities"? In the view of these critics, Marxism gains from its economic theory neither as a system of thought nor as a movement of social protest. No crowds are likely to be driven to storm the bastions of autocracy or capitalism because of Marxist *economics*. The legacy of the economic argument to the suceeding generations of Marxist leaders and intellectuals has been mainly the diversion of energy from concrete political and revolutionary tasks to the defense of a doctrine "so dull and illogical," as Lord Keynes phrased it. If Marxism could only have preserved the simplicity, immediacy, and revolutionary appeal of the *Communist Manifesto!*

Such criticisms are usually grounded in the opinion that Marx's economic theories can be divorced from his revolutionary message and that the surplus-value theory and what follows is merely an intellectual fabrication of one man's mind and not a theoretical expression of the revolutionary ideas current in Marx's society. In fact, the economic argument is, as we shall attempt to demonstrate later on, a sophisticated arrangement of commonly held notions, both liberal and anti-liberal, characteristic of Marx's period. The surplus-value theory may or may not be beyond the ken of a follower of Marxism, but the type of thinking about the economy that it represents will at times find a ready response in the minds of people quite unversed in economic theory. An economist in 1900 or 1950 may barely contain himself while struggling against the illogicalities of the doctrine, yet his predecessor in 1860 or 1850, even though equally anti-Marxist, would have had to admit how close Marxian economics were, in spirit and structure of argument if not in conclusions, to the then dominant school of political economy.

Marx's economic inquiry is characterized by three assumptions. First, that political economy is the science of the distribution of wealth in society and of its rationale; that the aim of economics is to find out "who gets what and why," a notion proceeding from the Physiocrats through the classical English political economists to Marx. Second, that the introduction of machinery, industrialization, constitutes the decisive fact of modern economy, around which all the forces of the modern economy turn. Industrialization is a decisive break with the previous pattern of economic development and will lead to an entirely different relation of man to material forces. Third, that the economic development of England, roughly in the first half of the nineteenth century, is a preview of eventual economic development everywhere; that the observable data about the economic behavior of various classes there have a fairly universal validity. England in the middle of the century is Marx's laboratory for economic analysis and for what we would call today the psychology of industrialization. His worker is the English worker of the forties and fifties, his capitalist is the contemporary English capitalist.

In his philosophy Marx always goes back to his German origins.

In politics he is always attentive to French developments. A man of universal interests, he comments perceptively on developments throughout the whole world. But in economics the contemporary (or rather the recently past, by the time the first volume of *Capital* appeared in 1867) English economic scene crowds out everything else. When, late in his life, he hesitates and inquires whether Russia may not skip the capitalist stage of development, he departs from his main economic point and is not a "Marxist."

Within the three above assumptions, shared by him with the leading intellectuals of that very unsociologically minded era, Marx's economics fall easily within the dominant tendency of the classical political economy (i.e., Ricardian economics), but with an anticapitalist bias. He asks, "What is value?"—a question to us scholastic in its flavor and unanswerable. But this question was asked and always will be asked in a society in which a dramatic transformation of the economy has prompted an inquiry into the sources of new wealth and the claims of individuals and classes to its apportionment. Marx's answer agrees with Ricardo, asserting human labor to be the sole source and the real denominator of economic value. One step further and human labor becomes the only commodity which, in process of its use, expends more value than it uses up. Thus, not as a figure of speech but as a hard fact, human labor becomes the only maker of value, the only magic of economic transformation. From labor is extracted capital accumulation and the capitalist's profit. Its magic propensity gives the capitalist, after he pays the laborers for their labor, the natural wages of any commodity, i.e., the cost of its production, the *surplus labor*. The worker may satisfy his wants by working, say, four hours, but the capitalist system forces him to work longer and to produce *surplus value*. The whole process is one of exploitation, in terms not of human volition (i.e., the malevolence of the employer on the one hand, the worker's stupidity or weakness on the other), but simply of the necessary mechanics of the system. The cupidity of the employer and the chains of the proletariat are alike ordained by the forces of history prescribing the inevitable stages of capitalism, and only these forces, once the system is fully developed, will decree its collapse. In the meantime there is nothing that charity, parliaments, or unions can do to alter the consequences of the law of surplus value.

The howling of critics, the agonized attempts of defenders, and the simple exasperation of men of common sense have followed the surplus-value theory down to our own day. How can you talk about labor or labor power as if it were a concrete substance? How about a ditch digger versus a man operating an atom smasher? How about the role of management, the value of inventors and innovators? How about factors of scarcity, noneconomic influences, and so on? The answer is that *in the context of its times and circumstances* Marx's surplus-value notion did not depart from the best economic thinking.

More than that. In his admirable rephrasing of Marxist economics, Mr. Paul Sweezy[2] has re-emphasized the importance of Marx's attack on what he called "fetishism," a cunning tendency of the bourgeois economists to picture the whole economic process as consisting of relations between *things,* as concealing the essentially *human* nature of social and economic reality. The surplus-value theory was a concrete application of Marx's "new materialism": there are laws of history and economy, but they operate through human beings. There are heroes and villains, exploiters and exploited, even though they are cast in their roles not by their own volition but by historical forces. The mechanistic aspect of the "dismal science" of economics is supplanted by live actors, and here lies the continuing human appeal of an awkward theory.

From the perspective of a modern non-Marxist, the surplus-value theory is a clear example of an ideology masquerading as a scientific theory. It is necessary to meet this objection by repeat-

[2] *The Theory of Capitalist Development,* New York, 1942.

ing how close the economics of Marx are to the British economic thought of the generation preceding their formulation. The notion of the capitalist's being the inevitable exploiter because of the mechanics of the industrial process is parallel, for instance, to Ricardo's picture of the landlord gathering, through no merit or labor of his own, the fruits of the growth of population and industry. If Marx was intruding an ideology into his system, so were the others. If Marx rejected the common-sense version of exploitation (i.e., the cheating of the worker by the capitalist) in favor of a more subtle one, he did so because he was convinced that the economic system is regulated by laws of its own, having all the rigor of scientific laws—if not so rigorous as those of physics then at least those of biology. As a matter of fact, the more Marx studied political economy and the structure and argument of the contemporary bourgeois society, the more he became engrossed in their spirit. The violent diatribes and vituperations that intersperse the theoretical sections of *Capital* give the impression not only of an indictment of bourgeois society and its apologists, but also of an inner irritation at the way the author feels himself drawn into the spirit and the way of reasoning of his opponents. It is not just the statistics, equations, and theorems that replace the simple communist appeal of Marx's youth; it is also, perhaps, the realization of how much of the capitalist spirit has entered into the edifice of his socialism.

The moving factor of the capitalist development is industrialization. It is difficult, if we follow the main trend of Marx's doctrine, to conceive of capitalism apart from industrialization, impossible to conceive of the capitalist except through his role in the industrial process. And to anticipate, socialism without industrialization is in Marxist terms simply a contradiction in terms, because it follows and is the logical culmination of capitalism. Marx expressed the connection unmistakably:

Except as personified capital, the capitalist has no historical value, and no right to that historical existence, which to use an expression of the witty Lichnowsky "hasn't got no date." And so far only is the necessity for his own transitory existence implied in the transitory necessity for the capitalist mode of production. But, so far as he is personified capital, it is not values in use and the enjoyment of them but exchange value and its augmentation, that spur him into action. Fanatically bent on making value expand itself, he ruthlessly forces the human race to produce for production's sake; he thus forces the development of the productive powers of society, and creates those material conditions, which alone can form the real basis of a higher form of society, a society in which the full and free development of every individual forms the ruling principle. Only as personified capital is the capitalist respectable. As such he shares with the miser the passion for wealth as wealth. But that which in the miser is a mere idiosyncracy is, in the capitalist, the effect of the social mechanism, of which he is but one of the wheels. Moreover, the development of capitalist production makes it constantly necessary to keep increasing the amount of the capital laid out in a given industrial understanding, and competition makes the immanent laws of capitalist production to be felt by each individual capitalist, as external coercive laws. It compels him to keep constantly extending his capital, in order to preserve it, but extend it he cannot, except by means of progressive accumulation.[3]

The capitalist is history's agent of accumulation, without which industrial development cannot go on. Without this development the necessary material basis for socialism will not be achieved.

We already find here more than a hint of the industrial fanaticism and the mania for production that has characterized the Communists of our times. But in the context of the economic argument, the immediate importance of the statement is that it pictures the capitalist as the unconscious agent of industrial progress. The logic of industrialization brings about major changes in the capitalist system. The capitalist's psychology fits in with

[3] *Capital,* Volume I [1867], edited by Ernest Untermann after the fourth German edition by Friedrich Engels (New York: The Modern Library, 1932), pp. 648-649. All subsequent page references to *Capital* in this book are to the Modern Library edition.

the inherent logic of industrial dynamism, although the latter will eventually bring about his demise when he is no longer necessary. He cannot help but go on accumulating, extracting surplus value from the worker, indulging in catastrophic competition for the market with his fellow capitalist, and thus speeding the day of his doom. The capitalists as a class may not—though isolated individuals may—cease their feverish pursuit of accumulation and more production; they cannot develop the tastes and ethics of other classes and simply let the economy stagnate. Thus the picture of the dynamics of the capitalist mode of production can be understood in terms of two general assumptions of Marxian economics that we noted in the beginning: that the increasing use of machinery is the central and universal characteristic of the modern economy; and (a much more debatable notion) that capitalists everywhere and always will behave the way the English capitalists of Marx's time in effect did.

The drama of capitalism has as its cast of characters the worker, the capitalist, and the machine. Economically speaking, they have no choice in their actions. The worker *has* to sell his labor for the wages oscillating around what in the given society is the level of subsistence. The capitalist has to extract surplus value and sink it into expanding the means of production. Finally, the machine is both the cause and the nemesis of the capitalist economy. Itself nonproductive of value, it increasingly displaces human labor and forces the capitalist to reduce his investment in value-producing human labor as compared with his investment in machines. The organic composition of capital, the proportion of constant capital (mainly machinery) to variable capital (wages), goes up as capitalism progresses. Thus the mechanics of industrialization, of capitalism, must force employers to use less and less surplus-value producing labor and more and more machines, which do not produce more value than they consume!

The triumph that this theory achieves over obvious, palpable common sense did not escape even Marx. He granted that his law contradicted all experience based on observation. Everybody knows, he wrote in the first volume of *Capital*, that a cotton manufacturer who uses a lot of machinery in proportion to workers does not receive less profit or surplus value than does a baker who uses little machinery and a lot of human labor. The logic of the wretched law would have all capital go into the most primitive forms of production, with the capitalists falling all over themselves in destroying machines! Undaunted, Marx observed haughtily that:

For the solution of this apparent contradiction, many intermediate terms are as yet wanted, as from the standpoint of elementary algebra many intermediate terms are wanted to understand that $0/0$ may represent an actual magnitude. (p. 335)

He eventually undertook the solution of the dilemma, in the third volume, while reproaching the bourgeois economists of the labor-value theory (i.e., Ricardo and his school) for simply capitulating before this crushing paradox.

By the time the third volume of *Capital* appeared in 1894 with its "solution" of the dilemma of price versus value, the type of economic thinking embodied in the labor theory of value was almost incomprehensible to economists. It has become difficult to appreciate that Marxist economics were not only a logical conclusion of the tradition of classical economy, but embodied ideas about the production and distribution of wealth in which many "practical" people quite innocent of economics believed. Not only many a worker or radical agitator, but quite a few manufacturers in England from about 1820 to 1860 instinctively talked and acted as if they were demonstrating the Marxist "laws." By the nineties, the economic situation and intellectual atmosphere that had produced Ricardian as well as Marxist economics had largely become things of the past for Western Europe. The imperfections of Ricardo's theory, the cul-de-sac to which his theory of value led, were treated tolerantly by the then dominant school of economics. Great men, after the passage of time, have the privilege of being proved partly wrong. But Ricardo did not place economics as a basis of an elaborate political philosophy, or so it seemed, and the full fury of the marginal-utility-theory economists fell upon Marx.

The "solution" that Marx offered to his own riddle provides at the same time his exposition of the dynamic development of capitalist economy leading to its self-destruction. Although the capitalist cannot derive any profit from the machine, he is increasingly forced to use it, because he is in competition with other capitalists and because a technological advantage translated even temporarily into a cheapening of the given commodity is to him a matter of life and death. A technical innovation, a more extensive use of machines, enables him to grab a bigger share of the market and to force his more backward competitor from the rank of capitalists. Hence, even at the price of reducing the proportion of human labor employed and, therefore, at the price of reducing his profit, he is drawn toward greater and greater mechanization. It is this process of competition, this toll exacted by the mechanizing propensity of modern industrial civilization, that distributes among the surviving capitalists at a fairly equal rate the total sum of surplus value exacted from all the workers. Commodities exchange not according to the amount of labor embodied in them, but according to that amount as modified by the constant competition among the producers. The machine, which is the blessing of modern civilization, is at the same time the curse of capitalism. It undermines profit; it threatens the producer, unless he is constantly in the forefront of mechanical progress, with removal from the rank of manufacturers. Since the capitalists as an order have to pay an ever-increasing ransom to the machine, their profit is bound to decline and their number is bound to decrease. Industrial progress is forever devouring its children—the capitalists.

It is immaterial, from the point of view of the analysis of Marx-

ism expounded here, to concern ourselves with the extent to which
Volume III of *Capital* contradicts Volume I, or with the question
of whether the organic composition of capital creates the tendency
for the rate of profit to fall continually. The important thing
to note is that Marx's exposition reflects a peculiarity of his
period: human perplexity at the effects of scientific and mechanical progress. We may sympathize with thinkers of the first half
of the nineteenth century, for, after having become quite used to
and blasé about mechanization, we have been confronted most
recently by the implications of automation and atomic energy.
It is perhaps easier for us than for someone in 1900 to visualize
resentment at forces of our own making that yet control our
lives, independently, as it were, of our will. The century and the
class that prided themselves on shedding the shackles of superstition and custom were confronted with progress itself as
seemingly defying human volition. In more prosaic terms, the
English economists and philosophers were confronted with the
necessity of formulating a theory—"laws"—for a constantly
changing situation, the necessity of prescribing a stable and
unalterable pattern of relations for an economy in a state of
revolution. The most profound of them, even while sharing in
the enthusiasm for progress and technology, could not but reflect in their theories the very human if unscientific worry:
"Where will it all end?" Full accommodation to the Moloch of
industrialization was beyond their vision, just as it is difficult
for us to visualize how the world will come to terms with atomic
energy. Marx shared their fascination and perplexity, but because of his premises, his new materialism, *he* knew how it would
all end. Advanced industrialism is incompatible with capitalism.
Mechanization by reducing the share of labor in a finished product
impinges on profit-capitalism. Yet mechanization is both
necessary and unavoidable because of competition among the
capitalists. The final result can only be the replacement of
capitalism by a system that does not need the profit motive and

hence can live and thrive on technological progress—socialism.

It is with an almost voluptuous delight that Marx sketches several aspects of capitalism's race toward self-destruction. Periodic crises of overproduction destroy the weaker strata of capitalists, but also plunge whole societies in misery. Whether Marx was an "underconsumptionist" or not is a question of primary interest to the economists. Certainly within the body of his writings there are several suggestions about how the pleasing prospect of capitalism's self-strangulation is to become reality. Concentration of capital to an absurd degree and on a world scale is one such possibility. The world reduced to a few capitalists and hordes of paupers is a vision sufficient in itself. The most frequent economic argument for collapse is more varied. The perpetuation of capitalism under conditions of technological progress means a continuous effort by the capitalist to squeeze more surplus value out of his diminishing labor force. He will attempt to cut his workers' wages closer to the minimum subsistence level or to prolong their hours of work or to work them more intensely or God knows what else. The worker has no option but to take work on the capitalist's terms, because the mechanics of industrialization, progressively decimating the number of business firms, increase the number of unemployed, the "reserve industrial army of the proletariat." Periodic crises of increasing severity shake up the capitalist economy until the final one spells its destruction. Capitalism is doomed because it cannot accommodate technological progress to the profit motive. It is doomed because it *creates* socialism in the sense of concentrating the means of production in huge units, thus making the notion of private property an absurdity as well as a fetter on the productive system. It is finally doomed because in its fight for survival it has to bring increasing misery, exploitation, and unemployment to the mass of the population.

Such is the culmination of Marxist economics, the elaboration of which took the great revolutionary a major part of his life. Economists have written voluminously about its obvious weak points: the inconsistencies concerning the relationship of value and price and the belief that industrialism under capitalism is bound to make the working class more and more miserable. The latter point, Marx's "immiseration" theory as Schumpeter called it, is a tenet of Marxism most decisively refuted by history. Nobody would claim that the worker in England or France today is worse off than was his grandfather a hundred years ago. One may attempt, as the neo-Marxians have done, to plead that Marx meant a "relative" as opposed to absolute worsening of the standard of life. Such an interpretation is not borne out by a study of all that Marx had to say on the subject, and its content has not come true anyway. By contrast, Marx has been praised even by his adversaries for predicting the trend toward the centralization of industry and, eventually, monopolies.

Both the defenders and opponents of Marxism have thus distributed pluses and minuses to various points of its economic analyses. To the defenders of the over-all system as a correct analysis of and prediction about capitalism and its development everywhere was left the unenviable task of stretching every conceivable line of argument: Marx was interested in discovering the "laws of motion" of capitalist society rather than in describing its operations precisely; Marxist laws still describe correctly the natural tendency of capitalism, although at times this tendency is held in check by countertendencies; the downfall of capitalism is postponed by such extraneous factors as the imperialism of the great industrial countries. It was claimed that the Great Depression of the 1930's was a vindication of Marx's analysis—comparable to the vindication of a doctor who predicted that his patient would die of cancer within one year, only to have the man die twenty years later of a heart attack! The devotion of the believers, and the attacks or condescension of the opponents as well, overlook, ironically enough, the clear moral of Marxism itself: the rather commonplace idea that no social doctrine or system of economics can transcend its historical and social circumstances. The main point about Marxist economics is not the correctness or error of this or that item of his analysis, even though such a question in itself is of great intellectual interest. More important to the historian as well as the student of contemporary society is to ascertain the social and intellectual forces that gave rise to the Marxist structure, and to see where in the modern world the same or similar forces endow Marxist economics with relevance and persuasiveness.

THE CLASS STRUGGLE

The eternal battle array of history always ranges the oppressor against the oppressed, most commonly the owner of the means of production against the man who works with them. Only in the very beginning of human society was there no class struggle, just as there will be none in its culmination. Between the most primitive tribal community and the socialist-communist era, "the history of all hitherto existing society is the history of class struggles." [4] Capitalism witnesses this struggle in the most simplified form: the proletariat against the capitalists. The victory of the proletariat will bring with it the abolition of the class struggle. The discovery of private property disrupted the social innocence of mankind. The full utilization of mankind's productive powers under socialism will restore it. With the disappearance of private property and of the class struggle, most of the social evils will disappear and with them the rationale for oppressive institutions, including the state.

This is the most clear-cut and internally consistent of all Marxist arguments. From its ringing formulation in the *Communist Manifesto* to the end of their lives, Marx and Engels never doubted that they had found the operating pattern of history, that the reality of social and political life is expressed, not in the

---

[4] Karl Marx and Friedrich Engels "Manifesto of the Communist Party," in *Capital and Other Writings by Karl Marx,* tr. by Samuel Moore, ed. by Max Eastman (New York: The Modern Library, 1936) p. 321. Page numbers given in all subsequent quotations from the *Manifesto* refer to this edition.

struggle of ideas, dynasties, or nations, but in the class struggle grounded in economic motivation. To their followers, the principle was a satisfactory explanation and a reliable guide to action, with none of the puzzling qualities of Marxist economics or over-all philosophy. Class struggle became, in effect, the major portion of the revolutionary appeal of Marxism. Workers do not strike or storm the barricades in order to abolish surplus value. They strike and revolt against oppressive conditions, against the capitalists. From the point of view of political action, the slogan of class struggle is the simplest guide. It is also the simplest, most convincing revolutionary explanation of politics and history.

A deceptive simplicity! It has misled both the critics and the followers of Marxism. It has led Marxist movements too often to identify Marxist politics with a simple posture of opposition to the exploiting classes. The dominant faction of the German Social Democrats before World War I defined their Marxism as hostility to the imperial institutions and middle-class parties of their country. It led the Bolsheviks, in the first flush of their victory in 1917, to believe that by destroying the capitalists they were destroying capitalism. It has led people versed in Marxism to express surprise that many secondary features of capitalism "suddenly" made their appearance in Soviet Russia in the 1930's. Marxism became identified with insurrectionary action or with hostility, open and uncompromising, to capitalism and to everything and everyone connected with it.

It is necessary to repeat (as it will be again) what is perhaps the most pregnant sentence in Marx's view of social revolution, describing the role of the capitalist: "He thus forces the development of the productive powers of society, and creates *those material conditions, which alone can form the real basis of a higher form of society,* a society in which the full and free development of every individual forms the ruling principle." [5] Nothing in the *main body* of Marx and Engels' writing suggests that any po-

[5] *Capital,* p. 649. (Italics mine)

litical development, even a seizure of power by the proletariat, can abrogate the laws governing the material development of mankind. From the earliest days of their association, the days filled with the most immediate revolutionary hope, Marx and Engels believed in the primacy of material factors over political action. It is always possible to find an incident or a statement by one or the other that would range them in the camp of believers in revolution pure and simple and hang the stage of economic development. (Thus the brief "Blanquist" period of Marx's early revolutionary activity, and, late in his life, his opinion that Russia might skip the full capitalist phase and pass into socialism from pre-capitalism.) But it is impossible to claim that such incidents or utterances represent the main tendency of Marxism or, as M. Rubel claims in his excellent biography, that Marx ultimately abandoned economic determinism in favor of unconditional faith in the ideal of human liberation.[6]

What bridges the gap between economic determinism on the one hand and class struggle and the call to the proletariat to seize power on the other is Marx's revolutionary optimism. In the 1840's and early '50's, he believed that capitalism was on its last legs, that the economic as well as the political conditions for its downfall were at hand. It is true, as M. Rubel reminds us, that Marx was a socialist long before he discovered his economic system. It is true that the fascination of political economy engrossed and captured him, pushing his thought in directions he had perhaps not envisaged as a young man. But his socialism and his "discovery" of the class struggle did not precede his distaste for the existing moralistic brands of socialism and the determination to place *his* socialism on a firm, materialistic, scientific basis.

Again, what is difficult for us to understand from the perspective of a hundred years becomes easier if we immerse ourselves in the feeling of the period. How could a man believe both that

[6] Maximilien Rubel, *Karl Marx: Essai de biographie intellectuelle*, Paris, 1957.

capitalism was a necessary phase of the development of mankind and that Western European capitalism circa 1850 had played its role and was ready to leave the stage? The simple answer is that Marx and Engels shared not only the expectations of many radicals and socialists of the day, but also the apprehensions of many capitalists and liberal economists. Social and economic unrest had risen in ascending proportion from the introduction of what are *to us* the rudimentary institutions of capitalism to the middle of the nineteenth century. Was it entirely unreasonable to expect a fairly early economic collapse as well as a political revolution? Or to see a democratic revolution as a far-reaching step toward socialism? Many revolutionaries live expecting their revolution to take place any day. In Marx the faith of a revolutionary was complemented by the analysis of a social scientist. It is easy for us to say that Marx was wrong: capitalism did not collapse in Europe in 1850 or in 1860. But he was also right, though on wrong premises: what he assumed were relatively late stages of capitalism in France and England were in effect the early stages of industrialization and modernization in those countries, and in those stages capitalism is most vulnerable to class struggle.

Without revolutionary optimism, the doctrine of the class struggle, when joined with economic determinism, is a somber and tragic lesson. Except at the turning points in history, there is nothing the oppressed can do against the oppressor. The slave cannot prevail against his master, the serf against the landowner; and one type of oppression disappears only to be reborn in a different form of exploitation of man by man. Class struggle is compounded in the character of law and civilization imposed by each dominant class. Systems of religion and ethics serve to reinforce and to conceal at the same time the interest of the dominant class. Ever since he had seen, as a young man, the diet of his province discuss draconic laws against the removal of timber from state and private forests by the poor, all of Marx's instincts rebelled at the myth of the impartial state, impartial law. The system of private property under capitalism embodies best the double deception by which each exploiting class masks its exploiting role. It protects the capitalist against any tampering with his property, and it seeks to create the illusion of equality and impartiality for all. The plea for democratic franchise that the bourgeoisie makes is likewise a weapon of its class struggle. It seeks to strip the landlords of the remnants of their power and to delude the proletariat into believing that the essential issues are political in nature. The principle of class struggle illuminates world history by stripping it of its theatrical aspects of national struggles or contests about principles, and by demonstrating its material nature. Marx's is the "inside story" of world history, with economic interest its moving principle.

The "exposure" of history and politics was not unique to Marx. The dominant role of "interest" in politics and recent history was a cardinal tenet of the liberalism of his time. The sense of politics consisted in the struggle of classes seeking the advancement of their material interests. Thus the political struggle in the England of the thirties and forties between the Whigs and the Tories was interpreted as centering around the contest between the agricultural and the manufacturing interests. Liberal economists saw in their doctrine a guide to public policies that would secure a "harmony of interests," but they were far from assuming that the correctness of their theories would of itself secure their adoption, or that a collusion of vested interests could not—as well as ignorance—hamper public welfare. The liberal version was already a "suspicious" theory of history, with the material interests of classes lurking behind the struggle for politics and principles.

Marx elevates this suspicion into certainty. Thus, for example, the Glorious Revolution of 1688 is not primarily a victory of parliamentarianism over royal despotism, but a harbinger of bourgeois domination, with the Stock Exchange and other rudimentary institutions of capitalism soon to be established. In a sense, the Marxist class-struggle interpretation of history is more "historical" than the liberal one. In the liberal outlook, history had been a period of darkness and superstition until the sixteenth and seventeenth centuries, and only then had scientific principle begun to assert itself in thinking about human affairs. To Marx, on the other hand, the class struggle provided the rationale of social systems and philosophies from earliest times; the pattern of history is always meaningful if we follow the class-struggle principle and its economic underpinning. The Middle Ages are thus not merely a period of darkness and obscurantism: their social and religious ideas are perfectly understandable in terms of the then dominant mode of production and system of property. Marxist historical analysis and methods of investigation have had an influence on many historians, some of whom would repudiate indignantly the charge of having anything to do with Marxism.

The class struggle under capitalism ranges the proprietors of the means of production against the proletariat. To a man like Marx with an acute sense of contemporary social reality, it was obvious that the picture was much more complicated than that. The class struggles in France, Germany, and England in the forties and fifties demonstrated the presence of other classes, as well as the differentiation of the two principal ones. The aristocracy, a remnant of the feudal age, was still fighting a retreating battle. The peasants had some characteristics of a separate class; from another point of view, they constituted a part of the petty bourgeoisie. The bourgeoisie itself had elements of the financial class as well as of the industrial one.

Marx cannot be reproached with having overlooked the differentiation and proliferation of social classes in his society. Indeed, ostensible political activity consists in various classes and subclasses playing for, or being played for, power in the state. But the essence of the class struggle and its eventual determination is much simpler. Only two classes really count—the capitalists and the proletariat. Other classes and subclasses play increasingly minor roles in the drama of capitalism. Sooner or later they retire into the wings, leaving the stage to the two great antagonists. Insofar as it is the logic of history, i.e., the development of productive forces, and not the temporary whims or affiliations of groups of population that ordain social stratifications, only two classes will remain, and they are "really" the only classes in the true sense of the word. Capitalism is already destroying the landowning nobility, and it will destroy the peasants.

Marx's conclusions about the class struggle, its character, and its participants make sense only if one keeps in mind his economic presuppositions. Like many philosophers of history of his period, he worked on the assumption that history operated neatly and always solved the problems it had posed. It did not occur to him that an advanced capitalism might still shelter a peasant problem or that a concentrated system of retailing might not completely replace the local grocer. Indeed, what "spoils" his analysis of society and his remarkable social acumen, so much more penetrating than that of his contemporary liberals, is precisely his analytical gift, his conviction that the observable tendencies in his society *must* work themselves out fully! History likes to chastise those who presume to understand it fully—a remark Marx would have classified as sheer obscurantism!

The two classes that are to square off in the last phase of the class struggle are quite dissimilar in many characteristics. The capitalist class is forever growing smaller in numbers; the proletariat, the exploited, ever larger. The rationale of the capitalist process, while it makes the capitalists aware of certain interests they have in common, still obliges them to engage in suicidal competition. The capitalist-industrial process makes the workers more and more unified in the realization of their common interest and in their class solidarity. The peasants, for instance, because of their dispersion, because of the peculiarity of their way of living, can never achieve real solidarity and a real community of interest and feeling; and thus, apart from their marginal economic significance, they can never constitute a true class. The workers, on the contrary, are disciplined by the circumstances of their work, brought together in great aggregations where they can feel the community of their privations and realize the logic of capitalism as leading to socialism. The *spontaneous growth* of class consciousness accompanies the growth of the capitalist-industrial system.

We shall see later how this concept of the spontaneous growth of class feelings and of its character was rooted in the experience of the early days of industrialization, and what trouble it brought to those followers of Marx who had to expound it under conditions of mature capitalism. Here we may observe certain interesting connotations of the concept. It is *rationalistic* in the extreme. The working class will not be distracted from the obligation and the realization of the inevitability of the class struggle by nationalistic or religious slogans and considerations. Only a degenerate, rootless portion of it, the *Lumpenproletariat*, may capitulate to the schemes of reactionaries and adventurers. The vast majority of the workers will understand their historical position and historical mission. The vision of the working class is Hegelian in its underpinnings. The proletariat is the universal class, carrying in its future the destiny of mankind, thus parallel in its function to Rousseau's General Will and Hegel's State. The loss of individuality caused and made inevitable by factory labor, the worker's *alienation,* carries in it the seeds of the fullest assertion of individuality under socialism, which comes as a Hegelian "negation of a negation." In more prosaic terms, the factory system is inevitably oppressive and inevitably felt by the worker as such. This oppression *inherent* in the system produces the class feeling. Capitalism = factory system = class consciousness is the line of argument, and a closer examination of each term of the triad

will illuminate the nature and conditions of the appeal of
Marxism.

The doctrines of the classes and the class struggle have, within
the context of the Marxist system, some further rather unex-
pected connotations. Take the class struggle between the bourgeoisie and the proletariat. The latter, through strikes and political action, resists the inevitable tendency of the capitalists to
increase the exploitation of the workers. Yet nothing is clearer
according to the logic of the doctrine than that the class struggle
cannot paralyze capitalism until the system is fully developed and
ready to pass on, or until the proletariat is fully capable of
wresting power from the bourgeoisie. What might be called guer-
rilla class warfare, endemic industrial strife, which would paralyze
the system, is clearly against the logic of Marxist thought, even
if paradoxically within its spirit: the worker has to get used
to the hated factory system, has to undergo exploitation, before
the material conditions of the society will allow the transition
to socialism. From the perspective of a hundred years, we may
appreciate how the Russian and Chinese Communists have taken
to heart the logic of the last proposition.

There is no *mystique* of the working class in early Marxism,
no extolling of humble material circumstances as being conducive to virtue. Workers are not asserted or called upon to be
heroic. They are asserted and called upon to be rational, to
develop class consciousness. To Marx, nothing would have been
more distasteful than the emotional undertones of later syndicalism. The ideal (in Weber's sense of the term) Marxist worker is
a curiously unemotional creature. He has no country, no real
family life; and his main objective in life is not an amelioration of
his condition, but the overthrow of the whole capitalist system.
His sense of suffering injustice, of being exploited, does not deceive him into immediate action against the immediate agents of
oppression—the factory and the employer—but into a *planned*
struggle against capitalism and the capitalist state. In his political

writings and speeches, Marx makes eloquent and emotion-tinged appeals, but the fact is that the main tenet of his theory about the worker and the class struggle is coldly rational in its logic. Human passion and generosity cannot in the last analysis prevail against the facts of history. The drama of the class struggle and the heroic exploits of the working-class revolutionaries are secondary to the working out of material forces. One cannot divorce economic evolution from the human drama that underlies it, but one must not ignore the laws of economics in revolutionary action. It is only a superficial reader of Marxism who would read into it the assumption that the proletariat may by political or insurrectionary action void the laws of history and avoid, say, by seizing power before capitalism is fully established, the hardships and privation of the factory system.

The idea of the class struggle serves to disprove the facile optimism of the liberals for whom, in all the clashes of interests, an "invisible hand" assured in a rationally organized society the harmony of individual and class self-interest with the general welfare. Marx's "invisible hand" is the very visible forces of production, which by their evolution confront each succeeding civilization with a different type of class warfare until, finally developed, they bring about classless society.

The centering of the social problem around the individual is, according to Marx, another pious hypocrisy of liberalism. Individual liberty and due process of law are, within a capitalist society, simply contradictions in terms. They are at most scraps of concessions thrown by the bourgeois state to deceive the proletariat, and in the circumstances of the workers' life under capitalism, they are of no value to them. This contemptuous attitude toward civil liberties, of such great historical significance to Marxism, is attuned to the circumstances of the worst period of the Industrial Revolution: with the proletarian working twelve and fourteen hours a day, and his wife and underage children also in unregulated industrial labor, the Bill of Rights did not, in fact, appear of overwhelming importance to the working class. The class struggle becomes the doctrine of total distrust of the capitalist state, with its laws, bureaucracy, and ideology. The violence of this distrust and opposition, the difficulty Marx and Engels experienced in acknowledging even the slightest social-welfare aspect of the bourgeois state, have often led to the optical illusion that Marxism was opposed to the state as such. It has enabled the revolutionary Marxists to denounce *the state,* with all the accents and conviction of anarchists, forgetting, for the moment, that the centralized state, like the capitalism of which it is a necessary ingredient, is an inevitable part of the historical process.

An alteration in the character of the capitalist state—such as the development of the workers' class consciousness into something other than the class struggle—is a possibility early Marxism cannot admit. "The civilization and justice of bourgeois order comes out in its lurid light whenever the slaves and drudges of that order rise against their masters. Then this civilization and justice stand forth as undisguised savagery and lawless revenge," [7] wrote Marx about the supression of the Paris Commune. The lures of legalism, of parliamentarianism, of social reform by the state are illusions and deceptions. When Marx or Engels admit the possibility of a peaceful transition to socialism under exceptional conditions, they do so grudgingly. Theirs is a theory grounded in the period when self-confident factory masters confronted the helpless workers, and the state backed up the masters with its police powers and philosophy of self-reliance. Like Marxist economics, the Marxist postulate of the class struggle ill fits the reality of full-grown capitalism—the reality of strong trade unions, social welfare legislation, and parliamentary socialism.

Here, then, is a theory attuned even more closely than other parts of Marxism to the facts and feelings of an early period

[7] "The Civil War in France," *Capital and Other Writings, op. cit.,* p. 421.

of industrialization. The class struggle is the salt of Marxism, its most operative revolutionary part. As a historical and psychological concept, it expresses a gross oversimplification, but it is the oversimplification of a genius. The formula of the class struggle seizes the essence of the mood of a great historical moment—a revolution in basic economy—and generalizes it into a historical law. It extracts the grievances of groups of politically conscious workers in Western Europe, then a very small part of the whole proletariat, and sees in it the portent and meaning of the awakening of the whole working class everywhere. The *first* reaction of the worker to industrialization, his feelings of grievance and impotence before the machine, his employer, and the state which stands behind the employer, are assumed by Marx to be typical of the general reactions of the worker to industrialization. What does change in the process of the development of industry is that the worker's feeling of impotence gives way to class consciousness, which in turn leads him to class struggle and socialism. Marx's worker is the historical worker, but he is the historical worker of a specific period of industrial and political development.

Even in interpreting the psychology of the worker of the transitional period, Marx exhibited a rationalistic bias. The worker's opposition to the capitalist order is a total opposition to its laws, its factories, and its government. But this revolutionary consciousness of the worker is to take him next to Marxist socialism, where he will accept the factory system and the state, the *only* difference being the abolition of capitalism. Why shouldn't the revolutionary protest of the worker flow into other channels: into rejection of industrialism as well as capitalism, into rejection of the socialist as well as the capitalist state? It is here that Marx is most definitely the child of his age, the child of rationalistic optimism: the workers will undoubtedly translate their anarchistic protests and grievances into a sophisticated philosophy of history. They will undoubtedly realize that the forces of industrialism and

modern life, which strip them of property, status, and economic
security, are in themselves benevolent in their ultimate effects
and that it is only capitalism and the capitalists which make
them into instruments of oppression. The chains felt by the
proletariat are the chains of the industrial system. The chains
Marx urges them to throw off are those of capitalism. Will the
workers understand the difference? And if they do, will they
still feel that in destroying capitalism they have a "world to
win"?

SOCIALISM

How different will the better world of socialism be from the old
one of capitalism? Marx and Engels have notoriously little to say
about the wonderful new world their criticism and theories imply. The wealth of observations and historical data illustrating
the nature of capitalism is paralleled by a skimpiness of reference concerning socialism: a few epigrammatic statements about
the general nature of socialist society, a few items of the political
program for the socialist parties, incidental references to the
contemporary socialist movements and such revolutions as the
Paris Commune, and that is all. The task of expounding the
Marxist canon in the very un-Marxist world of Western Europe of
the 1880's fell mainly to Engels. He wrote chattily and attrac-
tively, a fact that makes him, rather than his great companion,
the favorite of the popularizers of Marxism. His thought on the
main issues had, of course, for a long time merged with that of
Marx. There is in Engels, at the same time, a certain dilettantism
and a tendency to write around rather than to address himself
directly to the most important theoretical issues. At his death in
1895, the canon of Marxism was frozen, and the vital questions
of the socialist role in parliamentarianism, of the nature of transition from capitalism, and of socialism itself, remained to be
fought over by the Revisionists and the orthodox Marxists. The
fight, although accompanied by continuous invocation of the

scriptures, points up the really enigmatic and ambiguous nature of the Marxist argument as it touches the actual problem of socialism.

The apparent enigma disappears if one refuses to be distracted by the revolutionary phraseology of Marxism into believing that *from the economic point of view* the stage of socialism represents a drastic break with capitalism. Quite the contrary: socialism, once it assumes power, has as its mission the fullest development of the productive resources of society. Though private ownership of the means of production and the profit motive are abolished, the state takes on the mission, formerly performed by individual capitalists, of creating "those material conditions which alone can form the real basis of a higher form of society." The logic of the doctrine implies that in so doing the state will in no wise proceed differently from the capitalist: i.e., it will take the worker's surplus labor in the form of surplus value and will sink it in further investment. From the earliest, most revolutionary writings of Marx and Engels until the very end of their activity, there is no indication that society, until full material abundance is achieved (whatever that may be), can dispense with the organization of labor and production typical of capitalism. What, then, is socialism? *It is simply capitalism without the capitalists*. There is no need for elaborate descriptions of socialism. Except for the abolition of private property in the means of production (its rationalization), socialism continues and intensifies all the main characteristics of capitalism. The Bolsheviks and especially Stalin have been accused of perverting Marxism into state capitalism. Yet we need not burden Marx and Engels with the responsibility for Stalinism to perceive that the notion of socialism as state capitalism is found in the canon of Marxism under all the revolutionary and anarchistic phraseology.

When they wrote the *Communist Manifesto*, Marx and Engels were very young men. They could not deny themselves a certain youthful bravado ("Communism is already acknowledged by all European powers to be itself a power." (p. 320)—a ridiculous statement in the Europe of 1848) and a most literal attempt to *épater les bourgeois* ("The Communists have no need to introduce community of women; it has existed almost from time immemorial."—p. 340). Yet even in the midst of all this pathos, so typical of revolutionary manifestoes mushrooming all over Europe in 1848, there is a chilling reminder:

The proletariat will use its political supremacy to wrest, by degrees, all capital from the bourgeoisie, to centralize all instruments of production in the hands of the State, i.e., of the proletariat organized as a ruling class; and to increase the total of productive forces as rapidly as possible. (p. 342)

Even at the most revolutionary moment in their career, Marx and Engels do not envisage the worker getting away from the treadmill of the factory system, do not allow the industrial system other functions than the ceaseless race for more and more production, more and more accumulation. Nothing in *the logic* of Marxism should enable the worker to expect his standard of life to rise *immediately* following the revolution. Nothing in the doctrine extends to the worker the prospect of greater control over conditions of his work once socialism is established. The state runs the factories; and the socialist state, as much if not more than the capitalist, is interested in increasing production and productivity. The devices of workers' control, industrial democracy, and profit sharing by the workers receive in Marxism all the sympathy they would receive from an early nineteenth-century capitalist. To be sure, the worker will have the pleasure of seeing "the expropriators expropriated," and crises and unemployment will disappear once the profit motive is eliminated. Yet the worker remains subject to factory discipline. Socialism demands that everybody work, but it repudiates the idea that everybody should be paid equally. The emphasis on technology and productivity promises, as a matter of fact, that there will be a very considerable inequality in wages and salaries under Marxist socialism. How many proletarians would be likely to stir into revolutionary action if the logic of Marxism were thus expounded to them?

If there is a clear line leading from the logic of Marxism to certain central features of the development of the Soviet Union, we must still be on our guard against the gross and unhistorical tendency of reading into original Marxism a blueprint for Stalinism. Just as Marx's economic determinism and revolutionary activity are bridged by his revolutionary optimism, which makes him see *both* the economic forces and political action of the proletariat leading simultaneously to a revolution in the near future —so his rationalistic and democratic faith enable him to envisage a workers' state that continues some of the principal features of capitalism. The workers under capitalism hate the factory system with its discipline and monotony. Somehow, once the capitalists are gone, they will understand and approve the necessity of the very same system under socialism. They hate the centralized bourgeois state with its bureaucracy and police, yet under socialism they will accept and increase the powers of the state. Marx, in effect, promulgates an "abstinence" theory of the worker's socialism: once in power the workers are willing to forego the immediate fruits of their victory in order to build the material base for the next step, communism.

It was inherent in Marx's rationalist faith, a product of the century, to believe that the centralized state of socialism would somehow be drastically different from the bourgeois state just by virtue of being a workers' state. In commenting upon the Paris Commune of 1871, both Marx and Engels approved its democratic character, its "smashing" of the bureaucracy and the police, its making all offices, including the judicial ones, elective and revocable. *The Civil War in France* seemingly gives the lie to the accusation that Marxism under socialism means state capitalism and the old capitalist state. It praises the egalitarian character of the Commune's short-lived institutions and democratic instincts. Yet what is essentially a political pamphlet addressed to the political needs of the hour does not change the clear logic of the Marxist system. Marx approved the spontaneous democracy of the Paris workers after its suppression by the French government. Yet, had it survived, this democracy would have been expected to centralize the industrial system, to abandon its anarchistic undertones, and to recreate a society devoted to production. Marx could afford to be both a democrat and a Marxist because of his untested belief that the workers, having seized power under democratic and anarchist slogans, would willingly accept the Marxist, i.e., centralized, state and the industrial system and discipline of capitalism.

What would Marx have said of the Commune had it continued and expanded in power, but under the leadership and in the ideology of the Proudhonists and Blanquists who had led it in its failure? He was happy in his conviction that the absolute priority of building the economic prerequisites of the new order would be as evident to the workers once socialism won as it was to him now. He did not face the possibility that the worker who won power under anarchistic slogans might require an elaborate bureaucracy, secret police, and suppression of real democracy—in brief, totalitarianism—to make him submit to measures necessary for the creation of "those material conditions which alone can form the real basis of a higher form of society."

To approximate Marx's vision of the socialist state and socialist society, let us use a tangible example. Let us take the official theory and the constitution of the USSR, forgetting for the moment the *reality* of the political picture there. We see universal democracy, public officials freely elected and subject to recall. We see national self-determination and the fullest regional autonomy. Yet through the free working agreement of all parties concerned, Soviet Russia has a highly centralized planned economy. The citizens of their own free will, unanimously, forsake immediate improvements in their standard of living to build at a rapid rate the productive powers of the economy. This society has no desire for morbid introspection or highly personalized subjects in the arts and literature. There is no need, except in marginal cases, for the police or for oppression. Crime, when found, is a distant reflection of the pre-socialist past. The sense of creative partnership in socialist labor pervades everyone, and no one feels the presence of undue privilege or of a barrier to the full development of one's personality. This fairyland of Soviet propaganda probably comes close to what Marx imagined would be the reality of socialist life. He would not have approved some elements of even the official picture. No egalitarian, still he would almost certainly have been shocked at the extent and scope of the officially and cheerfully acknowledged disparities in pay and ranks, at the uniforms and official pomp. No model of intellectual tolerance, he was still a man of the nineteenth century for whom an officially approved theory did not put an end to a scientific discussion. But in general we shall not err by taking the romanticized self-portrait painted over the reality of Soviet life as coming close to the vision of Marxism. The logic of the doctrine found its fulfillment in Soviet Russia, but the accompanying dream of a democratic and humanitarian society found its place as window dressing.

That this should have happened is a peculiar irony of history. Marxism boasts of being scientific socialism, and the assertion is made with all the implications of being hardboiled, realistic, and done with all the moralistic nonsense that pervades other brands of socialism. Marx's revolution against the contemporary school of socialism is in fact more fundamental than his revolution against capitalism. Capitalism is a definite part of the historical process. Important elements of capitalism entered the blood stream of Marxism. The leading contemporary schools of socialism—those of Fourier, Proudhon, and Saint-Simon—

are, on the contrary, but secondary symptoms of the disturbance
and misery produced by capitalism and of no major historical
significance or revolutionary value in themselves. There is a
very human reflection of ideological rivalry in this appraisal of
Marx's. The story of his personal relations with other socialist
leaders is a partly humorous and partly pathetic tale of ex-
acerbated vanity, charges of plagiarism, and the confrontation
of the rigid and sensitive German academician with the easy-
going Gallic nature of a Proudhon or the Slavic disorderliness
of a Bakunin. These stories and the related one of Marx's anti-
Semitic vulgarity about Lassalle have provided excellent material
for those writers who feel Marx's chief failing to be his own and
his theory's lack of humor and other redeeming, if not dialectical,
human characteristics.

The major reasons for Marx's criticisms of other socialist
sects and their apostles are, however, more fundamental. In
the first place, there is the obvious criticism of the "utopian"
and other socialists for their belief that an amelioration of the
condition of the working class can come by good will, or by
propaganda, and without the realization by the proletariat that
only the full development of the productive forces of society as
well as the class struggle can bring about real socialism. For
instance, in his *Critique of the Gotha Program* (1875), Marx
assailed the newly born German Social Democratic Party for
the Lassallean phraseology of its program. Much of the criticism
is petty, a testimony to Marx's vindictiveness toward his colorful
contemporary. But there is also a sincere effort to teach the
German socialists that socialism is not merely vague talk about
equality and vague promises of social reforms, and that the
Socialist Party should teach its own followers a definite economic
and political creed grounded in the laws of historical development.
Even in a political program, one should not try to delude the
workers into believing that under socialism the total social
product will be distributed among them, with no deductions for

the communal needs, administration, and further investments. Nor should one equate socialism with complete equality. The first stages of socialist society will require considerable inequality, teaches Marx. "Right can never be higher than the economic structure of society and the cultural development thereby determined." [8] Even equality of pay according to the individuals' needs (an ambiguous formula) is left for that rather distant, "higher" stage of socialism—communism, in which the full abundance of material goods and the full development of the individual will permit the disappearance of the state and divisions of labor and allow the establishment of the principle, "From each according to his ability, to each according to his needs." [9] Only the remotest reach of the historical process is given over to the anarchistic dream of equality and no state.

What *loose reading* of Marxist politics would lead one to believe is that the immediate objectives of socialism are its distant by-products, according to the *Critique*. It is no wonder that the pamphlet, despite its brevity and compactness, has never been favored reading for the purpose of Communist agitation.

The other reason for Marx's revulsion against other brands of socialism is actually a variant of the preceding one: the revolutionary appeal of Marxism, despite its quite different logic, is essentially the same, addressed to the same instincts, as that of many contemporary socialist and anarchist movements. If "Property is theft" is the most effective Marxist appeal, it was also a slogan thrown by Proudhon; but in reality, of course, the Marxist theory teaches that property is something else. Had Marx been more cynical he might have urged his followers not to be carried away by their own propaganda. As it is, the revolutionary fervor of a Marxist is quite likely to carry him into anarchism, just as his sober realization of the material prerequisites of socialism may induce him to be patient with

[8] Karl Marx, *Critique of the Gotha Program*, New York, 1938, p. 10.
[9] *Ibid.*, p. 10.

capitalism. The secret of the proper blending of the two elements was something that the master tried to infuse in his followers. Thus, to apply the frightful semantics of the Communists, Marxism as a child revealed its parentage by being susceptible both to "right" and "left" deviationism. To Marx, the greatest danger came from the possibility of confusing Marxism with mere revolutionary socialism, with simple opposition to capitalism, and with the desire only for the destruction of the old order. Hence his intense irritation with his closest ideological relatives.

The vocabulary describing socialism and communism is as vague as it is rapturous. Following the destruction or collapse of capitalism, we are to get "the revolutionary dictatorship of the proletariat." The meaning of this celebrated phrase is quite obscure. Is it to be like the Paris Commune? Not likely, because, despite Marx's eulogy over the grave of the Commune, it had been dominated by the essentially anarchistic followers of Proudhon and Blanqui. We have said that Marx probably had in mind something on the order of what the Soviets pretend they have in fact. But the formula is certainly vague enough to accommodate a multitude of interpretations. All that Marx insists upon is that the essential features of the industrial system be preserved under socialism. Granted that it is difficult to see how "the revolutionary dictatorship of the proletariat"—which is helpfully defined as in fact being a democracy, because, unlike bourgeois democracy, it represents the domination of a vast majority over a small minority of ex-capitalists—could be very democratic. Would the dictatorship of the proletariat look kindly upon the formation of political parties demanding *immediate* equality of wages, workers' control of the individual industrial enterprises, or the abolition of factory discipline?

The next and final stage of historical development, communism, was painted by Marx and Engels in terms so nebulous as to suggest their relative lack of interest. We are told that com-

munism will come after the productive powers of the society
have been developed to their fullest and after human personality,
freed of the fetters of capitalism, has reached its highest growth.
Instead of the detailed constitutions of heaven offered by Owen,
Fourier, and Saint-Simon, the Marxists have to be content
with epigrammatic phrases about the passage from the realm of
necessity to freedom and about the fullest development of
everything. The practical sense in Marx scorned the easy task
of building utopias. The important thing is to get rid of capitalism without disturbing its industrial machine. The distant
phase of communism is simply everything that capitalism is
not, a consolation, perhaps, for the fact that socialism will have
to be so much like capitalism. It is a concession, an empty one,
to the anarchist in every revolutionary: the wondrous future
where there is no state and no division of labor.

Engels, in the famous passage in *Anti-Dühring,* was eager to
fill in some details. The abundance of goods under socialism
brings with it progressive attenuations of the repressive and
planning functions of the society. Labor becomes lighter and
less regulated, and various functions of the state superfluous.
Finally the state withers away. Human nature has been basically
transformed. It is only in this anarchistic and individualistic
paradise, which to a skeptic does not seem to afford much scope
for human activity, that Marx and Engels meet with Proudhon,
Bakunin, and Fourier and the subject of their quarrels, the
state, is finally laid aside.

Volumes have been devoted to the questions of whether socialism abolishes classes or class antagonism, what degree of material
influence must precede the passage from socialism to communism,
etc. Such disquisitions might best be left to the Communist
leaders and their philosophical attendants, who indulge in them
in the line of duty and as a relaxation from more practical
matters. In Marx's theory, the importance of communism, in
the technical sense of the term, is negligible. On the other hand,

in the Marxist movement, the propaganda value of the fact that
communism is often mistakenly read into the Marxist definition
of socialism has been enormous.

The relationship of revolution—i.e., seizure of power by the
socialists—to the stage of economic development of the given
society has justly been considered the most perplexing problem
of practical, as well as theoretical, Marxism. To young Marx, the
problem was relatively simple: capitalism in the most advanced
capitalist countries (particularly England) was drawing to the
end of its course; thus, there was no contradiction between the
political and the economic aspects of the problem. A democratic,
i.e., Chartist, revolution in England would soon be followed by
a socialist one: witness the strong socialist undertones of Chartism. This fantastic optical illusion, product of Marx's revolutionary optimism, that Western European capitalism circa 1850
had nearly reached its full economic as well as political development, could not withstand the experience of the three remaining
decades of his life. What Marx subsequently meant on the subject
but never quite brought himself to say was that a socialist revolution (i.e., the seizure of power by revolutionary socialists) and
the end of capitalism *as an economic system* need not coincide.
The socialists may—should—seize power if an opportunity war-
rants, even if capitalism has not reached its full development.
This is indeed clearly forecast in his *Address to the Communist
League* in 1850, which the Bolsheviks rightly considered almost
a blueprint for their tactics in 1917 in Russia.

According to the *Address,* a democratic revolution in Germany
is to be turned by the Communists to their own use and made
the starting point of a socialist one. Germany, no matter what
her stage of economic development, is to be seized by the socialists.
If capitalism has not fully completed its preparatory task for
socialism, then the socialist state should, first, finish the work
of capitalism. Thus, if small peasant holdings have not been

converted into huge capitalist estates, then it will have to be socialism rather than capitalism that delivers the *coup de grâce* to the independent peasant. If full state centralization has not been achieved, the socialists will have to press for it or accomplish it, and "they need not be misled by democratic platitudes about freedom of the communes, self-determination, etc." [10] Marx does not say, and the omission is understandable in a political address, that there are other tasks which socialism, in a country unripe for socialism, might have to perform in lieu of capitalism —breaking in the worker to factory discipline, discouraging the notions of the workers' control of industry, etc. Though the *Address* is principally tactical advice to the "workers" about what they should do after having overthrown, in alliance with the bourgeois democrats, the old regime, it is also a prescription for the socialists' measures after the death of "unripe capitalism." The revolutionary in Marx cannot quite wait for capitalism to die of old age, but the economic determinist in him knows that the necessary historical tasks of capitalism must be performed even under socialism.

The dazzling profusion of terms—capitalism, socialism, communism—each having a political as well as an economic meaning, and one shading into the other, may well induce the exasperation of the follower or critic. A witty British critic suggested that the title of a future book on the subject might well be *What Marx Really Meant, Actually*. The confusion is reduced if we remember that there are two consistent lines in Marx: one, of a revolutionary always against the status quo, feudal, capitalist, or whatever; the other, of a believer in the immutable laws of material development, which no *political* revolutionary could affect. At first, in Western Europe of the 1840's, it was easy to be both; later on it became increasingly difficult. It fell to his successors

[10] Karl Marx, "Address to the Communist League," in *A Handbook of Marxism*, edited by Emile Burns, New York, 1935, p. 70.

to try to reconcile the logic of the theory with its revolutionary emotion, in a world quite different from the one in which Marx and Engels had spent their formative years.

The circumstances of the times also dictated some secondary characteristics of the theory of revolution and socialism. To an age that was beginning to witness the stirring of subject nationalities, nationalism still appeared a passing phenomenon. The small politically minded element among the English, French, and German workers was internationally oriented, as were the middle-class democrats of these countries. If the fight against autocratic oppression by the Poles or Hungarians was felt by the enlightened men in the West to be a part of their own struggle, was the future fight against capitalism to be confined within narrow national bounds? And the national question was just a reflection of the economic and political oppression. With this oppression gone, nationalism itself was to find its fulfillment in internationalism, dictated by the ever-spreading network of industrialization. The logic of industrialization, which makes the workers into socialists, forbids them to become chauvinists. Hence the tasks and the natural inclinations of the proletariat are international in their character, and the bonds of the common chains infinitely stronger than the accidental ones of nationality or religion. This optimism, though it too did not remain unscathed by the developments after 1870 following the Franco-Prussian War, is never repudiated. And, sadly distorted as it has become in the main Marxist movement, it remains in Marxism an attractive reminder of the rationalist faith of the era when enlightened men believed that the conquest of the forces of nature would automatically banish injustice and intolerance.

An account of the original Marxist argument must close with a repetition of its major intellectual premise: history works out tidily, creating no problems it cannot solve. The observable economic forces of Marx's times must work themselves out fully to their logical conclusion, leaving no nooks and crannies of the social system where anachronistic economic phenomena lurk. Likewise, in individual consciousness no reflexes or instincts characteristic of pre-industrial society will be allowed to remain. Such is the Marxist world, into which generations of Marxists have had to fit their contemporary reality.

III THE SOURCES AND DYNAMICS OF MARXISM

If it seems illogical to follow a discussion of theory by detailing its sources, one must plead special justification in the case of Marxism. To see the main sources of Marxism is to explain its appeal. If the Marxist system as a whole strikes us as something too vast, overpowering, and complicated to exercise an immediate attraction on the minds and emotions of men, then the answer must be found in the character of some of its components. From Pareto to Schumpeter, unfriendly critics have sought the explanation of the appeal of a doctrine "so illogical and so dull" by consigning it to the realm of religion. An involved theology to amuse the intellectual and an appeal to the most primitive emotions to stir up the masses—such is the essence of Marxism under the veneer of its philosophical and economic system. If this were so, we would still be begging the question. Why Marxism rather than some competing religious system, also masquerading as ideology? To ascribe the cause of major historical events to human irrationality and the propensity to be duped does not explain anything except the underlying premises of the authors of such an explanation.

The source of the abiding influence of Marxism must be ascribed to the lasting character of human reactions to social change. These reactions may be rational or irrational, depending on one's definition of the term. But under certain conditions and at certain times, they will always characterize the human response to industrialization. The childhood and even the prenatal conditions of Marxism explain its fortunes as a mature doctrine and a fully grown political movement. The history of its sources is an explanation of its appeal.

INDUSTRIALIZATION

In the midst of revolutionary fulminations and economic theories, one postulate of Marx's may strike the reader with its unexpectedness: "Combination of agriculture with manufacturing industries; gradual abolition of the distinction between town and country by a more equable distribution of the population over the country." [1] This is a postulate of socialism, and the year is 1848. The modern reader will be puzzled. This is not the apprehension of an atomic war, or the answer to the spectacle of huge urban conglomerations creating insufferable traffic and supply problems. Even the "most advanced countries," to which the plan was addressed, presented in 1848, from our point of view, a picture of bucolic simplicity: overwhelmingly rural Germany, prevailingly rural France, and even England, where industrialization had not as yet destroyed the largely agricultural character of the economy. Why should a socialist basing his revolutionary expectations on the urban proletariat have reservations about the growth of the cities? And the apprehensions about urban civilization are balanced by a frank dislike of the countryside, of what Marx in the *Manifesto* engagingly calls "the idiocy of rural life." The misery and degradations of the cities and the primitiveness and lethargic condition of the country are constant themes of Marx and Engels. Socialism cannot be fully established nor communism begin to grow until the distinction between the city and the countryside is obliterated. Why?

The answer will go a long way to explain the assembly of

[1] *Manifesto*, p. 343.

interests and emotions that are the sources and the moving forces of the Marxist appeal. Marxism is *about* industrialism. It is not about equality. Even the anticapitalist argument is secondary to the concentration on the phenomenon of industrialization, with its destructiveness and its promises. The city is the symbol and the reality of modern industrial civilization. It concentrates people joined by nothing other than the accidents of employment and the necessity of earning a livelihood in industry or service. It is a visible demonstration of the soullessness and alienation of the machine age. Yet it is necessary, for without it there is no progress in industry, no progress in culture. Its crowded conditions, the friendless intimacy into which it forces the proletariat, the contrasts, visible to hundreds of thousands, between wealth and poverty, between crime and the protection afforded by authority to the rich and privileged, are in themselves lessons in the class struggle.

The countryside, on the other hand, presents the illusion of orderliness and social placidity. To the city proletarian, who has not yet lost his roots in the country, it is the place where he had status and stable livelihood, where the system of authority, being traditional, appeared less oppressive. Even the economic and political forces that destroyed the quiet of the village and made him come to Manchester or Lyons were somehow of city making, divorced from the natural mechanism of agrarian existence. For the actuality of agrarian pre-industrial existence, Marxism has nothing but contempt. Villages in the industrial age are locations of social torpor and superstition; and the peasant, unless stirred up by unusual exactions or distress, is a patient beast of burden, a potential tool in the hands of reaction. But for the ideal of human existence as embodied in the proletarian's dream of a "natural," stable, and egalitarian agrarian community, Marxism has the highest respect. That ideal, according to Marxism, embodies not only a temporary grievance and consequently an overidealized version of the immediate past,

but a constant element of the proletarian's psychology. It is
not merely a reflection of a period of adjustment and economic
distress, of sentiments that will pass or change once the economic
situation improves and a new set of values takes hold. The longing for the simple community and the nonindustrial life is a
constant source of revolutionary feeling and of the worker's unalterable opposition to the agent of the change, the capitalist.
Socialism, then, must mean extracting from the proletarian's
dream its justifiable human aspiration to a more dignified,
leisurely, and stable existence than that provided by the city—
the modern industry. But it must also mean the rejection of the
reactionary, utopian part of the dream, the idealization of the
coarse and unenlightened past of the peasant and the artisan,
and the illusion that that past may be recreated by rejecting the
machine civilization and its consequences, the city and the
state. Only the highest development of modern industrial forces
can bring about the ideal of human dignity and equality inherent
in the dream of the small agrarian community free from the
tension of modern industrial life.

The city and the countryside: two ways of life clashing—
neither of them in itself complete and adequate to the requirements of modern life—both of them having to undergo changes
and amalgamation before socialism can be established. Such is
the message of Marxism. Unlike some of his contemporaries,
Marx is not given to rhapsodies over the picture of model factories amidst green fields or to dreams of erecting little self-sufficient communities free from the taint of industrialism. Behind
the Hegelian phraseology of two opposites merging in a synthesis, there is evoked an acute intuition of the incompatibility
of two ways of thinking, two ways of life put in sharp contrast
by the rise of industry: first, the older agrarian order, based on
ancient traditions, providing if not material progress then a
modicum of economic and social security; second, the new
industrial order, whose only constant characteristic is change,

continual revolution in the productive forces, and consequent instability of employment and economic insecurity for the mass of the population. One appears "natural," sanctioned by long usage and habituation; the other "unnatural," bewildering in the variety of new habits, concepts, and skills it requires and constantly changes. This is the clash that makes Marxism and fills its formulas with life. The uprooted peasants and craftsmen recruited into the proletariat seek a personalization of the forces of change and disturbance. Marxism intuitively, though not without help, hits on a formula that explains and apportions blame for the destruction of a world which, as it recedes into the past, looks all the more—and unrealistically—stable and uncomplicated. Hence the proposal to combine the stability and simplicity of the past with unavoidable technological improvement. Hence the real meaning of "combination of agriculture with manufacturing industries" and "gradual abolition of distinction between town and country," which Marxism inscribes on its banners.

Across a century, a noted practitioner of Marxism restated the problem in more concrete if oversimplified terms. Wrote Stalin:

The problem of eliminating the antithesis between town and country, between industry and agriculture, is a familiar problem which Marx and Engels posed a long time ago. The economic basis of this opposition is the exploitation of the countryside by the city, the expropriation of the peasantry and the ruin of the bulk of the rural population by the entire process of development of industry, trade and the credit system, under capitalism. Therefore, the opposition between city and country under capitalism must be regarded as an opposition of interests. On this foundation a hostile attitude arose on the part of the countryside toward the city and "city folk" generally.[2]

[2] *Economic Problems of Socialism in the U.S.S.R.,* quoted in *Current Digest of the Soviet Press: Current Soviet Policies,* ed. Leo Gruliow, New York, 1953, I, 4-5.

We may amend the statement in some respects to get at the meaning of the conflict. The ruin of the countryside by the development "of industry, trade and the credit system"—in short, by industrialism—is the basis of the resentment, whether the development is done by capitalism or by any other system, as Stalin, of all people, had occasion to observe. Then the "hostile attitude toward the city and 'city folk'" is not a peculiarity of the peasants under industrialization; it is felt even more acutely by the mass of the "city folk," the proletariat. It is the basic, the instinctive form of Marxism among the dispossessed peasants, craftsmen, and unemployed workers who constitute the first waves of the industrial army.

Anti-industrial feeling is the basis of Marxist emotion, just as its opposite, worship of science and technology and faith in their limitless possibilities, is the basis of Marxist logic. Without the first, Marxism would not be a revolutionary movement, always relevant when industrialization hits a hitherto mainly agrarian and traditionalist society. Without the second, it would, like many of its contemporaries among socialist movements, spend its energies battling the unavoidable forces of modern life, unable to construct a working social system, even if it were to succeed as a revolution.

The anti-industrial feeling on which the Marxist movement subsists is not infrequently also the breeding ground of its elaborate theories. Human grievances do not indefinitely persist in abstract expression, as resentment against impersonal "forces." The anguish of industrialization finds a more advanced complaint in the proletarian's exaltation of the role of labor and in his hostility toward the visible agent and beneficiary of the economic revolution, the capitalist.

This was the plain sound, raw material of average working class opinion or instinct out of which, with the tools of Ricardian economics and the measuring rod of Patric Calquhoun's estimate that the wage earners received a bare quarter of the national income, scattered thinkers of that generation had constructed those theories of value, doctrines of the right to the whole produce of labour, which Karl Marx was subsequently to put into crabbed dialectical shape.[3]

The relationship is not that simple, and the genius of Marx consisted not only in distilling out of the proletarians' grievances their unconscious theoretical substratum, but in bending it into a system that harnessed the social protest to a philosophy and objective quite opposite to the worker's immediate aims. But anti-industrialism does find its practical meaning in anti-capitalism. In an industrializing society the appeal of Marxism rests on the fact that its *intermediate* aim, the overthrow of capitalism, coincides with the proletariat's instinctive reaction against industrialism.

Anti-industrialism and the most absolute faith in industrialization are the two interwoven themes of Marxism. They are so closely knit together that it is difficult to discern either in its full complexity or intensity. The anti-industrialism of the doctrine matches or surpasses in intensity the most violent anarchist sentiments. Its underlying faith in progress through science and industry sometimes leaves behind as pale and unsubstantial the most uninhibited liberal optimism about the benevolent effects of industry and free market.

It is necessary to explain more fully the phenomenon around which the two most actively operative parts of Marxism turn—industrialization. The setting is the first half of the nineteenth century in Western Europe. In our thinking about the phenomenon of industrialization, we visualize factories, railways, canals, etc. Or we think in more abstract terms about capital accumulation and the rate of growth. It is difficult for us—for we live in a highly industrialized society with more than a century of habits and techniques appropriate to it behind us—to realize the full complexity and meaning of the process. This is so even

[3] J. H. Clapham, *An Economic History of Modern Britain*, Cambridge, England, 1926, II, 477.

though in some of the most civilized societies there are still regions and groups, as in parts of the South, for whom the process is still going on. It is most difficult to understand the problem of human adjustment to the economic change, the revolution in values and habits that must precede and accompany the full functioning of the new society.

In Western Europe of that time, the process, although prepared for by the Enlightenment and by long commercial development, still manifested some elements of the shock that primitive societies, the "underdeveloped countries" of today's jargon, undergo when submitted to "Westernization." "Detribalization" may be too strong a term to apply to the situation of an English or Irish peasant whom combined economic and legal forces eject from his holding and force into a cotton factory, but it may not be too inappropriate a description of his situation and of his reactions to it. The bewilderment at the change, the confusion about its economic and political causes, and the shattering impact upon previously held beliefs are present in both cases. In the twentieth century, industrialization comes seemingly prepared by planning and buttressed by various devices (like social security) to ward off its most immediate anarchic and disruptive effects. But in the first half of the nineteenth century, Western Europe was at a disadvantage. Nobody, least of all the bulk of the industrial workers, was quite sure what was happening to the economy. Voices were heard quite late in the period questioning the veracity of official statistics that the population of England was growing under the Industrial Revolution, and maintaining that in fact the population was declining—this at the period of its greatest increase in history! A more serious debate divided those who saw further industrialization and depreciation of the agricultural interest as the surest road to economic ruin from others who urged manufacturing and trade as the only roads to salvation. The curious propensity of philosophers for seeing premonitions of disaster in the growth of material wealth was not escaped even by some of the most ardent advocates of the new age. The fear of mechanization as leading to widespread unemployment and the exhaustion of natural resources already exerted its gloomy fascination on some of the acutest minds of the era. How then could the common uneducated worker see the unmistakable proofs of progress in what was happening around him and to him?

Industrialization in the most immediate sense means an adjustment to the machine. This adjustment takes the form of the factory system, which in addition to the specific skills it requires of the workers, even at its most primitive, has the basic requirements of division of labor and industrial discipline. We need go no further to find the social basis and sentiment of Marx's "alienation of labor." Whether the worker feels that he produces the whole value or not, he will always feel oppressed by the discipline and monotony of factory labor. If the conditioning in industrialism, the immeasurably better terms of labor, and the immeasurably higher standards of living have not entirely erased these feelings among the workers in the most advanced industrial countries, how do the conditions of factory life strike those who are unused to it and who have to experience it under the most primitive and degrading conditions? Marx drew upon the reports of the Factory Inspectors to picture some of the worst cases of the worker's misery in the beginning phases of industrial capitalism. But any discussion of the excesses dulls the perception of the general shock that the shift to industrial life produces even *without* unreasonably hard conditions.

About labor migration and its connection with industrialism, a British historian wrote:

It is hard for one born in a mature industrial region, inhabited by a *race of patient and disciplined factory workers,* to realize the difficulties involved in the deliberate formation of a factory community, even where industrial habits and traditions are already well established among the local population. *In the course of a generation or two* it becomes quite "natural" for people to work together by hundreds in hot, humid, barrack-like buildings for a fixed number of hours each day, regulating their exertions constantly by the movements of tremendously powerful machinery. After a great war, or any other prolonged dislocation of industry, there may be some temporary restlessness among the "hands," but the routine soon reestablishes itself as part of the ordinary discipline of life.[4]

Before the *race of patient and disciplined workers* is created, it is not unlikely that these people experience their own version of what Marx tried to express by "alienation"; and it may take more than one or two generations before general anti-industrial feeling ceases to provide fertile soil for revolutionary protest.

The adjustment to the machine not only means the habituation of the worker to the factory existence. It means learning and accepting a whole network of ideas and customs. A commonplace feature of attempts at Westernization of backward areas has been the opposition often encountered among the population to the most ordinary and beneficial scientific or public health measures if they somehow clash with local customs and beliefs. The difficulties attendant upon the acceptance of science and rational criteria are compounded in the replacement of men by machines: this causes additional confusion and bewilderment, and, ultimately, in an agrarian society urged into industrialism, often results in revolutionary protest. Here again the recent experience of the more primitive communities in the process of seizure by modernization is helpful. Revolutionary movements are not infrequent when ancient superstitions, nascent nationalism, and distorted echoes of Western political ideas blend into a hopeless revolt against the new.

It is a far cry from an African territory of today, or the China of the Taiping rebellion, to even the most primitive area

[4] Arthur Redford, *Labour Migration in England 1800–1850*, Manchester, 1926, p. 18. (Italics mine)

of England or France at the beginning of the nineteenth century. But some of the elements of protest are similar. The Luddite movement, when, to the accompaniment of fantastic rumors, the displaced workers destroyed machines; similar developments of the first two decades of the century in France and elsewhere; the opposition to smallpox vaccination—these are but the most primitive symptoms of the incipient revolt of the simple people against the mysteriously changing circumstances of their lives. Progress and education may ride roughshod over uncivilized protests, but the shock of industrialization, instead of disappearing, will become greater even though the reaction to it becomes more indirect and subtle.

Beyond the machine and its consequences, the most important, though subtle, element of transition from pre-industrial to industrial mode of existence hinges on the notion of *property*. An agrarian society is built around the concept of property. Land is property, however much the concept may be attenuated by tenantship, serfdom, or membership in a commune. So is the artisan's shop and his tools of trade. The status that a peasant or craftsman acquires from the mode and quantity of his property is much more important than any other aspect of his social personality. What happens to the connection of status and personality under the industrial process is dramatically if exaggeratedly described by Marx in the *Manifesto*:

Hard won, self-acquired, self-earned property! Do you mean the property of the petty artisan and of the small peasant, a form of property that preceded the bourgeois form? There is no need to abolish that; the development of industry has to a great extent already destroyed it, and is still destroying it daily. . . . In your existing society, private property is already done away with for nine-tenths of the population; its existence for the few is solely due to its non-existence in the hands of those nine-tenths. (p. 335-337)

The process has not been that drastic or automatic, as Marxism has to its sorrow discovered. But the fact remains that one of the basic features of industrialization, transmuted into one of the most potent spurs to revolutionary feeling, is exactly the loss of "property"—hence, status—which the peasant or small craftsman experiences in becoming a proletarian. His previous existence or that of his father may have been, probably was, economically marginal, and his fresh status may mean a material advance. But as likely as not he will feel degraded, he will have the illusion of being impoverished, by the loss of his property. In a mature industrial society, where a man's status is measured mainly by the quantity of goods and services he commands, by his income, the social grievance caused by the exchange of a petty property inadequate to eke out a livelihood for the more varied and materially satisfying life will appear incomprehensible. But it will take more than one or two generations for the workers to lose the feeling of having been declassed just by the fact of being workers and of being cut off from their previous mode of existence and status.

The problem of the small producer, most commonly the peasant, so brusquely disposed of in the *Manifesto,* so readily assumed by Marxism to be solved by the very dynamics of industrialization and capitalism, has been both the crux of and the main impediment to the revolutionary appeal of socialism. Here it is sufficient to observe how varied are the revolutionary ramifications of the pressure exercised by the "city" upon the "countryside" during the initial, intense period of industrialization. Economic forces that make small-scale agriculture and crafts unfeasible or less and less profitable are at the same time the instruments for creating the labor force for the factories, the preconditions for science and sanitation, which lead, at first, to a prodigious growth of population. Economic crises and revolutionary stirrings reach not only the proletarian, but also the peasant or craftsman who is fighting, with the odds against him, against becoming a proletarian. Such is the initial impact of intense industrialization, and it is against this background that

Marxism drew its conclusions about capitalism and the class struggle.

Politically, industrialization means acceptance of the state. That the centralized and strong state is a necessary feature of industrialization may seem a paradox in view of the fact that the industrialization of Western Europe was carried through under the auspices of liberalism, which proclaimed as its political philosophy governmental noninterference with business and the fullest autonomy of the individual. Here the insight of Marxism shows more than historical appearances. A moment's reflection will show how much the laissez-faire state had to legislate in order to establish laissez faire; how the mass of regional peculiarities, of paternalistic laws, of pre-industrial customs had to be legislated away before the establishment of the legal and political prerequisites for the industrial order. When Rousseau wrote about the General Will and Hegel about the State's being the march of God in history, they were, in a way, giving expression to the longing for an authority strong enough to establish mores and an outlook for the whole society, something the most autocratic *pre*-industrial state could not do. There was no need for an English liberal to be lyrical or to engage in high-flown oratory about the state. The liberal state was legislating, almost unconsciously, a social and economic revolution, engaging, especially in the England of the thirties and forties, in what we would call today social engineering. The liberal ethos was finding its legislative expression, as in the New Poor Law of 1834. Not only the exclusive privileges of the land-owning aristocracy, but the whole network of legal and customary impediments to the business civilization, were being swept away by the action of the state. Politics was obediently doing the bidding of economic forces, of the ascending economic interests.

Even in the most mechanical sense of the term, industrialization means the age of regulation and a tendency to uniformity. Authority in a pre-industrial age may appear oppressive at the same time that it appears a part of the natural order of things. *Ideally* it does not interfere with the personal world of the lower orders: religion, family, "property," and daily life. Since nothing remains ideal there are moments of stress and rebellion, occasioned by unduly harsh exactions on the part of the authority, economic distress, or national and religious grievances. But in general a pre-industrial society will give a deceptive picture of placidity and harmony, for the natural radicalism of its typical member—the peasant—the product of his economic and legal helplessness, is held in check by his natural conservatism, by his attachment to and the belief in the permanence of his way of life. Once the "idiocy of rural life" gives way to the hustle and exactions of industrial existence, political authority appears in a different light. It is the state that somehow stands behind the forces disrupting the previous routine of life. It is the state that stands behind the factory owner and overseer. It is the rulers of the state who can decide whether food will be dear or cheap, who could, if they would, mitigate poverty and unemployment. To the disfranchised proletarian, there are no laws of economics superior to human volition; and if political authority has sanctioned the disruption of economic life, then it has the clear obligation to set it right, and its refusal to do so can mean only its unwillingness.

In the context of natural radicalism bred in the workers by the circumstances of industrialization, it is almost superfluous for Marx to teach the proletariat that the bourgeois state is the executive committee of the exploiting class. The state, in both its activity and its inactivity, as the policeman and the legislator, appears as the enemy. Perhaps the diagnosis is extended further. Authority of any kind, religious or political, is essentially a screen for economic oppression. Instinctive anarchism of the

large part of the proletariat is the legacy of the pre-industrial
age to the period of industrialization, of the "countryside" to
the "city."

ANTI-INDUSTRIALISM

"I have great pleasure in conversing with the lower part of
mankind, who have very curious ideas," wrote James Boswell.[5]
Boswell's pleasure might have been lessened had he foreseen
how within two generations the curious ideas of the lower orders
would come to affect the destiny of the more elegant part of
society. No sociological surveys enable us to ascertain exactly the
ideas of the French and English proletariat during the period of
the great economic transformation. The wealth of memoirs,
political reports, and even rudimentary economic surveys helps,
but the picture of the impact of industrialism is still like that
of the proverbial iceberg: a small part of it visible in the form
of theories, statistics, and political and social movements; the
greater part of it, the feelings and thoughts of the people affected
by industrialization, is submerged. We are forced to speculate
about the latter from an analysis of the former. But such deductions must be made with the caution that our asumptions about
the feelings of the proletariat are based on the opinions of a
small but very active minority. The historical and economic
literature of industrialization in the West supplements the raw
emotions of the political tracts.

To the affluent contemporary reader, the social historian pictures
the unspeakable horrors of the era which employed children as
mine workers and chimney sweeps. The economic historian adds
his reservations: for all the wealth of the data illustrating the
horrors, we must not conclude that the standard of living, say
in England between 1820 and 1850, was lower than before, that
the most intense period of industrialization was, as the agitator
and Karl Marx proclaimed, a period of unremitting suffering

[5] *Boswell's London Journal,* ed. Frederick Pottle, New York, 1956, p. 106.

for the worker.[6] Both the economic and the social historian may be right, each from his own point of view. Real wages may be on the increase and yet the confusing newness and lack of security of industrial life may create the illusion of a lowered standard of living and give the worker the feeling that the industrial process leads to his increasing misery.

The content of the "curious ideas" of the lower orders in the face of industrialization does not come readily out of the statistics or the contemporary parliamentary debates. It does not come with full freshness and directness from the plans of the reformers and system makers. The latter may infuse too much theory and logic into what is initially a spontaneous and bewildered reaction to a new world. It is best to approach the character of innate radicalism of the working masses by looking at earlier movements that embodied some of the angry bewilderment and opposition to industrialism. Their appeal to the masses may have been ephemeral because they have no well-thought-out reforms or even utopias to offer, or because what they demanded was clearly ruled out of order by the political and economic forces of the moment. But the very incoherence and temporary popularity of the protest help explain the abiding appeal of the more "artificially" constructed theories of reform and revolution.

A tangible example is the career of William Cobbett. Tory,

[6] "Again, the legend that everything was getting worse for the working man, down to some unspecified date between the drafting of the People's Charter and the Great Exhibition, dies hard. The fact that, after the price fall of 1820-21, the purchasing power of wages in general—not, of course, of everyone's wages—was definitely greater than it had been just before the revolutionary and Napoleonic wars, fits so ill with the tradition that it is very seldom mentioned, the work of statisticians on wages and prices being constantly ignored by social historians. It is symbolic of the divorce of much social and economic history from figures that, in a recent inquiry into the fortunes of one group of trades, the tradition of decline appears in the text, some corrective wage figures in an appendix and the correlation nowhere." J. H. Clapham, *An Economic History of Modern Britain,* Cambridge, England, 1930, I, vii.

then Radical, pamphleteer, and propagandist, he remains in history mainly as a colorful figure of English politics in the first third of the nineteenth century rather than as a major reformer or thinker. No primary, practical reform can be associated with Cobbett's name, as it can with Francis Place's. No specific socialist philosophy was developed by him, as it was by Robert Owen. And among those who struggled against and tempered the worst effects of the Industrial Revolution, he cannot be ranged at the side of Lord Ashley or John Fielden. Yet on the contemporary scene Cobbett was a man of considerable influence and of great appeal to the lower classes. His *Political Register* at times reached a circulation of sixty thousand— enormous, by the period's standards. The reasons for Cobbett's popularity must be sought, with all due allowance for his genius as propagandist and libeler, in his faithful portrayal of the common man's prejudices and grievances. No aspect of anti-industrial radicalism fails to appear in Cobbett's writings, which are a vast compilation of the emotions and prejudices on which radicalism, both left and right, feeds.

Cobbett's writings, from the beginning, when he was a Tory, to the end, when as a Radical he espoused the principle of universal suffrage, have the character of a criminal inquest on the subject, "Who is destroying the old England?" More specifically, what is destroying the most useful social class, the small farmers, "a set of men industrious and careful by habit; cool thoughtful and sensitive from the instructions of nature"? [7] At the foundation of the *Political Register* in 1802, the criminals were identified as domestic and foreign enemies of the Tory establishment: the political reformers and Napoleon. But the list soon lengthened to include the Tories, the system of government with its sinecures and corruption, and the royal family itself. Behind the outward agents of the change, Cobbett soon perceived the world of finance and industry which was taking

[7] *The Autobiography of William Cobbett,* London, 1948, p. 179.

over early nineteenth-century England: bankers, stock jobbers, rich Jews, and manufacturers. The oscillation from extreme conservatism and chauvinism, to radicalism is quite typical of the unreflecting radicalism aroused by the destruction of the allegedly simple, virtuous, and prosperous agrarian society. This radicalism was probably the secret of Cobbett's popularity among his countrymen. So was the idealization of the old: the love for the countryside, the harmonious life of the small cultivator, the virtues of family life on the land; and the defense of the traditional sports of bull baiting and fisticuffs. Farming, gardening, and animal husbandry receive from Cobbett almost as much attention as do the opprobrious inroads of the new civilization relentlessly defacing and destroying rural England.

At the later and more advanced stage of his activity, the simple picture of the clash of the two worlds was elaborated into an indictment of industrialism and of its social and political appurtenances. The enemy is now the machine, challenging the natural order of the world, which demands that "nine-tenths of the people should be employed on, and in the affairs of the land." [8] For the machine, as for such corresponding phenomena of modernity as smallpox vaccination, Cobbett had no use. The encroachments of science provoke a defiant reassertion of a number of popular superstitions (for example, horse hairs may occasionally turn into living things!).

In the same spirit, Cobbett, now a Radical, opposed any schemes for a national system of education. In brief, his radicalism became basically a passionate thrashing around in an anti-industrial fury. Compassion for the poor and exploited, and hatred of the exploiters and the privileged are not absent from his writings, but the driving force is uncomprehending hostility toward the new order.

The radical stage of Cobbett's activity coincided with the enhanced pace of industrialization and the intensification of

[8] *Ibid.*, p. 218.

social problems that followed the end of the Napoleonic wars. How simple radicalism and nostalgia for the idealized past may shade into political radicalism and a sort of home-made theory of class struggle becomes readily visible: "The march of circumstances is precisely what it was in France, just previous to the French Revolution. . . . The middle class are fast sinking down to the state of the lower class. A community of feeling between these classes . . . is what the aristocracy has to dread." [9] The formerly idealized landowner has now become an oppressor, only a shade better than the manufacturer or the banker, and the chauvinism of the earlier days gives way to the perception that the French wars were begun by the English ruling class to prevent reforms at home. Along with many other Radicals, Cobbett, who once objected to the King's dropping the "King of France" from his titles, now considered the victory at Waterloo as a sad defeat for the liberties of England.

Social indignation often turns into a generalized suspicion of the motives of the rulers, then into mistrust of the whole social and political system, and finally into the certainty that the system exists merely as a cloak over exploitation and oppression. It became necessary for Cobbett to illustrate how the last three centuries of English history had been, in effect, the history of the class struggle, how the Reformation had predestined the birth of the Stock Exchange and of the Bank of England, and how the Glorious Revolution had accelerated the race toward industrial towns and hypocritical political economists. The latter, headed by Malthus and Ricardo, were in Cobbett's view but the lackeys of the plutocracy, as were the greater part of the Liberal reformers headed by "Jerry Bentham, an egotist and coxcomb."

The indiscriminate attack upon men and institutions had one unifying theme—hostility toward anything and anybody con-

[9] *Rural Rides,* ed. G. D. H. and Margaret Cole, London, 1930, II, 665.

nected with turning England into an industrial society. A Protestant, Cobbett was driven into a eulogy of the Catholic Church, because that church was identified with the allegedly happy agrarian past and with the nonindustrial virtues of charity and toleration toward the poor. The full virulence of an extremely virulent pen is turned against those ethnic and religious groups that seem to thrive on industrialization and commercialism and that embody the virtues demanded by the new order of society. It is embarrassing for those who would claim Cobbett for a progenitor of English socialism to face his inflammatory language about the Jews and the Quakers. A relatively mild sample is his observation about the two groups:

Till excises and loan mongering began, these vermin were never heard of in England. They seem to have been hatched by that fraudulent system, as maggots are bred by putrid meat, or as the flounders come to live in the livers of rotten sheep. The base vermin do not pretend to work; all they talk about is dealing, and the government, in place of making laws that would put them in the stocks, or cause them to be whipped at the cart's tail, really seem anxious to encourage them and to increase their number.[10]

And the Methodist ministers are hardly better; they preach to the poor to be content with their miserable lot.

Writing at a much later date, Alfred Marshall employed the language of early liberalism in discussing the mental traits required of the pioneer capitalist entrepreneur. He had to have the ability to concentrate on the practical, an openness and alertness to new ideas, and a sense of proportion. Concludes Marshall, and the sentiment he expresses was a favorite motif of the great economist as it had been of the early liberals: "These are faculties which have been conspicuous in the Jewish race longer than in any other: but they were also such as could be, and

10 *Ibid.*, II, 512.

were, quickly and strongly developed in that sturdy English character, of which the foundation had been laid by the sea rovers." [11]

Industrialism and anti-industrialism are at opposite poles on the subject of the groups that seem to embody values destructive of the older order. In *On the Jewish Question,* young Marx gave proof of his affinity to anti-industrialism. The Jew expresses the essence of the bourgeois society; he is the carrier of the capitalist values. It is too much to read into Marx, or to explain his theories, by a species of masochistic anti-Semitism. The original, undifferentiated, anti-industrial radicalism is prone to anti-Semitism, for the the same reason that the liberal and business circles of early nineteenth-century England and France were filo-Semitic and pioneered in the social and political emancipation of the Jews. Over and above abstract principles and religious considerations, the dividing line was the acceptance or rejection of the civilization and its values, which the Jew (and, in England, some of the dissenting communities) appeared to symbolize. Cobbett's is the inflammatory language of anti-industrial radicalism. The element of ethnic hostility in it may become subdued or muted if that radicalism is assimilated into socialism. Or it may become expanded if the radicalism is absorbed into a revolutionary movement with nationalistic or fascist characteristics.

The stubborn refusal to recognize the facts of social and economic improvement is frequently a common characteristic of the conservative and the radical. The Marxist diagnosis of capitalism as leading to the worsening of the workers' standard of living is matched and surpassed by Cobbett's triumph over the facts in his assertion that population under industrialism tends to decrease. England's population during the Middle Ages must have exceeded her population of the 1820's.

[11] *Industry and Trade,* London, 1920, p. 48.

Populousness is a thing not to be proved by positive facts, because there are not records of the people in former times; and because those which we have in our days are notoriously false, if they be not, the English nation has added a *third* to its population during the last twenty years. In short, our modern records I have over and over again *proved* false. . . .[12]

The demographic revelations of Cobbett find a parallel in his historical discoveries. James II was a conscientious and freedom-loving king, his opponents scoundrels. History and economics of the past are frankly seen through the prism of the author's acknowledged biases. The rough and ready philosophy of history pictures it as a continuous story of trickery and exploitation of the ruled, engendered by the ascendancy of the materialist tendency ever since the Reformation. There is no well-conceived scheme of reform. The only solution is a return to the solid virtues of the past, the restoration of the yeomen class as the backbone of the nation, and a halt to industrialization and urbanization. Political reform, i.e., universal manhood suffrage and annual parliaments, is advocated by Cobbett in a spirit of pique at the upper and middle classes, rather than in a democratic spirit, of which he had very little.

The great agitator remains amidst the gallery of English politicians and reformers of his day as a uniquely naughty and biased, but thereby human, figure. His terrible prejudices are somewhat softened by a sense of humor, which made him ask of himself, in the midst of spouting historical nonsense, "Is this what you call writing a history?" The fact that he has appealed to people as diverse in their political philosophies as G. K. Chesterton and G. D. H. Cole shows the enigmatic character of the instincts and emotions of which he has been a spokesman. More than anybody else of the period, Cobbett with his likes

[12] William Cobbett, *A History of the Reformation in England and Ireland*, Philadelphia, 1843, p. 26.

and dislikes demonstrates the content of the "curious ideas" of the common man. "Cobbett and the people *felt alike;* that was the secret of his ascendancy." [13]

The stock of prejudices and superstitions and the blind opposition to the forces of modern life that Cobbett represents are merely the breeding ground of indiscriminate radicialism. There is not enough of systematic theory in his fulminations to classify Cobbett as anything but an anti-industrialist, but we shall not be far wrong if we borrow a term for the kind of response that Cobbett, the common man of the 1820's, evidenced toward industrialism and call it basically anarchist. Unyielding conservatism in the face of economic change, rejection of the most basic means of accommodation to the organizational and scientific requirements of modern life, what else is the basis of anarchist sentiment? This sentiment often masquerades under pretended reverence for the older and now impractical forms of authority and social organization, but it does not offer solutions for fitting the older values into the changed social and economic structure. Where can universal suffrage lead without a system of universal education? How can a class of prosperous small farmers be preserved, if there is to be no paper money, no centralized banking system, but on the contrary a positive discouragement of industry and technology? Insofar as it expresses anything, Cobbett's philosophy is simply the anarchistic radicalism of the displaced countryman, with its inconsistent but very human mixture of individualism and authoritarianism, of xenophobic nationalism and humanitarianism, a radicalism that can flow into a more practical political movement of the left or the right, but of itself can accomplish nothing because it negates the simple facts of life, because it is an emotion and not an ideology.

The idea of the "good old times" is in fact the springboard of as much revolutionary as reactionary feeling. Young Engels could write of the disappearing craftsman-peasant, whom he and

[13] G. D. H. Cole, *The Life of William Cobbett,* London, 1947, p. 269.

Marx were soon to classify as part of the passing "idiocy of rural life," in the following terms:

> True, he was a bad farmer and managed his land inefficiently, often obtaining but poor crops; nevertheless, he was no proletarian; he had a stake in the country, he was permanently settled and stood one step higher in society than the English workman of today. . . . They did not need to overwork. . . . They were, for the most part strong, well-built people. . . .[14]

The recovery of the lost virtues of the past through the most intense development of the new—such is the scheme of Marxism. And it is in the rejection and condemnation of the present that it strikes a sympathetic chord in the proletarian. In this sense, it is superfluous to seek elaborate proofs of the paternity of this or that theory of Marxism in Cobbett, the Chartists, or the contemporary French socialists. Marxism simply breathes the same air of half-nostalgic and half-revolutionary rejection of the bourgeois world and incorporates it in its revolutionary appeal.

By the time the *Manifesto* was published, the "Marxist" period of English politics was, in fact, drawing to its end. Cobbett had been its precursor, and Chartism its political expression. If Cobbett is sheer, unorganized, anti-industrial sentiment appealing to instincts only one step more advanced than those expressed in Luddite riots and smashing of factory equipment, then Chartism means a further advance: the grappling for political power. The Chartist movement was not, despite Marx's dictum, a working-class *party*. It was a movement, mass action, groping to become a party. Its antecedents were not unconnected with the feelings that gave rise to the kind of historical nonsense Cobbett propagated: a Chartist like Doubleday could say that universal suffrage had been the custom of the country until Henry VI, and since then the common people had been despoiled by the aristocracy and the middle class. The movement could still find its "practical"

---

[14] "The Condition of the Working Class in England in 1844," in *Karl Marx and Frederick Engels on Britain*, Moscow, 1953, p. 52.

proposals in schemes like Feargus O'Connor's proposed mass resettlement of the proletariat on land. But its unhistoricity and nostalgia are secondary to the two great prerequisites of the Marxist feeling: the identification of anti-industrialism with capitalism, and the idea that only political action by the proletariat can secure its economic emancipation.

Neither of these premises of Chartism is unblurred or true of the whole movement. Real Marxism obviously required a Marx, whom the Chartists did not have, while they did count a number of middle-class reformers and moderates in their ranks. But Disraeli expresses the opinion of a large part of the movement when he makes the worker in his *Sybil* say:

The Capitalist has found a slave that has supplanted the labor and ingenuity of man. Once he was an artisan; at best he now only watches machines; and even that occupation slips from his grasp to the woman and child. The capitalist flourishes, he amasses immense wealth; we sink lower and lower. . . . And yet they tell us that the interests of Capital and Labor are identical. . . .[15]

We are closer to the formula with which Marxism transmutes anti-industrialism into anticapitalism. In the speeches and writings of the radical Chartists, we repeatedly get the claim for the worker of the "whole product" of labor. The primitive statement of the labor theory of value (and the obvious deduction from it) had been something of a commonplace among radical pamphleteers and socialists before Chartism, but in the latter it became elevated into a political principle and a part of political propaganda rather than of theoretical disquisitions.

From the point of view of political action, abortive concepts of insurrections and general strikes, Chartism also impresses us as a harbinger of Marxism. Radical revolutionary movements up to that time were either conspiracies or demonstrations which, often to the surprise of the participants, turned out to be revolu-

---

[15] *Sybil, or the Two Nations,* London, 1927, p. 134.

tions. The latter had been the traditional pattern of French politics since the Revolution. In Chartism we get for the first time attempts at this "controlled spontaneity," which later on became so characteristic of the Marxist movement—attempts at the synchronization of revolutionary activity and awaiting the appropriate moment to bring out the "masses." The proponents of physical force in the movement (like James Bronterre O'Brien, who argued that usurping governments never abdicate of their own free will but only because of force or fear) had their counterpart in the advocates of "moral force," remote ancestors of the revisionists and gradualists of the Marxian movement.

The official platform of Chartism was, of course, the People's Charter, published in 1838 with its Six Points demanding universal manhood suffrage, equal representation, annual parliaments, no property qualifications for Members of Parliament, ballot, and payment of the Members of Parliament. The ostensible program was political and constitutional: a demand by the working class, or its politically conscious segment, for the extension to them of political power, which the middle class had secured in the Reform Act of 1832. As such, the movement was viewed sympathetically by some Tories, out of spite, no doubt, at the middle class, and even by some democrats within the business community. Essentially, Chartism soon took on the undertones of social radicalism and became a reflection of the workingmen's grievances at the new order established by the partial victory of liberalism in 1832. Chartism's high points of agitation—1839, 1842, and the final spurt of 1848—coincided with periods of economic distress for the working class and amounted to a near-revolutionary situation which certainly alarmed the possessing classes.

The triumph of liberal ideology and of the business interests, which in the mid-forties set England on the road to free trade, separated Chartism from many of its middle-class supporters. About the same time, the beginnings of protective legislation on labor put rudimentary curbs on the greatest abuses of laissez faire and thus set the stamp on the character of liberal society in England during the next fifty years. It was to be a society dominated by commercial and industrial values, buttressed by the liberal ideology. The gradual extension of the democratic principle to politics, and the very gradual and primitive adoption of rudiments of social legislation and recognition of unionism, were to temper the radical protest. And the development of industry and the rise in the general standard of living stripped this protest of its mainly anti-industrial character. The forces of social and economic development were going to thwart decisively the challenge to industrialism and liberalism that Chartism had represented at its most intense. They were to make sure that when socialism as a political force again came to England it was to come under different auspices and in a different spirit from that of anti-industrialism. "The Marxist situation" was gone forever from the English scene after 1850. With it went the possibility of developing a political movement of the Marxist type, toward which some Chartists like Harney and Ernest Jones had groped before 1850, but which when enunciated after that date was simply to be an eccentric political cult bypassed by the main social and intellectual currents.

The wrath of the working class as embodied in Chartism appeared to Engels in 1845 certain to "break out into a revolution in comparison with which the French Revolution and the year 1794 will prove to have been a child's play." [16] This wrath spilled over from behind the political petitions for the Six Points of reform into what appears in retrospect to have been the last desperate stand against industrialism and the modern state. The Poor Law Amendment Act of 1834 embodied the central points of the new liberal philosophy, with its mixture of philosophical radicalism of the Benthamite school, belief in the benevolence of free market and the virtues of self-reliance, and echoes of Malthus.

[16] Engels, *The Condition of the Working Class, op. cit.,* p. 52.

The Act abolished the old Poor Law, one of the remnants of the patriarchal notions of society dating from Elizabethan and preceding times, and substituted a "scientific" and "modern" principle of relief. Outdoor relief was, in effect, eliminated, and public support was to be extended only to those undoubtedly indigent, under conditions as strict as life in the poorhouses was to be unpleasant. The administration of the new law was centralized and nationalized. The premise seemed to be that unemployment and poverty were a sin if not a crime, and the liberal state took as its motto what was to become an echo of fundamentalist liberalism in Marxism: "Those who do not work, neither shall they eat."

For Cobbett, just before his death, the new law was the dissolution of the unwritten social compact by which the possessing classes held their wealth on the condition of help extended to the poor. For the radical Chartists, it was a device by which freshly triumphant capitalism was to create an industrial reserve army to do its bidding. "Yes, my friends, the New Poor Law is the last blood-stained prop by which the money monster hopes to sustain the tottering fabric of his cannibal system—of that merciless system, which first makes you poor in the midst of wealth of your own producing, and would then bastile and starve you for the fruits of its own barbarity," cried Chartist James O'Brien.[17] From the liberal point of view the law abolished an inefficient and antiquated system, promoted mobility of workmen and removed inducements to their idleness and reliance on public charity. This point of view was incomprehensible to the Tory anti-industrialists and proponents of the protection of the workingman, like the famous Richard Oastler, who openly incited to violence and defiance of the law. To the class-conscious Chartist leaders like O'Brien, the intent was all too clear, and only complete political democracy, whether arrived at peacefully or not,

[17] Quoted in *The Chartist Movement in Its Social and Economic Aspects*, by F. F. Rosenblatt, Columbia University Studies in History, Economics, and Public Law, New York, 1916, LXXIII, 51.

could prevent the fastening of the relentless yoke of capitalism on the British worker.

The richness and multi-varied character of radicalism as exhibited in Chartism still requires systematic treatment. What is important here, in this brief notice of its importance for Marxism, is exactly its partly contrived and partly spontaneous character. It is no longer merely a nostalgic look at the unreal past, nor is it yet an organized political movement with a theology and schemes of its own. Some Chartists persisted in die-hard opposition to the symptoms of the new—paper money and the factory —others want a managed currency and a central banking system to spur industrial production. There was the voice of the worker, too, still confused by what was happening around him but now asking questions. Thus, when the London Workingman's Association, led by the pioneer Chartist William Lovett, drafted an address to the American workers in the late 1830's, it congratulated them on having what the British did not, namely, a republic and virtual universal suffrage. But then it proceeded to ask:

Why have lawyers a prepondering influence in your country?— men whose interests lie in your corruptions and dissensions, and in making intricate the plainest questions affecting your welfare. Why has so much of your fertile country been parcelled out between swindling bankers and grinding capitalists. . . . Why have so many of your cities, towns, railroads, canals and manufacturies become the monopolized property of those who toil not, neither do they spin! . . .[18]

Why indeed? The stage is all set for Dr. Karl Marx to enter and provide the English workers with a precise answer why suffrage in itself is unavailing and what can be done about it. When in effect he does enter on the British scene with his answers, the London workers will no longer be terribly interested.

[18] William Lovett, *Life and Struggles of William Lovett in His Pursuit of Bread, Knowledge and Freedom*, London, 1820, I, 134.

It is too much to proclaim Marxism a child of Chartism. But it is not too much to affirm Marxism as being shaped by the *impression* of English politics and economics of the 1840's. In the course of a generation, the English working class appears to have progressed from uncomprehending protests against industrialism, through premature efforts at unionization, to the point of revolutionary action, to the point at which it asked questions about the relationship of politics and economics. It was not too much to expect that the next step must be a fuller understanding both of industrialism and of the necessity for socialism, and then a spontaneous revolutionary movement of the whole class. It is also not too much to read into the picture the universal and unavoidable characteristics of modern capitalism and of the effect it produces on the working class. Crude formulations of what later on become Marxist dogmas are commonplace in the mouth of the Chartist leaders: history as a panorama of the class struggle, progressive impoverishment of the worker under capitalism, the labor theory of value and its moral, the industrial reserve army of the unemployed and the monopolistic tendency of capitalism—they all find repeated expression, not as something the speaker announces as a discovery, but as something he assumes the workers know from their own experience. It is hardly important to trace these ideas to the French Revolution, to Ricardo or Robert Owen; the fact is that they appear to comprise what Marx was to call the class consciousness of the advanced worker of the Chartist period.

In observing the English scene in the forties and even the fifties, it was a pardonable illusion for the author of the *Manifesto* to believe that the industrial process under capitalism enables the worker, with barely any help from an agitator or economist, to approach his own *Weltanschauung* and to reach the Marxist conclusion. From this point of view, the English development between 1830 and 1850 was much more Marxist than the French one. In France during this period, one can observe a variety of revolutionary movements and stirrings, often of working-class origin, and a variety of socialist schemes and utopias propagated by individuals and sects. But there is little connection yet between the two, little evidence that *the industrial process in itself* educates the worker about capitalism in the way Marx and Engels believed it did in England. The revolt of the Lyons workers in 1831 was a reflection of misery pure and simple, and its only motto was "Work or death." Even the uprising of the Paris proletariat in June 1848 was caused mainly by indignation over the fact that the Second Republic had not ameliorated the worker's misery. In France, contrived socialist ideas floated on the surface of the revolutionary wave stirred by the misery and dislocation of industrialism and the general instability of the state. In England, socialism appeared to be generated by the revolutionary wave itself, but this wave beat impotently against the strength of the liberal establishment.

Marx and Engels did not become convinced of the strength of the latter until long after the demise of Chartism. For them the next step was to be a clearly socialist, clearly Marxist phase of the English revolutionary movement. The best commentary on such hopes is provided by the story of the individual Chartist leaders after 1848. Many of them who had fancied themselves before as the Marats and Robespierres of the coming English revolution spent their last days in pathetic Victorian middle-class respectability. Their revolutionary and reforming drive was channeled into petty and socially approved paths of reform, temperance, "elevating" the working class through education, and so on. The most typical worker among them, William Lovett, sought unsuccessfully to become a small businessman and toward the end of his life looked with horror upon socialism. He retained his belief that the British Museum should be open on Sunday, so that the workers could go there and "their vicious habits would yield to more rational pursuits." [19] The upper-class

[19] *Ibid.*, I, 59.

recruit to Chartism, Ernest Jones, whom Marx considered after 1848 as the most likely leader of the English Marxist movement and who was the most dashing and revolutionary of the left Chartists, ended as a candidate for a liberal nomination for Parliament. Jones, who for years after 1848 preached near-Marxist socialism and theorized about the monopolistic tendency for self-destruction of capitalism, finished his life almost as a Gladstonian liberal. Another left Chartist, George Julian Harney, lived as an inconsequential radical long enough to have his eightieth birthday fund subscribed to by, among others, the embodiment of big business and radicalism turned to imperialism, Mr. Joseph Chamberlain.

The stories are symptomatic not so much of men naturally abandoning the radicalism of their youth, as of the triumphant ascendance of the Victorian social and political spirit, which made the earlier radicalism simply unthinkable for later generations. Biographers of the Chartist leaders are often moved to ascribe to the movement the historical merit of initiating the democratic reform which eventually swept England and of setting up the foundations for the rebirth of English socialism in the eighties and nineties. This homage to men who, whatever they were "responding" to, were often courageous fighters against injustice confuses the nature of two socialisms. Modern English socialism, the product of Fabianism and the trade unions, is the result of mature industrialism, with few if any ties to the anti-industrial, anti-state feeling so important in Chartism. Of the older type, traces can certainly be found in the socialism of William Morris, in the early Independent Labor Party, and in the guild tradition. But the main current, as we shall see, is quite different.

As to democratic reform, it is interesting to speculate what would have happened had the Chartists' Six Points been in fact adopted, instead of the gradual approach to universal suffrage, achieved in practice in the middle eighties. One thing is fairly certain: the dynamic of England's industrialization and the formation of the "cake of custom" appropriate to it would have certainly been disrupted had a Chartist Parliament been installed. One can imagine reforms on the order of the National Workshops of France of 1848 being tried alongside state-supported schemes of land settlement. If acceptance of industrialization, in the social sense of the term, is a prerequisite to stable democratic institutions, then the victory of Chartism might not have benefited the long-term prospects of democracy and might have made the English development similar to that of France, or led to a situation in which Karl Marx's hopes would not have been entirely disappointed.

LIBERALISM

The term *liberalism* has faded to the extent that everybody in the West who is not a self-declared fascist lays claim to being a liberal of sorts and programs ranging from extreme conservatism to communism are advocated in the name of "liberalism." Something of the *original* flavor of English liberalism comes out in Francis Place's prophecy about the socialists in the Chartist movement:

As the best men in the working class proceed in their attainment of knowledge, they will cease to enforce their mistaken notions, and this will be called abandoning their caste by those who remain unenlightened; and these men, and such other men as have power over multitudes of other men, and have sinister objects to accomplish, will misinterpret to the many the actions and opinions of those who have become more enlightened. . . . In the meantime many of the incorrigible leaders and large numbers of their followers who are unteachable will be wearied out with continued and rapidly recurring disappointments, will draw off to be replaced by better men; and notwithstanding the times of inactivity and despair which will occasionally occur, the progress of actual improvement in right thinking will go on with increased velocity.[20]

[20] Quoted in Graham Wallas, *The Life of Francis Place,* New York, 1919, pp. 383-384.

Thus Francis Place, not a middle-class manufacturer or economist, but a radical political reformer sprung from the proletariat. What is "right thinking" is determined by the principles of Utilitarianism and of political economy. The "mistaken notions" are those of socialism, or of the power of the trade unions to affect the workers' wages in defiance of economic "laws."

The quotation is typical of the deterministic rigidity of the liberalism that ruled the intellectual climate of England from the 1820's until the end of the century, its greatest and most extensive reign over morals, legislation, and the economy occupying the first forty years of the period. The power and self-assurance of English liberalism dwarfed movements and opinions opposing it. Though there were no public-opinion polls at the time, it is not unreasonable to assume that the conglomeration of opinions and movements known as Chartism enjoyed at times in the forties some measure of sympathy from the majority of the nation. Yet the waves of Chartism beat ineffectually against the rising liberal establishment. The ideology or parts of it made the round of the world. At home all the animadversions of the Carlyles, Ruskins, and Newmans could not keep it from becoming the ascendant intellectual doctrine, any more than the Cobbetts, the Tories, and the Chartists could keep it from becoming the basis of English laws and institutions for nearly a century.

The content of early liberalism is not easy to decipher. We do not begin to describe it by seeing it, as did Mr. Laski, mainly as the philosophy of business civilization or as a cloak thrown over vested interests. Nor is it sufficient to center it around the belief in the self-regulating market, the belief which, according to Karl Polanyi, was the major historical error of liberalism and the source of all our troubles since.[21] We gain little in comprehension by reading our contemporary ideas and alternatives into the past. Complete determinism and its relative in historiography —"What happened had to happen the way it did"—are no worse

[21] Karl Polanyi, *Origins of Our Times: The Great Transformation*, London, 1945.

than their opposites, which, for instance, would tax Cobden and Gladstone with not anticipating the ideas of Keynes and Beveridge. There is no denying that liberalism became, par excellence, the philosophy of the bourgeoisie and a rationale of the laissez-faire system, and that the connection influenced the philosophy itself. But it was not invented for this purpose, nor was it merely a reflection of business interests.

In dealing with liberalism, it is again wise to recognize the distinction between the great body of theories and philosophies that comprise its basis and what might be called the liberal outlook characteristic of a class and a generation. The philosophers from Adam Smith to John Stuart Mill largely shape this outlook and express some of its most salient characteristics. But liberalism as a whole is not simply the sum of its parts. The liberal spirit is at once broader and perhaps less sophisticated than the theory or theories of liberalism. The distinction, though it may seem fanciful, is always an important one to bear in mind in the case of a social or political philosophy that is not only a body of theories but also the basis of a popular movement. In the theoreticians of liberalism we find not infrequently a note of pessimism about material progress, questioning of whether the ever-expanding productive capacity of society may not be arrested sometime or whether it indeed leads to human happiness. The father of liberal economics, David Ricardo, expresses this (heretical from the liberal point of view) doubt:

Happiness is the object to be desired, and we cannot be quite sure that, provided he is equally well fed, a man may not be happier in the enjoyment of the luxury of idleness than in the enjoyment of the luxuries of a neat cottage and good clothes. And after all we do not know if these would fall to his share. His labour might only increase the enjoyment of his employer.[22]

This line of pessimism runs through Malthus to the man who expresses the transition from earlier to latter-day liberalism,

[22] *Letters of David Ricardo to Thomas Robert Malthus,* ed. James Bonaro, Oxford, 1887, p. 138.

John Stuart Mill. Yet how unrepresentative this is of the general spirit of liberalism and of what the followers of Ricardo and Mill took to be the main tendency of their teachers. Their tendency was one of triumphant materialism, of continued and indefinite improvement of mankind through material progress. This unsophisticated confidence, which permeated the middle class and spread to the rest of the nation in a manner unmatched in any other European country, was necessary to beat down and then practically extinguish the almost equally massive surge of anti-industrialism, as exhibited in Chartism. The workman William Lovett, coming to abhor the anti-industrial socialism of his youth, is matched by the Tory statesman writing, "If you had to constitute new societies, you might on moral grounds prefer corn fields to cotton factories; an agricultural to a manufacturing population. But our lot is cast, we cannot change it and we cannot recede." [23] The nostalgic retreat of other viewpoints, the helpless acquiescence of other classes, would not have been possible without the solid and unbroken confidence of middle-class liberalism.

Liberal materialism, then, came to be identical with belief in industrialism. To the middle-class reader who cared but little about the constitutional schemes and devices of Jeremy Bentham, the practicality and iconoclasm of Utilitarianism became a social gospel. Distrust of sentimentality on social questions, of too abstract principles in politics, the questioning of every institution by the standard of usefulness—these were the basic instincts of practical men, who now found a philosophy telling them what they felt. Materialism, which to young Marx meant emancipation from the miasma of Hegelianism and endless philosophical discussions, and a road to finding out how people, classes, and nations really behaved, was to the middle-class liberal the concrete reality of his social and professional life. Progress in science and technology was an unqualified good, and the task of society was to sweep away all impediments to it.

[23] Sir Robert Peel to William Croker, quoted in *Croker Papers,* London, 1887, II, 383.

It is no wonder that this massive self-confidence in industrialism was to lead to England's industrial supremacy in the world, just as it was to lead to the squalor and ugliness of the English industrial cities. The liberal spirit considered mechanical works and other trophies of industrialism more aesthetically pleasing than castles and green fields. The humanitarian objection was swept aside as unreal. Place no impediments on material progress and other social goods will eventually be added: education and a higher standard of living for all. Tamper with industry in the name of the most elevated idea and everything will be jeopardized. Had he felt the need to justify his function, the liberal businessman would have subscribed to one part of Marx's portrait of the capitalist: ". . . he thus forces the development of the productive forces of society, and creates those material conditions, which alone can form the real basis of a higher form of society, a society in which the full development of every individual forms the ruling principle." [24] Compared with this function, what is that of a carping critic or a social reformer? How ridiculous it is to glorify the pre-industrial past with its long history of barbarity, superstition, and wars, or agrarian existence with its "idiocy of rural life"! And how mischievous it is to propose to turn political power to the as yet uninstructed masses, who would use it to destroy the only means of bringing them out of their present misery and ignorance, industrialization!

The liberal spirit made the same selective use of the economic theories of Smith and Ricardo as it did of the politics and social psychology of Bentham. From the latter it took its utilitarianism and iconoclasm and largely ignored its extreme democratic conclusions and bureaucratic hints. The economics of Smith and Ricardo were not unqualified endorsements of free trade and industrialism. They were born in the still prevailingly agrarian country, where manufacturing was of the small-unit variety and the most fundamental economic questions turned around fiscal

[24] *Capital,* p. 649.

and trade policy. The liberal spirit lost many of its earlier economic inhibitions in the worship of industrialization pure and simple. Here again, Marx is a reliable guide as to liberalism's appraisal of the task it was performing:

The bourgeoisie cannot exist without constantly revolutionizing the instruments of production, and thereby the relations of production, and with them the whole relations of society. . . . The bourgeoisie has through its exploitation of the world market given a cosmopolitan character to production and consumption in every country. To the great chagrin of reactionaries, it has drawn from under the feet of industry the national ground on which it stood. . . . It has created enormous cities, has greatly increased the urban population as compared with the rural, and has thus rescued a considerable part of the population from the idiocy of rural life. . . . Independent, or but loosely connected provinces, with separate interests, laws, governments and systems of taxation, became lumped together into one nation, with one government, one code of laws, one national class interest, one frontier, and one customs tariff. (p. 324-326)

And the famous tribute:

The bourgeoisie, during its rule of scarce one hundred years, has created more massive and more colossal productive forces than have all preceding generations together. Subjection of nature's forces to man, machinery, application of chemistry to industry and agriculture, steam navigation, railways, electric telegraphs, clearing of whole continents for cultivation, canalization of rivers, whole populations conjured out of the ground—what earlier century had even a presentiment that such productive forces slumbered in the lap of social labor? (p. 326)

The sober businessman could not have approached the lyricism of Marx in the *Manifesto*, but would have granted that the passionate German did justice to the historical task of liberalism. The meaning of Marx's words becomes more clear cut if for the "bourgeoisie" we substitute "industrialism." The belief in the all-encompassing, benevolent powers of industrialization is the central point of the liberal spirit, the belief which in its most fanatical and unconditional form is the legacy of liberalism to Marxian socialism.

The industrial orientation of liberalism combines with its class-interest component in the plea for state noninterference. In the fathers of liberal economics, there was never a clear-cut argument for *absolute* laissez faire. Bentham's political philosophy bears a bureaucratic tinge. Voices for factory legislation in the 1840's were raised not infrequently by liberal manufacturers, though more typical was the liberal member of the Commons who argued that his profit was made in the last two hours of his workmen's labor and that to cut off those hours would make him bankrupt and his men unemployed. Class selfishness, in other words, though prevalent, was not as strong as the industrial mania. The two coalesced easily in the belief that social reform and economic regulation were the devices by which the aristocracy was fighting a retreating action and would thwart the benefits of industrialization and free trade. The typical liberal, as in Morley's portrait of Bright,

. . . was carried along by vehement political anger and deeper than that, there glowed a wrath as stern as that of an ancient prophet. To cling to a mischievous error seemed to him to savour of moral depravity and corruption of heart. What he saw was the selfishness of the aristocracy and the landlords and he was too deeply moved by the hatred of this, to care to deal very patiently with the bad reasoning which their own self-interest inclined his adversaries to mistake for good. His invective was not the expression of mere irritation, but a profound and menacing passion.[25]

If we supplant, as the object of hatred, the aristocracy by the bourgeoisie, the description could be Marx's.

Moral anger aroused at the irrational privilege, at the fostering of what it considered economic superstitions, made the liberal

---

[25] John Morley, *The Life of Richard Cobden,* London, 1918, I, 209.

spirit suspicious of state action. Yet it is not entirely inconceivable to imagine, in different historical circumstances, the same men working to build industrial society, with the same passions and uncompromising vigor, as state-installed managers and bureaucrats, rather than individual entrepreneurs. But not in a society in which the British "are a servile aristocracy-loving, lord ridden people, who regard the land with as much reverence as we still do the peerage and baronetage." [26] Social antagonism can be a powerful spur in economic activity. The liberal industrialist, in his furious activity, was not without the grim comfort that his exertions were showing up the social uselessness and parasitism of the aristocracy. A century later, the same masochistic self-sacrifice on the altar of industrialization was to be urged upon the Soviet worker and manager.

If Marxism inherited much of the industrial mania of the early liberal spirit, then this spirit itself was not without a certain one-sidedness and intolerance for different standards of value. The source of this intolerance, again a paradox and an analogy to Communism, was not so much class selfishness but precisely the sense of social mission, of performing the necessary and inevitable task of industrialization and modernization, of rescuing England and then the whole world from superstition and backwardness. One cannot blame a contemporary observer like Marx for incorporating in his theory the conviction that industrial fanaticism and self-righteousness were indelible traits of the capitalist. That the capitalist would grow more humane, that he would slacken in his ceaseless pursuit of accumulation and expansion, were not impressions readily warranted by the English social scene of the 1840's and '50's. It appeared then equally unlikely that the capitalist would modify his values or submit without the use of force to the full panoply of the welfare state: state regulation, unionism, and high taxes. The continuously and increasingly dissatisfied worker facing the inflexible capitalist—

[26] *Ibid.*, II, 20.

this fairly realistic picture of early industrialization is taken by
Marx to express the eternal law of capitalism.

Sources of the ethos of industrialism have been sought in religion, more specifically in the Puritan tradition and Calvinism.
Theories of this kind, whether presented with the scholarship
of Max Weber or with the vulgar exaggeration of Cobbett, are
elusive of proof. It is equally difficult to establish related notions
of religious influence: for example, the often stated assertion
that Methodism had a quieting effect on the revolutionary turbulence of the masses. Industrialization and unbridled laissez faire
were both attacked and defended from the religious point of view.
There is no question that the spirit of liberalism was a secularizing
one, temperamentally antipathetic to excessively doctrinal and
ritualistic creeds; and yet no strict lines of religious divergence
can be established paralleling the defenders and attackers of the
new order.

What is more important here is attention to what might be
called the general assimilationist bent of liberalism and its
premises. It would not have occurred to the average liberal to
demand conformity, strongly addicted as the movement was
to individual freedom. Yet rationalism and industrial and political progress were equated in his mind. The spread of industrialization undermines the irrational institutions of the past,
in themselves reflections of obsolete economic forms. Industrialization and education will eventually impose the same rationalistic,
materialistic, middle-class stamp on men everywhere. The average
liberal would have thought it inconceivable that a fully industrialized and rational society would shelter such phenomena as
Catholicism, nonobjective art, Christian Science, militarism, and
socialism. Tolerance, which is justly associated with the liberal
spirit, was initially due to its invincible conviction that it was the
"wave of the future."

We might digress here and anticipate the discussion of Soviet
society. The startingly Victorian code of morals (if we omit the

religious element) and arts that the Stalinist period fastened on Soviet society flows rather logically from this fundamentalist liberalism ensconced in Marxism. What the liberals—and Marx —assumed would result automatically from the development of economic forces and the adjustment of social values to them was in the Soviet Union created by decree. Both early liberalism and Marxism carry in them the premise of conformity, even if this premise is coupled with the promise of the fullest flowering of individualism once the social environment (largely through this conformity) provides the appropriate material basis.

The passion for freedom in liberalism is not unconnected with this rather oversimplified—from our point of view—estimate of human nature. No doubt about man being formed by his environment, no doubt about material progress beneficently transforming human nature. The outook of Dr. Marx stares at us from many of the preconceptions of liberalism, but it is in vain that one looks for Dr. Freud. It is difficult to find a society so self-congratulatory for its virtues, for dissipating the darkness of the past, and for discovering the true principles of moral and social improvement, as English liberalism of the mid-nineteenth century.

. . . give me a sober Englishman possessing the truthfulness common to his country, and the energy so peculiarly his own, and I will match him for being capable of equalling any other man in the everyday struggles of life. He has a self depending and self governing instinct which carries him triumphantly through all difficulties and dangers. . . .

writes Cobden.[27] The drunkenness of the lower classes and the perversity of the upper ones were blemishes that the progress of education and of democracy would remove, thus eventually uniting the whole nation in the industrious and sober virtues appropriate to modern civilization. The note of nationalism was seldom chauvinistic. Industry and commerce would inculcate

[27] *Ibid.,* II, 26.

in other nations the virtues suitable to self-government and individual freedom. If liberalism did not aspire to build internationals, it was for the same reason that it disdained to legislate conformity. The forces of history would chase away militarism and despotism. Noninterference abroad was the concomitant of individualism at home. Revolutions abroad, if directed against the type of forces that had opposed the Reform Act of 1832, were justified. With a great deal of reason, liberalism considered itself a revolutionary force on a world scale; and, had it known the frightful semantics of the twentieth century, it would have classified upstart socialism as "counterrevolutionary."

The preceding statement is of necessity an oversimplification. Just as social historians have in this century poked holes in "capitalist realism," with its picture of steady material and national improvement, so novelists and biographers have penetrated behind the façade of monotonous virtue and optimism of liberal society. Contemporary critiques, both conservative and pre-Marxian socialist, take as their point of departure a simple dislike of the new order. More recent criticisms illustrate the inner doubts, psychic suffering, and pessimism behind the Victorian façade of self-assurance. But the oversimplified view brings us perhaps closer to the viewpoint of a revolutionary like Marx, to whom liberal society did not even pay the compliment of political persecution, and who spent the greater part of his life in England, unnoticed and ignored. In his absorption with drawing up a list of indictments against liberal society, Marx was carried a long way toward acceptance of its values and ethos.

The main accusation against liberalism is not the unreality of its values—industrialization, rationalism, and individualism—but the hypocrisy inherent in their being combined with the bourgeois system of property. The unreal Marxist worker does not reject the gospel of hard industrial labor, the aim of comfortable existence, the plea for democracy and education. His quarrel with bourgeois society is that through its institution of property it denies to him the realization of his essentially bourgeois and liberal values. Marx's technological and scientific enthusiasm and his acceptance of industrialism have often been compared or traced to Saint-Simon. The great French philosopher had a mania for science and technology and some interesting ideas as to how the world might be arranged to further their development. But the technological obsession of liberalism was expressed not in extravagant theories but in the actual development and transformation of French and especially British societies. Just as Marx's conclusions about the revolutionary propensity of the proletariat are affected more by the reality of contemporary *movements* like Chartism than by revolutionary socialist *theories,* so the technological and industrial component of his socialism owes more to the absorption in and the reaction to the reality of industrial life under liberalism than to any theoretical cult of industrialism.

The reluctance of Marx to draw up any detailed socialist utopias may be another reflection of the air of practicality that characterized political life of the prototype of industrialism, England. Chartism, for all its land schemes, concentrated on the struggle for political rights. English liberalism progressed from the day of Bentham, with his constitutional models ready down to the last detail, to practical matters of political and economic reform. This air of practicality, of ready and immediate application of broader principles to political action, which was to give Marxism its unsurpassed advantage in competition with other socialist movements, is a direct inheritance of a society and a period which, whether in reform or revolution, was given less to brooding about right, wrong, and the ideal than to action. The great moral of contemporary liberalism is that an ideology which cannot be translated into political action is pointless. Revolutionary movements in Europe of that day often had one strategy, *coup d'état,* and one aim, the realization of a particular political or social utopia. By observing English liberalism between 1830 and 1850, we can draw closer to the conception of the political party inherent in later Marxism: *a political movement in being,* having its ultimate aim (even a utopia) but going after its objectives step by step, if need be forming temporary alliances, compromising, but never abandoning its objectives. What in contemporary British society was the result of fortuitous circumstances becomes, in mature Marxism, elaborated into a conscious system: a political party with a rigid program and ideology, but capable of basing its political tactics on an analysis of shifting social and economic forces in the given country.

The earliest political Marxism of the *Manifesto* still has the revolutionary impatience and immediacy of the utopian socialists. Later Marxism, although Marx and Engels never lose their revolutionary optimism, is mellowed into conceding the possibility of gradualism. One may at least conjecture that this fact, which gives Marxian socialism staying power not possessed by its rival revolutionary doctrines, penetrates the doctrine from an impression of the triumphant ascent of English liberalism.

". . . and notwithstanding the times of inactivity and despair which will occasionally occur, the progress of actual improvement in right thinking will go on with increased velocity."[28] This is a sentiment that Marxism, in effect, enrolls among its own. Place's condescension toward those who do not see the world the way he does is repeated by Marx's, even though the latter expresses it with greater violence and bitterness. The "other side" of Marxism is in effect a kind of integral liberalism of the early variety, liberalism unmellowed by absorption in democratic politics and untempered by conversion to social legislation. The *intellectual* atmosphere of Marxism has that excessive rationalism, historical iconoclasm, and defiant refusal to go below the material surface to probe human motives which have often made early liberalism unmarketable to the masses while endearing it to the scientist, engineer, and social planner, all struggling

[28] Place, quoted in Wallas, *op. cit.,* p. 384.

against inherited irrationalities of every social system and all seeing in science and technology the only roads to human emancipation. Marx and Engels, by setting their industrial and scientific creed within the frame of a revolutionary movement, shifted the emphasis of the early liberals. To the latter, democracy and individualism were the end products of free development of social and economic forces. Even a reasonable degree of economic equality was not beyond the ken of the earlier liberals, but they envisaged this development as the end result of a free growth of capitalism. "Time is a great equalizer," Bentham said, while rejecting progressive taxation as a logical corollary of his "felicific calculus." The liberal's realm of freedom was, like Marx's, to follow the realm of capitalism, but there was no intervening period of socialism. Furthermore, liberalism soon underwent "secularization," i.e., adjustment to actual politics: political and social reforms soon became tangible measures of freedom and ends in themselves, and these ends had a suspicious correspondence to the aims of the middle classes. Just as the revolutionary side of Marxism is couched in the violent and bitter language of contemporary, essentially anarchist, socialism, its "positive" side is couched in the liberal idiom of the century, and its better world to come is described in the humanitarian, cosmopolitan, and democratic terms of the liberal paradise.

To repeat, unlike the conservative or anarchist critics of bourgeois civilization, Marx and Engels are not really shocked by the appearance of bourgeois industrialism, by its money grubbing, or by its bad taste. Bourgeois civilization is bad because its values can be realized only by a small minority of the population and because it is predicated upon the growing misery of the masses. Once the revolution is effected, the logic of Marxism parts company with such aesthetic protests against capitalism as those voiced by Ruskin, Herzen, or William Morris and finds a more congenial association in the values and the spirit of the early liberal entrepreneur.

Liberalism as an enthusiastic response to industrialization and modernization and then as a rationale of their most intense development is a direct ancestor of Marxism. We shall not be surprised to see Marxist revolutions, carried out under anarchist, anti-industrial slogans, turn around after victory and sacrifice on the altar of industrialization and its logical corollary, the centralized state, the slogans that brought them to power. Suppose we make the absurd assumption that the real objective of Marx and Engels was to wean the masses of the freshly created proletariat from their unconstructive anti-industrial feelings and to convert them to the necessity of an industrialized society and a strong state. What better ideology could have been devised than one that asserted the inevitability of thorough industrialization and centralization and that placed the blame for the miseries of the transition, not on industrialism as such, but on the anachronistic and hence vicious role of the capitalist and "his" state. This legend is helpful in making us realize how much of raw liberalism there is in the Marxist system, and how the industrial mania of his Communist followers was not unanticipated by the father of the movement.

Apart from inculcating on Marxism the industrial mania, English liberalism was instrumental in the formulation of other related points of the dogma. Economic determinism, although it had been proclaimed before by Marx and was implicit in contemporary socialist and liberal thinkers, could take on flesh and bones from the observation of English society and the ascendance and character of its liberalism. From a historical perspective, we can now say that Britain was not the norm, but one of the rare examples of a society where, for a time, economic forces, the prevailing social ideology, and political power supplemented each other and made possible a feat of economic transformation which in its completeness and relative speed was approached in the twentieth century only by a totalitarian state employing totalitarian means. The naïve complacency of a

Francis Place over the dying out of the anti-industrial spirit and its "wrong" ideas was not disturbed by the reflection that this was due not only to the inevitable assimilation of the liberal values by the nation, but also to England's advantage of being first in the industrial race, dominating international trade and finance, and not having, after 1815, major wars. The permanent ascendance of liberal values based on their healthy materialism and their eventual spread to all parts of the world were taken for granted by the early liberals. As young Marx, in this respect a faithful interpreter of the liberal spirit, asserted in the *Manifesto,* the growth of industry and rationalism everywhere would do away with wars, despotisms, and protection. At home the full flowering of industrialism would put an end alike to the pretensions of the aristocracy and to the illusions of the proletariat about trade unions. The road to domestic as well as international utopia lay through the forces of production, which (again Marx) "alone can form the real basis of a higher form of society, a society in which the full development of every individual forms the ruling principle." [29] The universal enthronement of individualism, enlightened democracy, and perhaps a world order were to liberalism the inevitable result of economic forces, just as to Marx the same forces were creating universal socialism. No national differences, no social or economic lags, could, in the long run, interfere with this process.

How close to our own feelings this aspect of early liberalism is; how evident it is, for example, in the whole program and plan for economic assistance to underdeveloped nations; and yet how unreal to us is the easy optimism that underlies it. Today a variant of this materialistic utopianism is found only in the official speeches of Communist leaders. But even they, in fact, are no more confident that material forces, unaided, can bring victory to their side than is a Western statesman when he declares that an improvement in the standard of living will bring democracy

[29] *Capital,* p. 649.

in Africa or Asia. Contemporary expressions of both liberal and revolutionary optimism sound hollow when compared with their original prototypes. We know now that no other society in the nineteenth century became so thoroughly industrialized, in fact as well as in spirit, as England. Furthermore, even a considerable degree of industrialization has not brought to many other societies the benefit of stable democracy. Rigid determinism of the Francis Place type showed itself to be an illusion based on the observation of one society during one period of its development, just as the related Marxist determinism misinterpreted even more fundamentally the social meaning of England's industrialization.

Professor Dicey traced to about 1870 the decline of the original individualistic liberalism and the shift to its collectivistic stage in England. The shift in the intellectual atmosphere is best epitomized by J. S. Mill's words in his *Autobiography* when he forsakes his earlier belief in the automatism of economic forces and qualifies his democratic belief by the need for state action to provide the framework for meaningful citizenship. There is a straight line from his avowal to Fabian socialism. With this later liberalism, so prone to turn into welfare-state socialism, Marxism has nothing in common. Neither its social analysis nor the chosen path of reform, through the democratic process, is understandable in Marxist terms. Nor did Marx and Engels foresee that at the close of the nineteenth century working-class socialism in England would arise from satiation with industrial values rather than as a reaction to industrialism and liberalism as had been true of earlier working-class radicalism. The industrial mania of earlier liberalism was mellowed and qualified by the achievement of industrialization and the subsequent realization that in itself industrialization did not provide all the answers to the social problems of mankind. The dogmatism and spiritual aridity of the earlier liberal spirit gave way to a variety of, actually, more tolerant, if also less self-assured and certain, liberal opinions. But Marxism persisted in seeing in the capitalist of 1900 his ancestor of 1850; in the democratic state the limited-suffrage institution dominated by the bourgeoisie; and in the social welfare philosophies the rationale of the class interest of the exploiters. With its anachronistic picture (insofar as the West was concerned) of its old enemy—liberal society— Marxism also preserved unimpaired its original characteristics— uncomplicated materialism, belief in economic "laws," and passion for industrialization.

SOCIALISM AND ANARCHISM

In considering the relationship of Marx to earlier and contemporaneous socialist thinkers and movements, it is well to keep several points in mind. Marx was a great synthesizer and a voracious assimilator of ideas and social facts. At the same time, his receptivity to new ideas and movements definitely slackened after about 1850, when the main outlines of his system were laid and he entered on the task of elaboration. Thus his thought, it is hardly worth repeating, bears the imprint of many minds and many movements. But beyond identifying the great intellectual traditions in which Marx and Engels were nurtured— Hegelianism, English political economy, and socialism—it is difficult as well as almost superfluous to trace this or that idea of his to this or that socialist thinker. Many of his most startling concepts to us were virtual commonplaces of the English and Continental radicalism and socialism of his formative years. Were the radical implications of the labor theory of value taken by Marx from John Francis Bray, William Thompson, or John Gray? It is fairly unimportant to decide, for not only they but a host of others, economists, agitators, and politicians, voiced rough and ready versions of the same theory. Modern economists, while assailing Marx's economics, praise him for foreseeing at that early date the future tendency of capitalism toward economic concentration and monopolies. To be sure, the classical economists of the period thought in terms of perfect competition and lived in the era of a multitude of small producing units. But predictions of the future bigness and concentration of business were not unique among the radical reformers and socialists. That most impractical of men, Charles Fourier, feared the coming of the era of "industrial feudalism." So did Sismondi, Blanc, and a host of others. The old academic game of "tracing the influence" of this or that thinker or theory does not go far enough in explaining the sources of Marxism or of its influence. To ascertain the doctrine's affinities to and differences from other socialisms, we must look at the principle of selection that Marx employed in taking and rejecting items from the common fund of contemporary radicalism.

It is also worth keeping in mind that Marxism is interested in "ideas in action," ideas that are not only the product of an individual's mind, but that are, or appear to be, postulates or practical demands of a class. Hence it has been asserted here that Marx was more influenced, both consciously and unconsciously, by Chartism on one hand and liberalism on the other than by all the productions of the plethora of individual socialists. The splendidly arrogant words of the *Manifesto* claim for Marxism this double advantage of being a part of actual life—of the thought and feeling of the working class—and of transcending that thought and feeling by understanding history and, hence, the future:

The Communists, therefore, are on the one hand practically the most advanced and resolute section of the working-class parties of every country, that section which pushes forward all others; on the other hand, theoretically, they have over the great mass of the proletariat the advantage of clearly understanding the line of march, the conditions, and the ultimate general results of the proletarian movement. (p. 334)

Other socialist theories, according to Marx, fall to the ground on either of these two counts: they are unthinking reflections of the *immediate* feelings of the proletariat and pay no attention to the historical causes of the given situation; or they are intellectual creations divorced from the life and aspirations of the worker. This self-proclaimed function of Marxist socialism as the vanguard of the working class has, of course, been established as the organizational principle of the Communist Party of the Soviet Union. It enabled Marx to view other socialist thinkers either as stragglers wandering off the road of the historical march of the working class, or as persons in the ranks, their view obstructed by the multitude around them, and thus unable to see clearly what the head of the column, i.e., Dr. Karl Marx and Friedrich Engels, saw. This vision persisted through the days when, inexplicably, the masses became separated from the vanguard, and the latter, instead of leading a victorious march, found itself doing scholarly work in the British Museum. History seemed to have punished Marx for the presumption of his youth; and when he was on his deathbed in 1883, his theory must have appeared to many just as "utopian" as those he and Engels had scorned.

From a longer perspective it must be admitted that Marxism's self-appraisal and judgment on the competing socialist cults contain a great deal of truth. No other brand of socialism was so insistently a blend of actual workingmen's grievances and acceptance of the logic of the system that had led to those grievances. Many of the contemporary socialists say, in effect: "Give me but a chance to put into effect my own scheme, and human grievances and dissatisfactions will disappear." Others are just as ready to lead a revolution without inquiring where it will eventually lead them. Fourier on one hand and Blanqui on the other, stand as examples respectively of the fanciful deviser of utopias and the unreflecting exponent of revolutionary action. Petitioning the great of this world to put their fancies into effect or storming the barricades, are the recipes of these early socialists for realizing their ideas.

A modern socialist may well conclude that Marx was right in his slighting condescension toward his rivals. Yet a more balanced judgment must acknowledge the tremendous importance of the early socialist thinkers. A closer look at them will explain not only certain points of original Marxism, but even more clearly the factors that influenced the acceptance or rejection of Marxism by sections of society in various countries.

To return to the simile: the claim to be both a part and the vanguard of the working class illustrates not only the strength but also a certain weakness of Marxism. One cannot have one's cake and eat it too, even if one specifies that the two actions are to be separate parts of the historical process. Marxism *has* to sacrifice a certain part of its sensitivity and appeal to the working-class grievances when it accepts the logic of industrialization, just as this acceptance *has* to be modified toward revolutionary appeal. To that extent, Marxism is a much less faithful reproduction of the actual worker's revolutionary feelings than that found in some Chartists (for the British worker) or in Blanqui or Proudhon (for the French). The absoluteness of the belief in the environment's shaping of man comes out more strongly in Robert Owen and the technocratic cult appears more forcefully in Saint-Simon than even in Marx. A brief consideration of some of the early socialists may bring out which elements in Marxism will appeal to which social force or intellectual tradition in a given country.

The dates of some of the great precursors of socialism give a clue to the characters of their doctrines: Saint-Simon, 1760-1825 —Robert Owen, 1771-1859—Fourier, 1772-1837. Their roots are very definitely in the spirit of the Enlightenment. Theirs is the temperament of the reforming *philosophe,* with his neat schemes and model settlements, and the unthinkability of achieving reform aims through popular or political action. It is the Englishman Owen who comes closest to the notion of political action among the working class and political agitation. But even Owen was ready to memorialize William IV, the monarchs of Europe, and Metternich on behalf of his scheme, and to preach conversion to his ideas through the example of model communities. And then there are the stories about Saint-Simon writing to Napoleon and Fourier pathetically awaiting a rich philanthropist to finance his phalansteries. Alas, our heroes lived before the age of the Carnegie, Ford, and other American foundations! But their delusions about the eventual appearance of an "angel" who would finance the one certain way to salvation are not just tragicomic incidents of their biographies. Nothing is more alien to their spirit than the Marxist dictum that the emancipation of the working class can be only achieved by the working class itself. Their mechanistic approach to the social problem and their expectation of patronage in the construction of a new political and social system separate them from the spirit of modern politics.

Equally outdated in terms of nineteenth- and twentieth-century politics, though in a different way, is the type of socialism represented by Auguste Blanqui (1805-1881). This is insurrectionism pure and simple, with but little thought of devising elaborate schemes for the day after the revolution. Blanqui's socialism lives entirely in the conspiratorial world. It is akin to the conspiratorial groups of revolutionaries, whether quasi-socialist or nationalist in character, that flourished on the Continent between 1815 and 1848 and constituted the backwash of the revolutionary and nationalist excitement stirred up by the French Revolution and the Napoleonic wars. The dazzling possibilities of a *coup d'état* on behalf of an oppressed class or nationality stirred up men's minds from Paris to St. Petersburg. The immature revolutionism that would persuade a group of students, young officers, or radical workers that political power in the modern state could be seized and consolidated by a demonstration or conspiracy is another, if more advanced, variant of the model-community-building mania of the earlier socialists. In neither case is there any idea of converting a large part of the nation to one's revolu-

tionary program or of fitting the program in with the postulates
and interests of a class. The realities of politics, especially of
Continental politics, make utopian expectations of conversion by
the example of a model community or romantic revolutionism
the only ways for those who would change the world. We are still
in the days of mass illiteracy, of no or limited suffrage and
parliamentary institutions. By the same token, the Leviathan,
the modern state, is still in the process of growing. It appears
not unthinkable that the course of a society may be changed
by the actions of an enlightened autocrat, the good will of the
great, or a determined action by a relative handful of men.

In the *Communist Manifesto* and in the activities of the
Communist League, we find numerous traces of romantic insurrectionism; in another decade after 1848 it is almost gone from
the European scene, and the last traces, barring distant echoes in
Russia, will be found in the Paris Commune. In pouring abuse
and ridicule on most of the contemporary socialists, Marx and
Engels were blind to the element of utopianism and insurrectionism in their own manifesto. The specter that haunted the
Guizots and the Metternichs of the day was not one of the little
group headed by Marx and Engels but of the general revolutionary
excitement unleashed by the forces of modern life upon the old
or slowly changing order: nationalism, schemes of social reform,
and democratic and liberal stirrings. The heritage of earlier
utopia-building, sheer revolutionary excitability, and conspiracy
thus becomes a part of early Marxism, but already because of the
British example it is subordinated to the study of the organic
growth of society and of its "laws." Thus in the edifice of Marxism, in addition to its exposition of the logic of industrialism
and its summation of anti-industrial grievances, are present unreflecting revolutionary enthusiasm and utopianism.

What lies behind them is the vivid recollection of the French
Revolution and the Napoleonic period. Continental socialism in
its beginnings was not a response to the social question. The

poverty of the most numerous class and the attempt to alleviate its lot were almost an afterthought, even with Saint-Simon. Socialism, even before it became harnessed to the task of revolution or reform or concentrated around the phenomenon of modern industry and the modern state, was born out of one central intellectual current and one great historical experience. The intellectual current was the scientific curiosity of the Enlightenment, which made men think of applying social engineering to society. Yet it would not have occurred to Rousseau, Mably, or Condorcet, any more than it would have to Sir Thomas More, to found a movement to push toward the realization of their ideas. The French Revolution and Napoleon provided the examples both of popular passion stirred up on behalf of political ideas and of attempts at social engineering on a vast scale, and a tangible refutation of the conservative thesis that social change is the work of generations and cannot be accomplished by a man or a movement. Socialism, which had always existed as an intellectual or religious fad or literary exercise, thus emerged in the form of schools of thought after the great historical experience. It was another and even more pervasive experience—industrialization—that turned socialism from utopian projects and schemes of *coup d'état* into political movements.

The France of Marx's youth and mature age provides the classical example of the evolution of socialism from intellectual fancies into a political movement. In England, the tempo of industrial advance catapulted the quasi-socialism of the Chartists into the political spotlight, only to grind it equally quickly under its wheels. In Germany, the national problem subordinated the social one. It was in France that socialism preserved longest its "academic" character: an individual's search for a solution to the puzzle of a changing world and the first attempts to anchor this solution to the feelings and interests of the people.

This really primitive phase of socialism has some interesting characteristics, which appear in unequal proportions in its leading exponents. One is the obsession with the religious problem. The religious mania, in the form either of defiant atheism or attack on religion as identified with and comprising the established order, is no more pronounced than the religious or quasi-religious character given by the critics to their own systems. With the liberals or with Marx, the whole matter of religion is definitely pushed to the secondary plane. For them religious values either fit the values of the rising industrial society or they are an anachronism, in the process of being removed by material progress and education. The preoccupation with the religious problem of a socialist or a radical thinker is an indication in itself that a basic prerequisite of industrialization, a certain secularization of thought and life, has not been achieved, and that *the problem of reform or revolution in itself appears as a religious one.* That a religious dogma might dominate a society practicing *his* system would be as inconceivable to Robert Owen as to Saint-Simon, Fourier, or Proudhon, for their systems are essentially religious cults.

This characteristic intolerance was partly inherited by Marxism but with much less intensity, for Marx also partook of the liberal assumption that the problem would solve itself, and, this being the case, why attack the obsolete remnants of a dying order while a more potent enemy was at hand? Thoroughgoing materialism in a materialistically minded society cannot be intensely violent or intolerant on the religious issue. The passion and energy expounded by some early socialists in their love-hatred complex about Christianity were devoted by Marx to the assault upon capitalism, and by a liberal to a concrete political, economic, or religious reform. But enough of the older socialist tradition rubbed off on Marxism so that, in some future "underdeveloped" society, Marxism will appeal to a young intellectual as a liberating religious cult. Actually, the main interest of the doctrine lies elsewhere.

The preoccupations of the fathers of socialism tell us a great deal about their underlying premises. Politics was still viewed from the religious standpoint; the way of putting their theories into life, apart from the immediate instrument of a benevolent patron, lay essentially in indoctrination in the given cult. The mantle of a prophet was needed, for it covered the authoritarian conviction that the masses would never achieve or learn anything through the actual circumstances of their lives, but would have to be taught like children through example, authority, and indoctrination. The essential goodness of man and his perfect malleability by the environment were the common sentiments in the profuse socialist literature. But what could be done to lift from the masses the dead weight of superstition and traditionalism, abetted and exploited by kings, aristocrats, and priests? Only the moral passion of a new religion or doctrine could accomplish the task, not ballots or the forces of production.

It might seem that this irrationalist view of human nature and the consequent authoritarian premise would be absent in Saint-Simon. Admirer of science and technology, praiser of British parliamentary institutions who wanted a parliamentary confederation of Europe, lover of liberty, Saint-Simon seemingly stands as an exception to what has been said here about pre-Marxian socialism. Yet, what this apparent rationalist recommends in the end, is a religion of science and social welfare—and the word *religion* is employed not as a figure of speech but in the literal sense. "Princes, listen to the voice and God, who speaks through my mouth . . ." proclaims the author of New Christianity. In his new Christian society, the preachers will "make their audience tremble by painting the horrible situation which is the fate in this life of a man who has incurred public disesteem; [they] will even show the arm of God raised against a man, all of whose feelings are not dominated by those of philanthropy." [30] The poets will be required to help the "preachers" by writing their poetry in what might be called "new Christian

[30] *Nouveau Christianisme,* Paris, 1832, p. 68.

realism," and so will the musicians with their music. The
Catholics and the Protestants are heretics for reasons that are
spelled out by Saint-Simon with more eloquence than coherence.
How rationalist and scientific is the spirit of this cult of rationalism and science?

The same question might be addressed to Robert Owen, with
his inflexible conviction that "each ˙individual is so organized
that he *must believe* according to the strongest conviction that
is made upon his mind; which conviction cannot be given to him
by his will, nor be withheld by him." Hence the positive evil of
all religions.

It is necessary, therefore, that all doubt respecting the fact stated in
this law of our nature should be forever removed from the human
mind and until this shall be effectually done, it will be impracticable
to train man to become rational in their thoughts, feelings, and
actions, and equally impossible to form arrangements to train them
to become intelligent, sincere and permanently happy.[31]

The same note appears in Fourier and others and culminates
in Proudhon's interminable tirades about religion and his own
exposition of the essence of Christianity. Though none of the
great precursors of socialism advocated the use of force—which
appears in nineteenth-century anarchism à la Blanqui—their
authoritarianism is unmistakable. Mankind will see the light
and somehow extinguish the old superstitions and adopt the right
principles of behavior. Yet, their disciples will ask, what if the
superstitions cannot be removed simply by demonstrating their
error because they are abetted by powerful vested interests?
Isn't the moral fervor of early socialism eventually bound to flow
into these socialist movements, which take a less optimistic but
a more activist view about the propagation of their doctrine?

The reverse side of the religious obsession of the early socialists

[31] Robert Owen, *The Book of the New Moral World,* London, 1842, p. 39.

is their scientific mania. Here again, the actual meaning of their use of the term *science,* like that of "religion," has to be carefully considered. When we spoke before of the cult or religion of science and technology inherent in early liberalism and taken over from it by Marxism, we used a figure of speech describing the intensity of the feeling and wonder about the freshly demonstrated powers of science and industry. But the wonder at all those things (which today we can appreciate only by recalling our reaction to the harnessing of nuclear power) in liberalism or even Marxism never takes the form of an *actual* religion, with the appurtenances of worship, saints like Newton and Descartes, or confusion of one's own dogma with the law of gravitation— in brief, the form of obscurantism. A doctrine that worships science against the background of industrial development is unlikely to get unhinged and enthusiastically incoherent on the subject, just as a materialistic doctrine does not get violent on the subject of religion if it is posed against the background of a materialistic society. Industrialization makes a society absorb its original wonder at science. If it proceeds rapidly, science becomes an accepted and unsensational part of daily life. The anti-industrial obscurantism of a Cobbett is no more characteristic of the period of transition than the scientific obscurantism of the early socialists and their attempt to base their theories, whether pro- or anti-industrial, on "science." The pitiful complaint of Fourier expresses this spirit:

Philosophy maintains that God has not made the code for our industrial and social relations, that his providence has not provided for them; but he made this code for creations infinitely greater and smaller than we are; the stars and the insects. Is it not possible that the Revelator of these laws of attraction should be destined to fulfill this role for mankind? Opinion of the world extols Newton who began the calculus of attraction and has luminously treated the material world: would it not be advisable to accord a test to the continuator of Newton, the man who has explored other branches of attraction and whose theory follows on all points that of Newton . . . ? [32]

—that is, to Fourier himself! Science is something wonderful and magical. It is not integrated with any specific economic or social force. In the name of science, Saint-Simon demands centralization and economic planning; and in the same name, Fourier and Robert Owen demand small autonomous communities of essentially agrarian character. This reception of science is really quite "unscientific"; and the strange ideological concoctions which in a backward society are often the products of the impact of a technologically more advanced civilization, the mixtures of scientific, traditionalist, and religious ideas, are somewhat of the same order.

It may be that this view of the use of science in earlier socialism does injustice to Saint-Simon. In his sensitivity to scientific progress, his plea for government by a scientific and managerial elite and for international organization, some have found a remarkable preview of the main tendencies of modern life. His appreciation of the development of history has been favorably compared with that of Marx. Engels' laudatory comment in *Anti-Dühring* sets Saint-Simon alongside Hegel as a great thinker. It is impossible at the same time to dissociate Saint-Simon from the general characteristics of which we spoke before. On many counts he shows a remarkable intuition and insight; but the total effect is a bewildering profusion of schemes, plans, and associations, most of them bearing but little relationship to the actual or the possible. If he is a pioneer and prophet of modern industrialism or of modern science, then he is so only in the sense that one could consider Jules Verne the pioneer of the idea of space travel, or H. G. Wells of the use of atomic energy. The story of his followers, the Saint-Simonians, is instructive in this respect: after participating in a sect which in

[32] Charles Fourier, *La Fausse Industrie,* Paris, 1836, p. 17.

religious eccentricity and obscurantism far surpassed their master's ideas, many of them turned to amazingly successful careers in finance, business, and engineering. The original dogma could attract men of the speculative and enterprising spirit and could intensify as well as channel those abilities. But it was entirely incapable of creating a movement that would affect in the slightest the destiny of a modern society. The parallel to, as well as the difference from, Marxism is striking.

What is the general significance of the precursors of socialism, and what is their importance in explaining the future course of the development and appeal of socialist movements? The nexus *religion-science* demonstrates amply the fertile soil provided socialist theories by a society in the process of modernization, in which the traditionalist religious ideas are being upset and science and scientific thinking have not yet been integrated into modern life. We are still one step away from the full impact of modernization and industrialization, but their prerequisites, science and secularism, already create confusion and the consequent attempts at a synthesis—explanation of the old and new, some of them being socialist in character.

If we feel too condescending toward the fantasies of the early socialists, if we feel like scoffing at Robert Owen's theories because of his spiritualism, or at Fourier's because of his undoubted madness, it is well to keep in mind the variety of similar phenomena that have quite recently accompanied or ushered in the nationalist movements of the formerly colonial nations. Or it is unnecessary to go that far: one can think of the profusion of new religious cults in America in the nineteenth century, many of them bearing the imprint of the same reaction to the bewildering onrush of modernity: the cult of withdrawal into small communities separated from the whirlpool of industrial life, a combination of science and religion, evangelism, or communal living as a protective device against the too rapidly changing, too oppressive forces of modern civilization. There is no thought here of attributing all these to one main cause or of studying why in this country religious or quasi-religious activity has often been the response to industrialism. But it is well to keep them in mind as a corrective to the idea that the usual response to the onrush of industrialism consists in the reading of John Stuart Mill, or, at the present time, in the study of plans of economic development.

Why should socialism, and eventually Marxist socialism, be the main legatee of the strivings for reform produced by the chaos of the intellectual and industrial revolutions? The answer can be suggested by a look at some of the proposals of the precursors. Owen and Fourier are essentially advocates of cooperation, Science, they assume, has enabled mankind to live comfortably and, by their lights, virtuously, without the misery and oppression of the former ages. Societies should and will be transformed into vast networks of self-sustaining communities, living according to the right principles, tolerating no exploitation or superstition. It is unimportant, from our point of view, to go into details, to consider how egalitarian or authoritarian those societies are to be, or who is to direct them. The important thing is to note how, despite all the worship of science and industry, despite even an exaggerated view (for the first quarter of the nineteenth century) of their potentialities, the basic appeal is to the anti-industrial and pro-agrarian instincts. Owen's actual cooperative colonies and Fourier's projected phalansteries are to be islands of harmony and natural life, away from the turbulence of commercialism and competition. Their members achieve status and functions as partners in an organic community, not as single individuals tossed to and fro by the mechanism of the market, requirements of the industry, or command of the state. Despite his madness, Fourier expresses, for instance, the very basic and universal objection to industrialism: the abhorrence of division of labor. His fantastic community will fit jobs according to each man's aptitude and tastes. Furthermore, no man or woman will be tied down to one job any more than to one spouse: there will be pleasing alternation and variety in both respects.

In the name of science and industry, Fourier and Owen dispense with those central or accompanying factors of industrialization: the centralized state, the market mechanism, and "bourgeois" morality. The strictly regulated "freedom" of a small community liberates man from the nauseating influences of society at large. It gives him the full life denied by the hurried pace of modern economy. It frees him from the shackles of church and state and restores him to the vocation of human being. Let it be added that, as behooves a Frenchman, Fourier is much more explicit on the sensual joys of communal living. The man who made the undeniable discovery that the "English influence," i.e., industrialization, was injuring the French cuisine devoted an inordinate part of his writings to the gastronomical question. Who, living in the day of business lunches and ready processed food, can deny Fourier the credit of foreseeing and denouncing one of the most devastating effects of industrialization?

That the visions of Owen and Fourier attracted devotees and even practitioners not only in the countries of their origin but in places as far away as America and Russia, and that, for all their impracticality and often absurdity, many practical men throughout the nineteenth century were drawn to these doctrines, is proof of the strength of their underlying appeal, of the vision of a world freed from competitive individualism, commercialism, and political compulsion. Yet in time Owen's and Fourier's ideas lost their meaning as a *practical* protest against the organization of the modern world. What movement and what party was to embody the same elements of protest while linking them to a more realistic appraisal of social and economic forces and a concrete program of action?

And a somewhat similar process affected the propagation of the ideas of Saint-Simon. The mere cult of technology did not change the social reality. Passion for science, the conviction that through technology one can solve the problems of poverty and backwardness were united with the desire to accomplish actual improvement in the life "of the most numerous and poorest class." But the road of petitioning of princes and bankers appears ridiculous and unavailing against the reality of nineteenth-century Europe. The Saint-Simonians in France, after disbanding their cult, entered upon individual careers of active technological and industrial endeavor, but in another society less industrially developed, less subject to the liberal spirit, the doctrine appeals not as a plea for a scientific and managerial elite but as a rationale for political and social revolution. Even if the early socialist ideas are propagated in the spirit of non-violence, even if those socialists admit the most scrupulous regard for private property, their effect in the turbulent Europe of 1830-1850 is most often revolutionary. Their critique of the existing society and their common reverence for labor make them the basis of the actual socialism of the radical movements.

The net effect of the socialist theories of Owen and Fourier, and to a much lesser extent those of Saint-Simon, is to appeal to the inherent anarchism of popular response to industrialization. Taken out of the context of model communities, the feeling underlying the cooperative idea is one of protest and revolution. Even the implication of the technological cult of Saint-Simon is twisted in this direction. Science, he said, has now enabled mankind to put into practice the only true principle of Christianity: "love each other as brothers." Why don't governments and princes put into effect schemes of social betterment? Why do industry and the state ruin or displace the peasant, crush the craftsman, rather than enable him to lead a freer, more dignified and stable existence than that of the proletarian? The practical significance of the early socialist ideas lies not in the experiments attempting more or less literal application of the original models—New Harmony, Brook Farm, or the Saint-Simonian church—but first in their symptomatic importance as some individuals' response to the social malaise of the transition, and then in their reception in wider circles as surrogates of a revolutionary response to the actual political and economic environment. People grasp at fantasies because they do not quite understand, but they do dislike, what is happening. The moorings of the old system, with its agrarian economy and its traditional Christian belief, were slipping, and the new industrial and secular psychology was far from having penetrated the mass of people, who refused to accept it on the word of a middle-class economist or capitalist.

The next step in socialist thought is focused, not in the schemes of philosophers and inventors, not in isolated cults and discussion groups of intellectuals, but in the more immediate sentiments of certain segments of the laboring classes. As observed before, the connection between socialist theories or feelings and the actual sentiments of the working class is never as straightforward in France as it is in England during the period under discussion. In England between 1830 and 1850, the advanced section of the workers reached *almost* the level of the Marxist revolutionary analysis of capitalism, and Chartism behaved *almost* like a Marxist movement. In France during the parallel period, which lasted until the Commune of 1871, the revolutionary protest remained at the lower form of socialism (from the viewpoint of the Marxist measuring scale). The protest against industrialization, unlike that of Chartism, did not begin to be transmuted into a straightforward revolution against capitalism. French socialism fought not only the capitalists but even more the Industrial Revolution, and it never quite stopped refighting some old battles of the Revolution of 1789. Because French capitalism was weaker, because the industrial ethos of liberalism never acquired the absoluteness of domination that it acquired over English society, socialism in France was, from the Marxist perspective, less socialist and more primitive that the socialism that seemed on the point of emergence from Chartism.

By the same token, French socialism, whether it is the unreflective philosophy of the *coup d'état* of Blanqui or the free-ranging, universal social critique of Proudhon, is a "purer" form of socialism. It represents a more instinctive form of the reaction of the radical part of the working class to industrialization. It is less affected by the arguments borrowed from the armory of its enemy, liberalism, and its proponents are less likely to end up in submission to the spirit of liberalism.

The main tendency of French socialism is perhaps best found in Proudhon (1809-1865). He is a generation or two removed from the utopia builders, in some respects a continuer of their thought, but, in accordance with the new age, not so much an individual philosopher in search of patrons and disciples as a spokesman for popular radicalism. It will not be unfair to Proudhon to assert that the most striking impression produced by his writings is one of incoherence. This is produced not by the derangement of the author, for in contrast to Fourier or even Saint-Simon, Proudhon was eminently sane, nor by the inevitable inconsistencies of a writer who deals with everything under the sun. Proudhon's inconsistencies were produced exactly by a sense of reality and practicality and intelligence, combined with a vivid dislike of whatever was practical in terms of nineteenth-century politics and economics. (This, to digress, has not been atypical of French politics down to our own day.) The man who is best known for his (perhaps borrowed) aphorism, "Property is theft," was a great believer in private property. A proponent of equality and democracy, he adjudged the people a quiet beast interested only in eating, sleeping, and love-making. What could a sober liberal or Marxist socialist do with the social reformer and moralist who at one point dismissed all "long-run" theories and wrote, "On the contrary, profound moralists have held that life consists exactly in those brief moments when the soul and senses are engrossed in desire and voluptuousness, and he who has known this intoxication with life for a single moment, has lived ! " [33]

Born a peasant, becoming a craftsman and a self-taught philosopher whom Marx never forgave for the presumption of claiming to understand Hegel, Proudhon stands as the personification of the attachment to peasant values which are under the impact of industrialism being transformed into socialism. The family and small property are the anchors of human existence. But something has happened to property in the modern world. It now appears as an antisocial force. On the family, Proudhon has, as an Anglo-Saxon writer would put it, very Continental views. The father of anarchism has the peasant's ideal of a harmonious household ruled by the father. Proudhon's opinions on women, which scandalized many of his foreign admirers, were very definite. Woman's place is either in the kitchen or on the streets. The housewife and the prostitute are the two vocations granted to women by nature. To demonstrate woman's inherent inferiority, Proudhon goes into some very weird mathematical exercises. The same *petit-bourgeois* spirit pervades his views of morality. The main source of his abhorrence of the Fourierists and Saint-Simonians, one feels, is their views about the equality of women and their dissolution of the family. The man who believed that woman is inferior to man in proportion 28 to 7 and that the institution of marriage is the model of justice could yet hold love to be an unnecessary element in marriage and extol the father's absolute authority over children. Enemy of authority of all kinds, Proudhon shows a similar inconsistency in opposing the softening of laws against sexual deviants and the legalization of divorce. In brief, one feels that Proudhon does not need a phalanstery or any other model of ideal community. His utopia is the small household with its plot of ground, and his enemy everything

---

[33] Proudhon, *Systeme des Contradictions Économiques, ou Philosophie de la misère,* Paris, 1850, II, 146.

that intrudes upon this idyllic unit: the state, industrial economy, the religious power of the Church, and the socialist who would centralize and dissolve the family.

The religion-science obsession of the earlier socialists is still at its full strength in Proudhon. In addition to the family and land, religion is the third natural element of the order from which he arose. But Christianity has become perverted from its original ethical precepts and the Church has become an ally of the vested interests. The language of a secularist alternates with that of a passionate atheist, the Hegelian phrasing of the religious problem with the almost pagan accusations against God for leaving man in uncertainty and enduring human misery and suffering. Nothing can be done in France except through religion, he says in one place, only to return to his leitmotiv elsewhere: "And I say that the first duty of an intelligent and free man is to chase unceasingly the idea of God from his mind and conscience." [34] This is something that Proudhon, no more than many another revolutionary of his type, never completely succeeded in doing. God appears almost as the unjust father of mankind, the prototype of all tyrannical authority. The Church is the originator of one of the main evils of civilization: centralization. It has no place for science, for democracy, for the true feeling of brotherhood. The catalogue of reproaches links Proudhon's feelings to the religious obsession of early socialists. But there is a marked difference in tone. To Saint-Simon or even Owen, religion was an ethical problem, and the aberration of churches denoted the betrayal of their social mission toward the masses. The intensely religious feeling which underlies Proudhon's atheism has in addition something else: the primitive man's intimate personal dialogue with God. Education and radicalism may transmute that feeling into atheism—never into secularism or liberalism.

Hence the other divinity of the early socialists—science—

[34] *Ibid.,* I, 382.

never appears with the same intensity as the religious problem. Yet it is "science" that the workers need more than democracy; and, somewhat in the manner of Saint-Simon, a palace of industry, a permanent exposition is to regulate economic life. What this "science" is, in what sense economics is science, is never, needless to say, systematically explained by Proudhon. He dabbles happily in Hegelianism and its phraseology, but the total sum of his philosophy of history and nature comes to the already met postulate that "science" now enables men to live freely, without the superstitions and economic misery of the past. That science and technology go hand in hand is not readily admitted by the proponent of the thesis that mankind has reached the age of science. The machine and the division of labor are the permanent sources of misery. The establishment of railway lines in France is the beginning of economic perturbations and the cause of the ruin of the agricultural workers.[35]

"Though very much a friend of order, I am in the full meaning of the word, an anarchist," wrote Proudhon.[36] And the avowal helps us to understand what anarchism is, for the two parts of the statement are really complementary. The "order" is the stability of beliefs and of economy of a pre-industrial household. If the anarchist dislikes compulsion and authority of any kind, ranging from the old types to the ones created by industrialization—the authority of the centralized state, of factory discipline —then by the same token he is quite ready to erupt into violence against destroyers of this "order." The most pacific of men, who reproved Marx for his dogmatism and lust for bloody revolution, Proudhon was drawn at times to programs of violent uprisings, to plans for arrest of the "reactionaries," forcible dissolution of convents and monasteries, and expropriation of bankers and industrialists. Democracy and government by the majority held

[35] P. J. Proudhon, *De La Justice, Dans la Révolution et Dans L'Église,* Paris, 1858, III, 542.
[36] Edouard Dolleans, *Proudhon,* Paris, 1948, p. 218.

little appeal for the anarchist convinced by the plebiscites of Napoleon III that the majority of people were idiots and universal suffrage a delusion.

It is customary to ask what a given thinker or school "stood for." In the case of anarchism, the question is extremely difficult to answer. Anarchism has excellent critical sense: the logical corollaries and weaknesses of competing creeds, especially social-istic, are pointed out with great perception. The inherent authoritarianism of the Marxist doctrine was seen by Proudhon with the acumen displayed later by Bakunin in characterizing Marxism as, essentially, state capitalism. The authoritarian im-plications of Etienne Cabet's communism, Saint-Simon's elitism, and the hollowness of democratic slogans amid an ignorant and destitute population were all lucidly exposed by Proudhon. Proud of being French, he was at the same time an inveterate enemy of militant nationalism and an advocate of disarmament. Yet what is *his* response, *his* plan for the solution of the social prob-lem? Here anarchism falters, for it is much more a feeling, a sentiment of protest rather than an ideology. Proudhon's *mutual-ism* envisages a network of productive associations of producers. The political state withers away while the autonomous associa-tions happily trade with each other. But mutualism is as hazy in its administrative detail as it is paradoxical on its economic side. The enemy of savings banks and insurance, believer in "demonetization" of money, Proudhon calls upon, horrible to say, a centralized institution, a national bank to provide cheap and then free credit for his associations. Land is to be excluded from mutualism, because the private property of the peasant is to be guaranteed and passes by inheritance. The problem of politics and administration in the mutualist society? No such problem will exist, since public and private conscience, formed by the "science of right," will suffice to maintain order and guarantee liberties. This is the constant answer of anarchism to such impolite questions.

The anarchist *sentiment,* which underlay much of Chartism, never crystallized into a definite philosophy. Proudhon epitomizes the step forward from the mass of anti-industrial and anti-state prejudices, the inheritance of the peasant and craftsman psychology into a distinguishable, if hazily detailed, philosophy. From his socialist predecessors Proudhon is distinguished by his belief in revolution. The echoes of the older tradition, the search for a patron, Rousseau's "legislator" to put the new system into effect at one blow, are not entirely missing: at times Proudhon is not above putting his hopes in Louis Napoleon, or even Louis Philippe. But the main stress is on emancipation by the enlightenment and if need be by a revolution on the part of the proletariat. The anarchism of Proudhon becomes perhaps the most influential branch of socialism among the French workers. The incomplete victory of industrial values, when coupled with political instability, did not let the anarchist sentiment die out among the French proletariat, and the progress of industrialization reproduced this feeling under the new form of syndicalism.

One explanation for the victory of the industrial spirit in England and the persistence of anti-industrialism in other societies is suggested unwittingly by a man not credited with great theoretical insight:

. . . not only at the end of the last century but even today no other country attained the degree of development of capitalism and concentration of production in agriculture that we observe in Britain. Despite the development of capitalism in the countryside, other countries still have a quite numerous class of small and medium property owning producers in the countryside whose future would have to be decided in the event that the proletariat takes power.[37]

It is the existence of the peasant in society, the unerased peasant background of the proletarian, that makes him susceptible to

[37] J. V. Stalin, *Economic Problems of Socialism in the U.S.S.R.,* in *Current Digest of the Soviet Press: Current Soviet Policies,* ed. Leo Gruliow, New York, 1953, I, 3.

anarchism, which in its modern form is the revolt against industrialized life and its corollaries, the state and urbanization. In
England, through several circumstances, the peasant was practically eliminated; elsewhere the peasant problem often remained
as the breeding ground for the appeal of anarchist and syndicalist
philosophies.

And of Marxism. For while the theory of Proudhon, of Blanqui,
or of Bakunin is as antithetical to Marxism as it is to liberalism,
the anti-industrial anarchistic sentiment that underlies their
doctrines can often find its *effective* expression in revolutionary
Marxism. The latter as *protest* has almost everything that explicit anarchism can offer: it attacks the state and the possessing
classes and reaffirms the dignity and the sole value-producing
capacity of human labor. But Marxism has something else that
is missing in anarchism. Anarchist feeling is too formless, too
much divorced from the dynamic of economic development, to
create objective conditions and organization capable of absorbing
the economic facts of life. The anti-authority premises of anarchism hardly allow it to form an efficient political movement to
compete for power.

The anti-industrial tradition in which French socialism not only
had grown (as had all other socialisms) but also persisted thus
enabled Marxism to play the leading revolutionary role in
French politics, albeit Marxism in France appeared at times
closer to syndicalism than to the doctrine of Karl Marx. By the
same token, the persistence of the anti-industrial ethos has been
in France, and in other countries under similar circumstances,
a fertile soil for the revolutionary movements of the right. The
persistence of this psychology in society is thus both the cause
and the effect of radical and antidemocratic forces of both the
left and right.

Marxism is the type of socialism that believes in industrialization, but can live as a revolutionary movement of importance
only in symbiosis with a widespread anti-industrial feeling. As

such it is unique among socialist systems of the nineteenth century. We might exhibit a case that is *almost* an exception to demonstrate the point. Among the leading socialist thinkers in France at the time, Louis Blanc provides a striking example of modernity. In reading his *Organisation du Travail,* first published in 1839, one receives the impression of a style, argument, and method more characteristic of an English Fabian or a German revisionist socialist of the end of the century than of any of the socialist effusions of the time in France, England, or elsewhere. There is no opposition to the state, very few of the tiresome tirades about religion and science. Believer in large-scale industry and probably the first exponent of the collectivization of land—not to provide escape from industrialization in the form of little, self-sufficient colonies, but precisely to apply the full advantages of large-scale planning and technology to agriculture —Louis Blanc strikes one as being quite modern in his preoccupations. But if Blanc writes in the spirit of what later became known as "democratic socialism," his analysis of the future of capitalism does not transcend contemporary radical opinion. The theory of "immiseration" is stated as clearly as in Marx. "But who would be blind enough not to see that under the regime of unlimited competition [*concurrence illimitée*], continuous fall of wages is a necessarily general fact, and not an exception." [38] That big capitalists will eventually devour smaller ones is as certain to Blanc as it is to Marx.

But even Blanc, who in some ways anticipates Marx and in other ways the revisionists of Marxism, suffers in return from the early socialists' illusion that a mechanical contrivance, a model institution, can in itself effect a political and economic revolution. His National Workshops, run by the state, are to demonstrate the superiority of socialism over capitalism. In a very Fabian way, he writes: " . . . the state step by step will become master of industry, in place of monopoly we will have

[38] Louis Blanc, *Organisation du Travail,* Paris, 1850, p. 27.

as the result of [our] success the defeat of [capitalist] competition, association." [39] But the state that is to plan the economy
is not the kind of state that later in the twentieth century
could perform planning and social welfare. The worker who is
to be secured employment has but little liking for division of
labor and industrial discipline, to which he is now assumed to
submit out of a sense of social obligation rather than because
of want or fear of unemployment. In the context of a society
in which industrial values have not been assimilated, Blanc's
socialism is almost as utopian as Fourier's.

The great synthesis performed by Marx, a synthesis based
not only on theories and movements, but also on intuitive appraisal of social and political psychology of various classes, has
given his doctrine an unusual power of survival and influence.
After 1850 there will be many societies and countries where
similar economic and political conditions will bring forth ideas
and sentiments similar to those found in Chartism or in Saint-
Simon or Proudhon. But the would-be innovators and revolutionaries will be presented with a doctrine and movement that
already expresses some of their aspirations and revolt. *Complete*
opposition to industrialization or its opposite, *complete* acceptance of industry and the state, will almost always confine the
influence of Marxism to that of a small sect, while other types
of socialism attract the majority of the working class. But in
societies where anarchism has ceased to be a practical response
and trade unionism of the English type has not yet been firmly
established, Marxism will in fact become the vanguard of
socialism.

[39] *Ibid.*, p. 77.

IV THE DIVERGING PATHS: DEMOCRACY AND MARXISM

Let us return to one utopia produced by the onset of the Industrial Revolution that has in a large measure been realized: the liberal utopia. It is the dream of society where men are imbued with virtues appropriate to industrialism, where they do not long for status, brotherhood, or the intimacy of a small community or organization, but where they set their sights in terms of income (i.e., the quantity of goods and services they can command), and where they will move from one end of the country to the other, from one profession to another, if they can materially gain thereby. It is a society where men are too busy cultivating their materialistic garden to get profoundly excited over doctrinal differences, be they in politics or religion. Science is equally and unexcitedly accepted as part of daily life. No beating of the head against the wall of facts of industrial life: division of labor and the factory system are equally accepted, and a rising standard of life makes them less and less of a nuisance. The citizen accepts the state, not because of Hegel, but merely by paying taxes and accepting its regulations. Where is democracy in this scheme? It is simply a by-product of the acceptance of industrialism, education, and a high standard of living, of the withering away of superstitions, and of the irrational longing for the "status" and "property" of the disappearing

agrarian society. Again, it is not the General Will or any
metaphysical business that inclines, say, 45 percent of the people
to submit to being ruled for a time by persons elected by 55 percent; it is the realization of the essential *sameness* of political
values pervading the whole society. A man is entitled to vote not
because of any moral or Christian equality but because an advanced material and educational level makes the majority of
people qualified to exercise intelligent citizenship.

In the first half of the nineteenth century, this dream would
have appeared to the conservative and radical alike a nightmare,
a contemporary version of Orwell's *1984*. To young Marx, it
would have appeared *inconceivable under capitalism*. Yet when
the co-founder of Marxism was on his deathbed in 1895, the
liberal utopia seemed close to realization. Historical hindsight
shows 1895 exhibiting some other portents too, but to a social
observer in the year when Engels died and Vladimir Ilich Lenin
joined what was to become the Bolshevik Party, liberalism,
granted all its imperfections and limitations, appeared on the
road to a triumphant fulfillment in the West and eventual spread
elsewhere in the world.

The economic and social atmosphere in Western Europe has
made irrelevant both the earlier types of capitalism and anti-
capitalism. Industrialization brought a higher standard of living.
The state had begun to concede to the worker the right to
organize and to press for his economic postulates, just as the
ballot had given him the power to press his political aims. The
capitalist found himself being curtailed by the state with its
rudimentary social legislation, with its beginnings of progressive
income and inheritance taxation. Again, the situation in the
1890's, which looks so old-fashioned and capitalistic from our
vantage point, would have struck an observer looking back to
fifty years before as incomprehensibly collectivistic. What radical
in 1850 would have believed that the capitalists would submit
without a death struggle to the progressive income or inheritance

tax, social insurance, curtailment of political power through universal suffrage, or extension of the state's economic activity? Yet the seeds of all these measures or their beginnings are plainly visible in the 1890's. By the same token, what conservative would have believed in 1850 that a democratic electorate would tolerate vast inequalities of inherited wealth and income, or indeed the perpetuation of the industrial system? Both liberalism and the worker have changed. One has shown itself not exclusively based on extreme individualism and the inflexible belief in economic "laws"; and the other's psychology has been shown to be not exclusively grounded on anti-industrialism. The corrosive influence of economic improvement softened the doctrinal rigidity of the two opponents. The apparent triumph of liberalism, even if that liberalism had changed and softened, called for a new synthesis. The old battleground between capitalism and socialism, the battleground of industrialization, seemingly disappeared forever.

In dealing with Marxism during the period, we no longer deal with the thought of two men or with small groups of devotees. Marxism is now an international movement, the major inheritor of all the strains of socialism that were previously discussed. The doctrine has hardened into a dogma. The small groups of sympathizers and correspondents have developed into parties, some with mass followings. In the international socialist movement, Marxism is clearly the dominant tendency. The heavily intellectual doctrine becomes the official expression of the aspirations of workers throughout the world. The catholicity of the doctrine has surpassed even Marx's expectations. In it the German worker will express not only his economic grievance but a political protest against militarism and the Junkers, the Polish worker his protest against national oppression, and the Russian against absolutism and the lack of rudimentary political rights. To the intellectuals and large segments of the middle class, Marxism provides a "scientific" theory of society, a way out of social inequities through a rational organization of community, a much more practical expression of the instinct that led people to follow Saint-Simon, Fourier, or Owen.

Was the spread of socialism and especially Marxism a demonstration that the triumph of liberalism and the stability of capitalism were an illusion, or was it in fact an indication that socialism is the logical culmination and fulfillment of the other two? This is the question that dominates theoretical Marxism in the nineties. In the original canon there are arguments for both answers. But Marxism is now an international movement and a dogma buttressed by vast literature, theoretical journals, and the like. Whatever interpretation is given, its exponent will be reluctant to admit that the answer must be a relativistic one, that, taking the original premises of Marxism, it has completely different meanings in England and in Russia, that the logic of the argument would lead to revolutionary action in one case, to constitutional and democratic means in another, and to the abandonment of socialism in still another. Conflicting views of Marxism become engrossed in the exegesis of the scriptures. The doctrine becomes encrusted with heavy layers of historical, economic, and other commentaries to the point where its original outlines become almost unrecognizable.

We are here interested in one aspect of the problem: the uses of Marxism. To what groups, interests, and sentiments in the given society does the conglomeration of theories known as Marxism appeal, and why? And the obverse of the question: What instincts and interests does Marxism instill in those who consider themselves Marxists? How does Marxism "make a difference" between an average worker and the worker who considers himself a Marxist? To men who find themselves in absolute control of a society and who think of themselves as Marxian socialists? To a secular analyst, it is not necessary to connect answers to these questions with what "Marx really meant." The conglomeration of theories, facts, and predictions that is Marxism has a life of its own, and some of its uses and effects were as unanticipated by its authors as was the kind of world in which it was to score triumphs and suffer defeats.

THE ENGLISH EXCEPTION

Like the failure of the hound of the Baskervilles to bark, the failure of Marxism to take root in England provides a key to the mystery. The country which alone of European societies reached an absolute preponderance of industry over agriculture by the end of the nineteenth century, which pioneered in the development of modern industry and of social and political institutions appropriate to it, should have been, by a literal application of the Marxist analysis, the first place to have a Marxist revolutionary movement and a socialist revolution. Yet actually the Marxist situation in England had passed before Marxism was formulated. Neither the theory nor the practice of Marxism found many adherents in the country in which Marx and Engels were residents. The Social Democratic Federation, founded in the 1880's, and the activities of a handful of English Marxists, like H. M. Hyndman, toward the end of the century, provide the very small exception that proves the rule.

The luxuriant growth of Marxist movements everywhere in the 1890's and the first decade of the twentieth century is not paralleled by anything in England. Of all the many strains and theories that went into the building of English socialism, the influence of Marxism was the slightest. We do not get in England even the phenomenon observable in similarly industrialized countries (for example, the Low Countries and Scandinavia), i.e., a socialist movement that is *officially* Marxist in name and paraphernalia, but non-Marxist in behavior. In the revival of socialism in England among the generation, roughly speaking, before World War I, all kinds of socialist theories and movements are propagated. The weakening of England's economic position in the world, her loss of economic dynamism, bring forth socialist recipes ranging from the evolutionary socialism of the Fabians to the faint echoes of anarchism and syndicalism represented by Guild Socialism. But interest in Marxism, whether by the intellectual or the worker, is practically nil. The ability of Marxism to assimilate and give political expression to various strains of socialist thought and movement is conspicuously absent in Great Britain.

What produced the modern socialist movement in Britain? The same thing that led to sizable socialist movements elsewhere: the worker's search for a party and movement that would represent his interests and give a theoretical formulation to his aspirations and grievances. The success of industrialism in allaying the first anarchic response of the worker, the work of education and democratic institutions in allaying his sense of "alienation" do not permanently remove the opportunities for socialism. A mature industrial society will be faced with socialism in two distinct, though often merging, forms. One will be in the inevitable tendency of the modern industrial state to grow more complex and more collectivistic, assuming, because of the factors of sheer size and technology, a greater and greater role in the field of economy and social relations. This is socialism inherent in the very process of industrialization and democratization beyond a certain stage. In that sense, but not in the way he meant, Marx's prediction of socialism's emergence from capitalism is correct.

But this is socialism only in a limited sense of the word. It is socialism from the perspective of nineteenth-century economic individualism, the kind meant by a liberal chancellor of the exchequer when he said in the 1890's: "We are all socialists now." It is conceivable to have all kinds of collectivism and bureaucratic planning of economic life without the slightest advance toward social and economic egalitarianism. And the other kind of socialism is produced exactly by a certain egalitarianism fostered by industrialism and democracy. The rise in the standard of living kills off the earlier, anti-industrial type of socialism, with its anarchistic undertones. But the slackening of economic dynamism of an industrialized society, or a prolonged economic crisis, bring forth the kind of socialism that, in much purer form than other socialisms, is anticapitalist. Anticapitalism is no longer an expression of hostility to the whole complex of industrial and political institutions; it is a specific protest against large conglomerations of economic power and wealth in a society which no longer believes in unlimited opportunities for success and economic advancement for everybody. The proletarian of earlier socialism is the trade unionist of the later phase. The perspective of overthrowing the "system" and reverting to some real or imaginary pre-industrial situation no longer has any appeal for him. But the presence of class barriers, the lack or the slow pace of economic improvement puts him in the state of mind receptive to the kind of theory that presents socialism as merely a step forward from democracy, the reduction of existing inequalities, and the subjugation of economic to political power, which is already mainly democratic.

It is easy to see how badly Marxism fits the bill. The revolutionary appeal of Marxism rests on the worker's sense of grievance and alienation from society as a whole, the kind of grievance that had little relevance in England even of the 1890's. To assert that the electorate is being hoodwinked by the capitalists in power is not the same as to assert that the state is the executive committee of the exploiting class. The class-war appeal loses its emotional tone if you have to argue that because of the democratic franchise the class enemy is at your mercy. And under those conditions, the other side of Marxism, its technological enthusiasm, its indoctrination in the necessity of the industrial system, has likewise very little meaning. The industrial worker has reached the position where he is neither uncomprehending nor exultant over the facts of technology. Trade-union activity and political action are viewed by him as the means of both translating the technological progress into a higher standard of living and avoiding or tempering unemployment.

English socialism was thus likely to flow into other forms. It is misleading to view the problem of Marxism versus English socialism in terms of the dichotomy, revolutionary versus evolutionary socialism. The picture of the years before World War I is filled with major strikes, and with socialist theories which were quite revolutionary in their implications and at times sounded like echoes of the earlier anti-industrial opposition. The tenor of English politics of the period—the possibility of civil war in Ireland, the constitutional crises, and the social and fiscal legislation of the liberal administration of 1906 to 1914—created a situation which to contemporaries was fraught with revolutionary possibilities. But the response of the English working class was the creation of a labor movement and party, which, though led by socialists, did not commit itself to socialism until 1918. And even then this socialism was to be amalgam of egalitarianism and social welfare, with the nationalization of the major means of production as one of its main practical postulates. English socialism arose when the society was indeed far from a liberal utopia. But the saturation with industrial values was already sufficient to make both parts of the Marxist synthesis irrelevant to the British worker.

It is instructive to see both the essence and the extent of this adjustment. The oldest element is the fact of political democratization, the right of the worker to vote, the distracting practical effect of political activity upon the revolutionary utopias and dreams of reconstructing pre-industrial society. The revolutionary spirit, the blend of romantic protest and social utopianism, does not easily survive involvement in the prosaic business of actual politics. The spread of parliamentarism, the extension of suffrage, had been viewed by Marx and Engels with what was almost a nostalgia for the bad old days of their youth, when the state was definitely "they"—the upper and middle classes—and the worker had no right to suspect that perhaps he was also a wielder of political power. Marx's comments on the Gotha Program of the German Social Democratic Party of 1875 reveal a conflict of attitudes: one, a tone of pride at socialism becoming embodied in a real mass party; the other, a tone of irritation at the almost inevitable prospect of the watering down of the revolutionary spirit by the trappings of legalism and "constructive" social legislation. Equally threatening, though more distant, was the likelihood of the seduction of socialist leaders by ministerial posts and of the workers' "acceptance" of the state. Though the German Social Democratic Party "purified" its program of the Lassallean elements in 1891, the logic of legal political activity was in fact to justify some of Marx's apprehensions.

In the case of British socialism, the absorption in actual politics was, of course, a much more potent antidote to doctrinalism and revolutionary romanticism. Even Chartism had already found its outward focus in political demands. The much more democratic situation toward the end of the century imperiled even more the revolutionary protest of socialism. The road to revolution became a series of elections and legislative enactments. The final aim of socialism could not be awaited with the impatience that is the springboard of revolutionary action if indeed its postulates were being accomplished step by step. Democracy, an adjustment to industrialization, emasculated socialism of its revolutionary enthusiasm.

The other element of adjustment is inherent in the growth of English trade unionism. The union in its genesis is a product of anti-industrialism. To the early liberal and Marxist alike, it is the outcome of the "illusion" of the worker that through a conspiracy he can mitigate the effect of economic laws, raise his wages, improve his conditions of living in defiance of the market. To the historian of trade unionism the early unions represent something else: a desperate, often illegal attempt by the proletarian to regain status through association, to reproduce, often through odd ceremonies and vocabulary, the feeling of "belonging," to restore the previous peasant and craftsman existence —a defense against not only economic but also social individualism imposed by industrialization. To the liberal, unionism, once legalized, would wither away with the worker's realization that it was impotent to change his bargaining position. To Marx, unionism, as tried by some Chartists, would also lose its early illusions and become the weapon of the worker in class warfare. Yet unionism grew, after initial setbacks and persecutions, but in a way which confounded both early hopes and fears. Like the cooperative movement, trade unionism, originally the product of the impetus to erect an artificial barrier or preserve against industrialism, did become in time an integral part of the more mature industrial system, an agency through which the worker arrived at his compromise with the system, and, up to a point, a school of industrial and democratic values.

The growth and character of English unionism in the 1860's and '70's alarmed and disgusted Marx and Engels. To them it seemed to foster the petty bourgeois character of the more prosperous segments of the working class and to transmute the class struggle against capitalism into minor skirmishes for higher pay and shorter working hours.

The conservative type of unionism, uniting essentially the aristocracy of the working class, was considerably changed by the rise of "new unionism" and the organizations of unskilled workers in the 1880's. But the result was still far from the Marxian vision of spontaneous organizations of the working class, exuding class warfare and basically and impatiently opposed to the bourgeois state. Trade unionism as it looked to Lenin in 1902 *was* in fact the spontaneous form of organization of the worker, but the trade-union mentality was the negation of the Marxian revolutionary pattern.

The atmosphere of unionism is in fact representative of the mentality of the worker. But in its English version this class

mentality settles at a point equidistant between what Marx and
the liberals had predicted. It is neither a revolutionary reaction
against the alienation and poverty inherent in the industrial
system nor the loss of the feeling of class separateness and individualistic economic endeavor. The class mentality is that of
the acceptance of separateness, but not of alienation; of the
acceptance of the industrial system, but not of capitalism; of
individualism, but not of economic insecurity postulated in the
earliest laissez faire. The complexity of the worker's adjustment
parallels that of the English capitalist, who is no longer the ceaseless entrepreneur and revolutionizer of economic life, self-right-
eous and unyielding in his prerogatives and ideology. The more
involved economic reality traps and minimizes the sources of
the revolutionary confrontation of the worker and the bourgeois
state. The revolutionary optimism that Marxism exuded earlier,
when the acute antagonism between capitalism and the working
class had seemed to augur similar developments everywhere,
gave way in the 1890's to a parallel apprehension: what if a similar rise in the standard of living and progress in representative
institutions were to bring to the workers in other European countries, despite their present penchant toward Marxism, a similar
trade-union mentality?

The defense of Marxian orthodoxy, of the essential correctness
of the visibly disproved tenet of the continuous impoverishment
of the working class under capitalism, became for the Continental
socialists something of a psychological necessity in view of the
English experience. The contrast between Marx's formulation of
the misery of the workers under capitalism and the defense of this
thesis by his disciples half a century later is quite striking.
Marx expressed in an overly theoretical form what most of the
contemporary radicals and advanced workers around the middle
of the century firmly believed; but the German and other Marxists
faced the exactly opposite task of telling the working class that
what their senses told them was an illusion or a temporary freak.

The German worker's genuine dissatisfaction with his country's political system and with capitalism as a form of organization of economic life had to be supplemented by the unreal feeling that *somehow* his economic situation was getting worse. Indoctrination was called upon to help class consciousness. The self-imposed task of orthodox Marxists on the Continent became, one feels, not so much struggling against capitalism and authoritarianism as guarding the worker against falling for the "illusion" of economic progress and peaceful democratization. The threat posed to Marxist orthodoxy by historical facts was dismissed by Engels, shortly before his death, in an ingenious prognosis: despite all the growth of the socialist parties and democratization of political life, Marx's revolutionary prediction still holds true; it is now the capitalists who will strike first to prevent a peaceful transition to socialism. Yet how much sophistry and real apprehension of the extinction of the revolutionary impulse is in this view as contrasted with the primitive but self-assured and elemental appeal of the *Communist Manifesto*.

English socialism, by contrast, was never faced with a similar task of fitting reality into the uncomfortable confines of a theory. It never attempted to decide the correct pattern of the unfolding of history or the correct interpretation of the views of two deceased thinkers by vote of party congress. Socialism in England is fed by theories, some revolutionary, others evolutionary; some moralistic and religious in their anticapitalism, others pragmatic and utilitarian in their tone. But when the sum of influences jells into a movement and a parliamentary party, it reflects the acceptance of liberal society and the tendency to "stretch it" into socialism, the reflection not so much of any theory or group of theories but of the instinct of the British working class.

The attenuation of anti-industrialism as the basis for socialism —and hence the irrelevance of Marxism under English conditions —is best studied by observing the content and influence of two schools of socialist thought of the generation before 1917: Fabianism and Guild Socialism. Fabianism is a socialist descendant of Utilitarianism, the acceptance of liberalism with a collectivistic proviso. Guild Socialism is the last cry and formulation of anti-industrialism, the rejection of the state, an attempted escape from the fact of centralized economic and political life into vague schemes of workers' control and of guilds. Fabianism, for all its intellectual origins and attitudes, became the dominant tendency in English socialism. From it runs a fairly straight line to the Beveridge Report, the welfare state, and the philosophy of the Labour Party of today. Guild Socialism, for a period before and immediately after World War I, found some echoes in the sections of organized labor, but it vanished as a major influence and plays no part in contemporary English socialism. It failed to turn trade unionism in the syndicalist direction, and it left a much greater imprint on literary and intellectual life than on the ideas of the "lower part of mankind," which, whether in a democratic or nondemocratic society, ultimately decide the future of political movements.

Fabianism flows from the *Fabian Essays,* published in 1889 by a remarkable group of writers and reformers engaged in socialist propaganda. There is no echo in them of the theories of Karl Marx or of the presence in English society at the moment of Friedrich Engels. There is a small deposit, but very small, of what might be called the aesthetic protest against capitalism and industrialism, which will loom much more importantly in Guild Socialism. The early Fabians included Bernard Shaw and H. G. Wells, and there is something of Fourier in Shaw and an element of Saint-Simon's scientific utopianism in Wells. More generally, there is in the *Fabian Essays* a common-sense objection to the cultural and spiritual aridity of late Victorian life and an exasperation with conventionality and conformity and with the drab reality of the dominant lower-middle-class standards. This protest can be found vividly in H. G. Wells' novels of lower-middle-class life, with their revolt against the all-encompassing materialism

and "propriety" of middle-class civilization and its choking effect
upon human individuality. Unlike the earlier aesthetic critiques
of industrialization and bourgeois values by Carlyle and Ruskin
and the later ones by Chesterton and Belloc, this element of
protest in the *Essays* is not a basic rejection of the new scale
of standards by thinkers standing apart from politics and simply
grumbling about materialism. Rather, the protest denotes a
genuine disappointment at the unfulfilled promise of the new
civilization; it is a critical re-examination of industrial civilization, symptomatic of the slackening of material progress, rather
than of a fundamental hostility to the civilization.

The main theme of the *Essays* and indeed of Fabianism as it
grew up was that its brand of socialism was simply the logical
continuation and fulfillment of industrialism plus democracy.
It is not an attempt to *épater les bourgeois,* but to convince
them as well as the working class. The vision of industrial evolution is in the spirit of unemotional Marxism. The growing concentration of industry and business, and the depersonalization of the
ownership of the means of production, makes their assumption
by the state the next logical step. But despite some hints to the
contrary, the take-over from the capitalists is generally assumed
to come through "honest purchase" rather than expropriation.
The expanding sphere of collectivistic action by the state as well
as by the municipalities is quoted as a proof that the tendency
is already evident and inevitable.

The approach to the realization of socialism assumes the reality
of the democratic process. In fact, the Fabians were to use propaganda and education rather than any attempt at "mass action."
The road, according to Sidney Webb, must be (1) democratic, i.e.,
"acceptable to a majority of people and prepared for in the
minds of all"; (2) gradual, causing no dislocation; (3) not regarded as immoral by the mass of the people, and thus not
subjectively demoralizing to them; and (4) "In this country at

any rate constitutional and peaceful." [1] This is socialism that has accepted the premises of liberalism but no longer believes in the realizability of the liberal utopia. There is no wide-eyed enthusiasm over the powers of science and technology, no great concern with religion or the aristocracy. Fabianism is an unenthusiastic, matter-of-fact acceptance of industrialism and a plea, but again with very little emotionalism in it, for socialism.

Nothing illustrates the frustration of anti-industrial type of socialism in England better than the fate of Guild Socialism. In the years preceding World War I, Guild Socialism forged to the fore of socialist thought. In perspective, the period before the war represents a striking but short-lived rebirth of socialism grounded in the anachronistic protest against the overwhelming elements of political and economic reality: the state and centralized industry. It is no accident that the same period witnessed the questioning of the intellectual and political basis of liberalism. The rationalist tradition encountered a critique at the hands of Bergson, William James, and Freud. The reality of representative democracy was scathingly analyzed by Ostrogorski, Michels, and Pareto. The variety of criticisms of the foundations of liberalism was at once a proof that the intellectual underpinnings of liberal civilization in the West had passed their heyday and a tribute to the extent of achievement of the liberal utopia. A critic in the spirit of Hegel would see the varied movements of the generation before 1914 as a proof that the liberal synthesis had been established and that an inevitable challenge was forthcoming. A Marxist would observe the slackening tempo of economic expansion and the end of the revolutionary role of capitalism and would note the appearance of movements and theories questioning the basic premises of capitalism as the result of these changes. A secular explanation sees liberalism running "out of steam," unable to impose the pattern of industrialization and modernization,

---

[1] *Fabian Essays in Socialism,* London, 1931, pp. 31-32.

which had seemed to have come of itself in the West, on the world at large and on international relations.

In the English context, Guild Socialism is a rather distant echo of the general perturbation. The very name chosen by the movement indicates that what was implict in the original anti-industrial socialism is made explicit in this socialism as it fights a retreating action against the state and "wagery": a certain medievalism of outlook, the hankering after a society where everybody has his "place." From its beginnings, it was a hopeless political venture. The vision of the state transformed into a conglomeration of guilds, unions of workers, and professions, each running its own affairs, joined by something "non state," whether called the Commune or the Industrial Guilds Congress, has only to be put into words to show its utter unpracticality. The very need that Guild Socialists like S. G. Hobson and G. D. H. Cole felt to formulate their political schemes in detail shows the enervating influence of the British conditions upon anarchism and syndicalism. In France, Italy, and Spain, syndicalism of the period was widespread, but its exponents did not usually feel called upon to spell out what they would put in the place of the hateful realities of the state and capitalism. It is a sad day for syndicalists and anarchists when they feel compelled to produce positive proposals and organization charts!

The protest underlying Guild Socialism again links it to the critique of capitalism from the conservative viewpoint. The social passion of Guild Socialism pits it against the inequalities and competition of capitalist society. It harbors aesthetic grief over society's loss of organic unity and over the disappearance of the instinct for workmanship in pre-industrial crafts. These have been the traditional materials with which Christian socialism has been constructed. In Guild Socialism there is an additional echo of the revolutionary excitement of Continental syndicalism, of the worker now enmeshed in modern industry but still antagonistic to industrialism as such. We are reminded once more how anti-industrialism, if widespread in society, is the breeding ground of indiscriminate radicalism, how the former syndicalists often found their way into postwar communism, but also how a residue of syndicalist ideas found a place in National Socialism and Fascism. The struggle against concreteness, the urge, in one's irritation with the facts of the industrialized state and the "apathy" of the working class, to plunge into irrationalism, are not entirely absent in Guild Socialism. There is even a furtive approach to mystical nationalism. The state makes a reappearance, in S. G. Hobson, to express the spirit of the community and "the abiding truths" of the national interest as against selfish interests of particular segments of the community.[2] G. D. H. Cole, in one of his earlier books, toyed with the Rousseauistic conception of the state and with that "elusive but fundamental reality which he [Rousseau] named the General Will."[3]

But how awkward and unconvincing does the phraseology of "higher" interests and of the "real" state sound against the pattern of prosaic economic pursuits and aspirations of the actual industrial worker. The points of real appeal in Guild Socialism— its protest against the class system; its plea for more power for the unions and for social and economic democracy—flow more naturally into other socialist movements. Barring an economic or political catastrophe which disrupts the habits of a century of industrialism, the worker's response to the slackening of economic dynamism of liberal society takes the form of laborism. World War I, with its shattering impact on the domestic and especially what there was of the international liberal order still does not constitute that catastrophe. The British labor movement becomes more consciously socialistic, but it finds its socialism in the Fabian version rather than in other forms. What there is of communism in interwar England comes mostly, insofar as the workers are concerned, as a reflection of the much oversimplified

[2] *National Guilds and the State,* New York, 1920, p. 143.
[3] *The World of Labour,* London, 1920, p. 28.

notion of Soviet Russia as a "workers' state." In retrospect, the weakness of Marxism in England had been ordained by the same forces and habits that made for the insignificance of anarchism and syndicalism in the working-class movement and for the acceptance of liberal collectivism by society as a whole.

THE CONTINENTAL PATTERN

The epoch-making intellectual achievement of the English technologists and their like, who prepared the Industrial Revolution and have afterward worked out its consequences in technology and the material sciences, is not so much that they gained a new manner of insight into the nature and working of material things, as that they were, by force of circumstances, enabled to forget much of what was known before their time; by atrophy of the habitual bent for imputing anthropomorphic qualities and characters to the things they saw, they were enabled to interpret these things in terms of matter of fact.[4]

Veblen's characteristically involved statement contains its own insight about the mechanics of adjustment to industrialization. The ability to forget is important not only, as Veblen thought, in reference to the habit "of construing material phenomena in occult, magical, quasi-personal, spiritual phenomena." It is also the ability to forget the previous artisan and peasant existence. In England, the working class was already demonstrating this ability at the end of the nineteenth century. On the Continent, the tremendous development of industrialism, in the strict sense of the word, was not accompanied at an equal pace by the institutional and social appurtenances of the process.

But the ability to forget has yet another dimension. In a study of Marxism, it is easy to fall into the temptation to believe that the reality of politics is expressed exclusively in terms of "eco-

[4] Thorstein Veblen, *Imperial Germany and the Industrial Revolution* [1915], New York, 1957, p. 190.

nomic forces" and indices of industrial production. One may neglect the emotional factor in the adjustment of the worker to the political system. In England, the labor movement has always had some difficulty finding an appropriate group of martyrs to symbolize its opposition to the bourgeois order. The "Tolpuddle martyrs"—the group of laborers who in the 1830's were sentenced to transportation for illegal union activity—figure rather faintly compared with the hundreds of executions that followed the suppression of the Paris Commune of 1871. The long delays and legal obstacles that preceded full recognition of the role and functions of English trade unionism are again not of the same order as, say, the suppression of the German Socialist Party under Bismarck.

The facts of economic improvement or deterioration are but part of the story of the adjustment to "industrialization." The early irritants of loss of status and factory discipline may become dulled with the passage of time and the rise in the standard of living. The workers will not be able to forget their earlier grievances and express their present ones, if the state stands as the symbol of authority, apart and against them, if, for all the right to vote, there is an unbridgeable gap between them and the machinery of the bourgeois state. In England, the self-professed task of the Socialist Fabian society was, first, propagandizing not so much the working class as the middle class about the necessity of socialism and, second, infiltrating the civil service with collectivistic ideas. This, under Continental conditions at the beginning of the twentieth century, would have been the height of naïveté. The French worker viewed his *patron* and the German worker the imperial civil servant as class enemies. Though England in 1900 was less advanced in social legislation than Germany, though France was a republic, the two continental centers of socialism had elements in their political and social systems that gave more than superficial reality to the concept of the class war, and to the persistence within the working class of hostility toward the state and the ruling class on a scale unmatched in the country that originated the industrial system.

What Veblen wrote in 1915, trying to explain the dangerous character of German nationalism by the lag of social development in comparison with industry and technology, may be used (and not only in regard to Germany) to explain the acceptance of Marxist rather than laboristic socialism by a community with a high *technical* culture:

As a cultural community the Fatherland is at present in an eminently unstable transitional phase. Its population is in the singularly untoward position—untoward, that is, in the present immediate bearing—that they have come out of an obsolescent cultural situation so recently as in effect not to have forgotten what is necessary to forget, at the same time they have not been in contact with the things of the modern world long enough or intimately enough to have fully assimilated the characteristically modern elements of the Western civilization.[5]

The "obsolescent cultural situation" has already been defined many times in our earlier pages as simply the lack of adjustment to industrialization in some important political or social respect. It hardly needs to be added that, taking England as a model of such adjustment, large areas of Europe in 1900, or in 1915, were in an "obsolescent cultural situation," and that the survival of anti-industrial and antistate attitudes against the background of the centralized state and rapidly industrializing economy was creating favorable conditions for the flowering of Marxism. It is tempting to play with categories and types. At one extreme is a society industrialized in spirit as well as in fact (England), where socialism, when it appears, assumes the character of laborism. Further down is a country (Germany) where socialism is cast in the official Marxist mold, but where the rapid pace of industrial advance makes the mentality of the workers, if not

[5] *Ibid.*, p. 236.

the phraseology of their leaders, less and less responsive to the slogan of the class war. France before 1914 can be used as a model of a country where the anti-industrial protest is still so strong that even the official Marxist ideology of the socialist movement serves as a veneer over the essentially anarchist and syndicalist mentality of the radical element of the working class. At the other extreme is, say, Spain, where the low level of in- dustrialization makes the worker express his radicalism in anarchism and syndicalism pure and simple rather than in their subdued version of revolutionary Marxism.

If this pattern is examined, and if all the qualifications are al- lowed for, with an eye to the "catching on" of Marxism as a move- ment rather than as a theory, two things will be apparent: first, the tremendous ability of Marxism to fuse into itself, and to become the organizational expression of, other forms of socialism, mainly anarchism and syndicalism; and, second, the unstable character of the Marxist appeal to the working class. It is most effective at a specific period of the given society's development. But no sooner does Marxism replace anarchism and syndicalism as the official ideology than the same forces that had made the worker abandon the mere spirit of opposition to the state and industry, the mere principle of the workers' association as a substitute for any more comprehensive philosophy of politics and society, make him chafe under doctrinaire Marxism and push him toward a more pragmatic and evolutionary type of socialism. The ideal society for revolutionary Marxism is the one that is "arrested" in its response to industrialization; where large-scale industry and urbanization make simple anarchism obsolete and syndicalism unavailing from the point of view of the radical worker; where the relative newness of industrialization has not entirely killed off the peasant mentality; where a large part of the population consists of peasants tilling their small holdings; and where the political process and class divisions, whatever the official form of the state, do indeed give the worker the impression of the state as the "executive committee of the exploiting class."

We may observe the "in-between" character of Marxism by focusing for a moment on two writers of the period who attempted to rephrase socialism in terms of what they conceived to be the logic of social development and the character of class consciousness of the worker. At first glance, no two writers seem so many worlds apart as Eduard Bernstein and Georges Sorel. The German, a graduate of orthodox Marxism, a man who then attempted to modify Marxism to fit in with the genuine democratic creed, is the epitome of liberal values and the humanitarian approach to politics. The Frenchman, a proponent of irrationalism, without solid moorings in any political movement, later on an admirer of Lenin, a man whose writings found discordant echoes in syndicalism, Fascism, and Nazism, epitomizes the breakdown of the liberal values, the hankering after myths and violence—politics, in brief, as a form of excitement. The titles of their books, *Evolutionary Socialism* and *Reflections on Violence,* emphasize the contrast.

And yet how both of them turn to Marxism and invoke its thought in support of their quite contrasting conclusions! Neither is a "complete" Marxist, but each grasps one element of Marxian synthesis and disparages the other. To Sorel, Marx is the anarchist, the ancestor of syndicalism and the spontaneous revolutionary movement of the workers. To Bernstein, Marx is *primarily* the social democrat and humanitarian. If one discounts the revolutionary phraseology of Marx's younger days, obsolete under the conditions of socialism in twentieth-century Europe, one finds, holds Bernstein, the real Marx, real scientific socialism. If one discounts the deposit of the earlier socialist theories and utopias, retorts Sorel, one finds the real Marx: the revolutionary, the proponent of the violent take-over by the workers. Both the democrat and the believer in violence find in Marxism what they are seeking. Both the acceptance of industrialism and the democratic state and the rejection of industrialism and contempt for democracy which is syndicalism invoke Marx.

Bernstein and Sorel testify to how much the Marxist synthesis was made possible by the mid-nineteenth-century conditions under which it was generated, and how the breakdown of this synthesis fifty years later compels the Marxists to seize one or the other side of Marxism, for industrialism and anarchism can no longer be combined. Either, like Bernstein, you accept the logic of the doctrine as leading toward an industrialized state and democracy, or you seize the spirit of revolution and forget about the "stages of material development." Sorel portrayed with almost comic nostalgia the breakdown of the original Marxist analysis and the seductive power of industrialism and democracy:

In a society so enfevered by the passion for the success which can be obtained in competition, all the actors walk straight before them like veritable automata without taking any notice of the great ideas of the sociologists: they are subject to very simple forces, and not one of them dreams of escaping from the circumstances of his condition. Then only is the development of capitalism carried on with that inevitableness which struck Marx so much, and which seemed to him comparable to that of a natural law. If on the contrary, the middle class, led astray by the *chatter* of the preachers of ethics and sociology, return to an *ideal of conservative mediocrity,* seek to correct the *abuses* of economics, and wish to break with the barbarism of their predecessors, then one part of the forces which were to further the development of capitalism is employed in hindering it, an arbitrary and irrational element is introduced and the world becomes completely indeterminate. This indetermination grows still greater if the proletariat are converted to the ideas of social peace at the same time as their masters, or even if they simply consider everything from the corporative point of view; while Socialism gives to every economic contest a general and revolutionary colour. Conservatives are not deceived when they see in the compromises which lead to collective contracts, and in the bargaining between employers and labour the means of avoiding the Marxian revolution; but they escape one danger only to fall into another, and they run the risk of being devoured by Parliamentary Socialism.[6]

And Sorel's source of apprehension—bad old capitalism is gone and with it may go the real revolutionary spirit of the workers—is Bernstein's source of hope: "The movement means everything for me" and what is *usually* called the final aim of socialism "is nothing." The "movement" for Bernstein is the movement toward democracy; for Sorel, toward revolution. The German wants to extirpate in the workers the last of revolutionary intoxication, imbue them with the feeling that they will get everything they want by swimming with the tide of industrialism and democracy: "The conquest of political power by the working classes, the expropriation of capitalists, are no ends in themselves but only means for the accomplishment of certain aims and endeavors."[7] The Frenchman wants to preserve the struggle against the state *as such,* against the capitalist as the instrument of the worker's enslavement and alienation: "Syndicalists do not propose to reform the State . . . they want to destroy it, because they wish to realize this idea of Marx's that the Socialist revolution ought not to culminate in the replacement of one governing minority by another minority."[8]

Bernstein's *Evolutionary Socialism* (1899) and Sorel's *Reflections* (1906) are works by intellectuals, shaped, no doubt, by their personal predilections and idiosyncrasies. But they reflect much more than that, as witnessed by the great éclat that greeted them at publication.

Bernstein's Marx is the Marx of the German worker who has forgotten his anarchistic antecedents. His increasing well-being, the social legislation and protection by the state, the power of

[6] G. Sorel, *Reflections on Violence* [1908], New York, 1941, p. 87. I have substituted "bargaining between employers and labour" for the translator's "corporative particularism" as the former is obviously Sorel's meaning.

[7] Eduard Bernstein, *Evolutionary Socialism,* London, 1909, p. xv.

[8] Sorel, *op. cit.,* p. 123.

the unions—all these change the character of class antagonism on which German Marxism at first had grown. But the ideology remains in name, for it is the focal point of the still vivid anti-capitalism and the resentment of the arrogance of the ruling class and essentially nondemocratic government. But why a violent revolution if successive elections to the Reichstag bring a greater and greater socialist vote and open up the prospect of a peaceful victory of Marxism? What Bernstein wrote must have been felt by many: "As soon as a nation has attained a position where the rights of the propertied minority have ceased to be a serious obstacle to social progress, where the negative tasks of political action are less pressing than the positive, then the appeal to a revolution by force becomes a meaningless phrase." [9] If the German worker had not "forgotten" as much as his English counterpart, then, Bernstein believed, he soon would. And because in one sense he was still a good Marxist, he believed that he was describing the universal tendency of the working movement in the civilized world.

Sorel, never formally a Marxist, writes and speaks for syndicalism. The latter in its French version can be translated simply by "workers for themselves." The state, what is to be done the day after the revolution, how industries are to be run by the workers —these are problems on which syndicalism does not spend much time. Its French version reflects the specific French political and social conditions and the "memories" of the French working class. The roots of syndicalism lie in Proudhon and Blanqui. Its appeal to the *camaraderie* of the proletarian spirit and its protest against the *embourgeoisement* of the worker that is implicit in the more prosaic versions of socialism reflect the spirit of estrangement from the whole complex of the middle-class state. There is in Sorel a yet more extreme note—the rejection of the whole rationalistic and democratic tradition which Bernstein tries to read into Marxism. It is no longer a question of finding a refuge

[9] Bernstein, *op. cit.*, p. 218.

from the all-devouring state and industry: it is a masochistic delight at the forthcoming collapse of the whole mass of false values, the worship of action, admiration for all kinds of irrationalist theories showing up the "professors" and socialist bureaucrats. It is like much of *early* socialist thought, the instinctive reaction of the petty bourgeois striking up heroic poses in the face of the material forces that threaten his status and dwarf his self-esteem; but this instinct is now harnessed not to the scientifico-religious utopias of the pioneering socialists, but to the potentialities of the mass movements of the workers.

Sorel and Bernstein stand at the point of highest interdependence between socialist theory (and especially Marxism) and the Continental working-class movements. There is nothing yet of the ambiguity of the postwar situation, when one branch of the socialist movement will become an extension of the Soviet state and "its" ideology the result of decrees laid down in Moscow. The period before the war is one of *genuine* internationalism in the Marxist movement. The Second International, founded in 1889, is dominated by the Marxist parties; Marxism is acknowledged, in one way or another, to be the chief socialist tradition. Bernstein's revisionism, directed primarily to the awkward orthodoxy of the German Social Democratic Party, is also directed to the international socialist movement. Thus, its implications would read into international socialism the same meaning that Bernstein would read into the domestic form: it is the true heir, under twentieth-century conditions, of the cosmopolitan, democratic, and humanitarian tradition of nineteenth-century liberalism.

The pathetic strivings of the Second International to lay a basis for a world-wide pacifist movement to curb the rising tide of nationalism and militarism, to block the approaching war, are well known. Sorel's book provides a somber commentary on this count. Its exaltation of violence and irrationalism, its constant use of military figures of speech, augur the movements that will combine the socialistic appeal with racial and nationalist arguments. It is the sum total of Western bourgeois civilization which is to him odious: not only its state, its materialism, its industry, but its international order and rationalism.

The fears of Bernstein and the hopes of Sorel are alike symptomatic of the breakdown of the original Marxist synthesis—socialism coming in obedience to economic laws and fulfilling all the promises of rationalism; an international order and humanitarianism. This rationalistic optimism is missing in both writers. To Sorel, socialism will come only as the result of the abandonment of rationalism and a resolute stand against material progress: ". . . use must be made of a body of images which, *by intuition alone,* and before any considered analyses are made, is capable of evoking as an undivided whole the mass of sentiments which corresponds to the different manifestations of the war undertaken by Socialism against modern society." [10] Bernstein's abandonment of Marx's automatism of economic laws is equally pronounced, though it leads him to quite different conclusions: "Social conditions have not developed to such an acute opposition of things and classes as is depicted in the *Manifesto.*" [11] Socialism, then, does not *have* to come in the way that Marx imagined it would. It can come only through democracy: "democracy is a condition of socialism to a much greater degree than is usually assumed, i.e., it is not only the means but also the substance." [12]

An irrational myth on one side—"the whole of Socialism in the drama of the general strike"—a refinement of democracy and liberalism, on the other: such are the paths recommended for a reinterpretation of Marxism.

And yet, if the original synthesis of Karl Marx had broken down in the face of the facts of the world of 1900, he might well have reproached his interpreters with failing to provide a new and more realistic road to socialism, with being as much under

[10] Sorel, *op. cit.,* p. 130.
[11] Bernstein, *op. cit.,* p. x.
[12] *Ibid.,* p. 166.

the spell of the "inevitable" patterns of development within their own societies as he had been under the spell of the conditions of Western capitalism in the 1840's and '50's. It was naïve, he would have rejoined to Sorel, to ignore the logic of development of material forces, to imagine that socialism can come as an act of will, and to believe that the peculiarities of French and Italian capitalism, and hence of the working movement in these countries, represent a universal pattern. It was equally naïve of Bernstein to discard Marxist determinism while implying the acceptance of liberal determinism, to think of an uninterrupted growth of material well-being and democracy as leading rather easily to socialism, to believe the English pattern to be, essentially, the universal one.

It is easy to see, in historical perspective, how the contrasting interpretations of socialism were grounded, as the original had been, on the confusion of a particular socio-economic situation with a universal pattern and how they tried to preserve as universally valid an ideology which has drawing power under particular circumstances at particular times. Bernstein and Sorel rejected *literal* Marxism in favor of one part of the doctrine because one said, in effect, "Where are your terrible economic crises and the worsening lot of the worker?" and the other, "Where is your socialism after more than fifty years of capitalism?" But the success or failure of Marxism does not depend on its passing the test of historical prediction; it depends on the existence of conditions in which the questions and answers that Marx give appear both important and convincing to the working class.

This was not the case in Germany, or even in France. As mentioned before, the Marxist doctrine was like an ill-fitting suit of clothing worn over the actual working movement in both countries; if German socialism had outgrown it and was chafing under it, the French one had never quite fit into it. When Bernstein came out with his revisionist bombshell, he was gently reproved, so the legend has it, by an "orthodox" colleague, who said that, although they all felt the way he did, it was highly indecent to question the orthodoxy in public! In France the official Marxist tenor of the socialist party, created out of previous groupings in 1905, had to contend with syndicalism of the working movement. The C.G.T. (*Confederation Générale du Travail*)—the French trade-union congress—in its official declaration at Amiens (1906) spelled out its syndicalism in definitely non-Marxist terms:

But this task [of immediate practical protection of the worker] is but one side of the work of syndicalism: it prepares complete emancipation [*l'emancipation integrale*] which can be realized only by an expropriation of capitalism, it recognizes the general strike as a means of action and it considers that the union, today an organization of resistance, will be in the future the unit of production and distribution, the base of social distribution.[13]

It is natural that the trade-union movement should be more pragmatic, more related to the worker's nonphilosophical interests, and usually less radical than the corresponding socialist movement. It is thus all the more interesting that the French unions found themselves, by and large, on the left of the political movement and the German ones on the right.

The problem must be posed, though it cannot be discussed at length here, of the relationship of Marxism to the development of trade unionism. One pattern has been observed in Great Britain, where a party and a philosophy of socialism emerge from the structure of unionism, which represents the more active part of the working class, if it is not synonymous with it. In France, the much less numerous union movement (in proportion to the total industrial force), as represented by its major organization, the C.G.T., officially eschewed Marxism and professed syndicalism; and yet, because of practical exigencies, namely, the impossibility of expressing syndicalism in organizational political terms, it tolerated what might be called a liaison between the politically conscious worker and Marxism. In Germany, the

[13] Paul Louis, *Histoire du Socialisme en France,* Paris, 1950, p. 287.

relationship was more that of an uneasy marriage between the worker's party and his professional organizations. The relatively sudden and rapid onset of industrialization in Germany determined a correspondingly sudden and rapid growth of unionism and of political socialism. From their very beginning, the unions grew under the auspices of socialist theory, first that of Lassalle and then that of Karl Marx. While much is made of the differences between the two thinkers and of Marx's antipathy toward his colorful contemporary, the fact remains that Lassalle's socialism was essentially Marxist, even if it went further in explicit recognition of the role of the state and pragmatic use of unionism. German unionism was thus at an early stage divorced from its anarchistic roots. The socialist ideology grounded in Hegelianism and the large-scale character of German capitalism combined to uproot the remnants of anarchist feelings and to account for the weakness of syndicalist impulses in German trade unionism.

Was German *capitalism* helped in its rapid growth because the German worker, after industrialism hit Germany, never experienced a prolonged phase of "pure" anarchism and syndicalism, but found himself under a doctrine that, perversely acknowledged (and still does) the state and the benefits of industrialism? Or, on the contrary, was the character of German *socialism* determined by the rapid growth of German industrialism, by the visible benefits of the state and large-scale industry? There is, one feels, a great deal of logic to both hypotheses. Intense syndicalism is both a cause and an effect of a rather unenterprising small-scale capitalist development. A comment on French unionism may illustrate this rather involved point:

Only in France, Italy and Spain were there strong syndicalist movements, and only in France was it the prevailing doctrine of an important trade union movement. . . . The slow rate of economic development, the continued prevalence of small workshops, the lack of entrepreneurial daring gave French workers the feeling that they had little to expect from gradual processes. Such were their employers and such workers' expectations from the state of the economy, that revolutionary change was easier for many to envisage than day by day gains in their conditions of life and work. A revolutionary solution held greater attractions and risked less than in countries where capitalism was more dynamic. Even as they expressed their alarm over the spread of the Taylor system and the speed-up in France, C.G.T. leaders wished they could exchange their own unenterprising anti-union employers for no less anti-union but more enterprising employers of the United States. With such employers, they thought, French Unionism would itself take on greater force.[14]

We end up with a truly paradoxical picture: a vigorous growth of capitalism helps the growth of Marxist socialism among the workers; but, also, a speedy extinction by Marxism of syndicalist and anarchistic feelings among the workers can be a contributing factor to the flourishing development of capitalism! The lesson of Marxism has been absorbed by the worker: he works more efficiently since he accepts the inevitability of industrial labor and its appurtenances; his class hostility does not find expression in sabotage of the industrial and political system that he expects to inherit. The prospect of an *eventual* revolution removes the need for the strike, except as a struggle to win concrete professional benefits. One paradox leads to another: if capitalism is set within democratic or even semidemocratic conditions, the Marxist socialist movement will grow because of its undoubted organizational superiority over competing socialist movements. And under conditions of universal suffrage it may eventually come to power. But will this victory of the Marxist *movement* be the victory of Marxism, as Marx postulated? If the state has been conquered constitutionally, where are the state and the ruling class to be smashed? If, in the very process of gaining power, the working class, because of the lesson of Marxism and the rising standard of living, has learned to accept the industrial

[14] Val R. Lorwin, *The French Labor Movement,* Cambridge, Mass., 1954, pp. 36-37.

system, labor discipline, and centralization of economic life, where, in fact, is the revolutionary impulse? What remains, in effect, to revolt against? The contradictory parts of original Marxism are held together by one thing: the conviction that the growth of capitalism, of the industrial system, leads to the worsening of the worker's position. If that tenet is disproved, economically as well as politically, the very growth of the Marxist *movement* will lead to the worker's acquiring what Lenin called trade-union mentality; to his socialism being (for all the doctrinal references to the class war and revolution) essentially evolutionary and laboristic.

Revolution killed off by the growth of the Marxist movement, Marxism becoming the school of the middle-class values for the worker—these were the terrible possibilities faced by the leaders of the German Social Democracy. Ever since the party at its Erfurt congress in 1891 had purified its official doctrine of the Lassallean accretions, it had been considered *the* Marxist party in Europe, the official representative of the legacy of Marx and Engels. It was to the German socialists that the budding Marxist movements in Eastern Europe looked for leadership and guidance. It was the almost uninterrupted growth in union and party membership, in election votes cast for the socialists, that warranted optimism that Marxist socialism was the wave of the future. German socialism, like the rest of German society, patted itself on the back for its "theoretical" quality, as contrasted with the vulgar pragmatic of British socialism and the irrational adventurism of the French movement. For all the theoretical acumen displayed in the plethora of well-footnoted books and articles, for all the verbal fireworks with which the German socialists protested their contempt for bourgeois values and imperial institutions, the social democratic Karl Marx began to look suspiciously like Sidney Webb.

Bernstein's argument would have accepted and approved the similarity. German socialism, according to him, would have reaped the dividends of doctrinal flexibility and realism by attracting greater middle-class support in its struggle against the imperial government; it would have benefited from a more realistic and politically attractive policy on the peasant problem; and it would have had a greater possibility, even before a full electoral victory, of affecting German politics. The formal history of revisionism is well known: the party condemned Bernstein's thesis, reproved him, and clung to orthodoxy. The whole issue led the theoretical discussion farther and farther toward stretching the economic facts on the Procrustean bed of the original doctrine. Karl Kautsky's attempts to show that although the theory of "immiseration" may be *literally* incorrect, it is true in a *relative* sense, and that although the *natural* tendency of capitalism is toward the worsening of the worker's lot, a countertendency keeps it temporarily in check, are fine examples of the ideological calisthenics with which the leaders of the party attempted to keep the revolutionary spirit alive, if at a low intensity. The ingenious attempt of the left wing, represented by Rosa Luxemburg, to maintain Marx's theory of the catastrophic breakdown of capitalism by attributing the survival of capitalism to the exploitation of the noncapitalist segments of world economy, e.g., through imperialism, also falls in the same category.

It is customary to view the whole struggle within the German Social Democracy in terms of personalities: mild and democratic Bernstein, professorially unrealistic Kautsky, and revolutionary-minded Rosa Luxemburg, all struggling for ideological dominance in the spirit of German theoretical pedantry. An alternative is to refer the whole issue to the conservative habit of the party bureaucracy, which forced them to hang onto the doctrine with which they had grown up and with which they felt comfortable. But what underlies the conflict, the desperate refusal of the center and left wing of the party to acknowledge the facts, is an instinctive feeling that orthodoxy, with its absurd "immiseration" theory, is the last barrier preventing the worker's accommodation to the system and his *embourgeoisement*. And, under German conditions, if you give up revolution, do you guarantee that you will obtain democracy and representative government? We are discussing the period of irrationalist theories and movements, the period of the growing strength of nationalism, with its attendant phenomena of militarism and imperialism. It is ironic that the main Marxist party and movement, by its insistence upon an outworn theory, by saying in effect *"credo quia absurdum,"* ranges the Marxist tradition in the irrationalist camp and prepares the ground for its role as a theology in the Soviet system.

Orthodoxy versus revisionism in Marxism has its immediate meaning in the concrete tactics and problems of the German Social Democratic Party. A historian has outlined the theory under which the doctrine and reality reached a stalemate in the official posture of the German Marxists between 1900 and 1917:

> In terms of the divergent groups composing Social Democracy, Kautsky's theory may be viewed as a proposal for a truce under which the trade unionists and revisionists would give up their attack on revolutionary theory and their effort to come to terms with the ruling class, while the ultra radicals would cease their drive for a revolutionary tactic. The theoretical concept with which the truce was to be sealed was that of the passive revolution. Under it Social Democracy would move neither toward further acceptance of the existing order, nor toward action to hasten its collapse. It would organize and agitate, and maintain its moral integrity while waiting for the ruling class to destroy itself. Thus the effort to reconcile antagonistic political and intellectual tendencies led Kautsky not so much to a synthesis as to a stalemate.[15]

It is easy, with our historical hindsight, to project from this tragicomic predicament of the German Marxists—their inability to see things as they are because Marx had said they should be otherwise—a sequence of events from the German Socialists'

[15] Carl E. Schorske, *German Social Democracy, 1905-17: The Development of the Great Schism*, Cambridge, Mass., 1955, p. 115.

acceptance of the war, through their growing impotence in the Weimar Republic, to their all too easy destruction by Hitler. It is also easy to urge, depending on one's point of view, that either of two extremes, Bernstein's liberalism or Rosa Luxemburg's revolutionism, would have brought better results than the "muddle of the middle" in which the party stuck. But theoretical formulas are not magic incantations capable of changing political reality.

Industrialization in Imperial Germany had gone far enough to strip the actual socialism of the working man of its revolutionary component, but not far enough, on its political and social side, to make this socialism mostly pragmatic, democratically and liberally minded. A society in which feudal concepts were still rampant, in which a large part of the population remained in peasant status, and which was not a democracy, did not offer a completely plausible setting for Fabian socialism. "The 'social problem' that was so puzzling to our fathers, how to organize a capitalist-socialist society, is in reality solved at the end of the nineteenth century. It means that its principles are laid down. Their execution will constitute the difficult task of the technique of statesmanship," wrote a representative of "academic socialism." [16] This was an illusion. But so was Rosa Luxemburg's expectation that the collapse of the liberal and capitalist order would of necessity result in a revolution both democratic and socialist. History was to show that Marxism could come to power not as the heir of democracy or as the receiver of bankrupt liberalism, but only under the same conditions that had made it the ideology of the working class, *as the heir of anarchism*.

Had the international order not broken down with World War I and the international implications of early liberalism been shown illusory, the story might well have been different. The cardinal point of liberal internationalism was well stated in the *Communist*

---

[16] Werner Sombart, *Die Deutsche Volkwirtshaft im Neunzehnten und im Anfang des 20 Jahrhunderts,* Berlin, 1921, p. 455.

Manifesto: "National differences and antagonisms between peoples are daily more and more vanishing, owing to the development of the bourgeoisie, to freedom of commerce, to the world market, to uniformity in the mode of production and in the conditions of life corresponding thereto." [17] Had Marx and the liberals been right, then the spread of Marxism might well have followed Bernstein's prescription and Kautsky's expectations: socialism as the logical successor and culmination of liberal democracy. But the destruction of liberal internationalism, the fatuity of the rationalistic dogma of the liberal utopia exposed by the holocaust of the war, again made Marx the revolutionary and anarchist a more convincing prophet than Marx the liberal and democrat. A new synthesis of Marxism—at the time of its formulation, the creed of a small body of fanatics issuing from a backward and despotic society—was to become the dominant strain of revolutionary socialism. When in 1918, at Lenin's prompting, the Bolsheviks decided to change their official title from Social Democrats to Communists, they were, like Marx and Engels in 1847, eschewing the nonrevolutionary and parliamentary connotation of the term "socialist." But there was a more profound, though at the time not entirely perceived, element of continuity with the original thought of Marx and Engels. That thought had been revolutionary; it had combined wonder at the material forces transforming men's life with protest against the destructive effects of industrialization. The same combination reappears in Communism and explains the sources and main locations of its appeal.

A NEW MARXIST SYNTHESIS—LENINISM

The history of all countries shows that the working class, exclusively by its own effort, is able to develop only trade union consciousness, i.e., it may itself realize the necessity for combining in unions, to

17 P. 340.

fight against the employers and to strive to compel the government to pass necessary labour legislation, etc.[18]

Lenin, when he wrote these words, set the basis for the Bolshevik party and for the movement which within fifteen years of the writing of *What Is to Be Done* was to seize the Russian Empire and inaugurate a new phase in the development of Marxism. In retrospect, it is truly amazing that a turgidly written pamphlet concerning an obscure conflict between two minute groups of Russian Marxists came to be the foundation of an ideology and a movement that was to conquer Russia and become a leading force of the century. It is as if an article written in 1944 concerning a dispute between two branches of the American Trotskyites were the foundation of the political movement in power in the United States in 1960, and thirty years later the basis of the ideology officially enthroned over one third of the population of the world.

What Is to Be Done is the basis of Bolshevism. It is the argument of Bolshevism, the formulation of the concept of the party, so essential to Communism. It is the *style* of Bolshevism—the tedious, repetitious, pedantic argument that makes the original works of Marx and Engels shine like great literature in comparison. One is drawn to wonder how the Russian revolutionary movement, initially so romantic, nurtured on so much literary inspiration, came to be expressed in a document having all the external romance and excitement of a doctoral dissertation! And the problem is more fundamental: how a movement capable of inspiring people to both heroism and cruelty, to tremendous feats of construction, and to an appalling subservience, can have as its set of scriptures a dismal collection of undigestible scholasticism. Why of all branches of *literary* Marxism was the Russian one destined to be the dullest, seemingly most drained of the feelings and emotions that excite people to revolutionary action; and

[18] V. I. Lenin, *What Is to Be Done* [1902], New York, 1929, p. 32.

why of all Marxist *movements* was the Russian one to emerge
as the heir of the most elemental and violent of revolutions? Why
has the same movement been the beneficiary of assorted revolutionary strivings all over the globe, of economic grievances of the
worker, of the peasant's desire for more land, of national and
anticolonial aspirations, of the intellectual's search for order and
creed?

Those are the questions that can be addressed to the version of
Marxism known as "Leninism," which in its simplest formulation is found in *What Is to Be Done*. The work is ostensibly a
variation on one main theme: Marxian class consciousness, political class consciousness, socialist consciousness, call it what you
will, can come to the workers only from the *outside*. As spelled
out in the opening statement, by themselves the workers can
reach only trade-union consciousness, the desire to improve their
economic status and to obtain better working conditions, etc.
Although the argument is directed at German revisionism and its
alleged Russian followers, there is this basic agreement between
Lenin and Eduard Bernstein: the forces of history are not making
of the workers a *revolutionary* class; the spontaneous organization
of the workers leads them not to revolution but to the struggle for
economic and professional improvement. Why, then, is Bernstein
a "revisionist" and Lenin an "orthodox" Marxist? Because Bernstein believes in the workers' party following the inclinations of
the workers and bowing to the inherent laborism of the industrialized worker, whereas Lenin believes in forcible conversion
of the worker to revolutionary Marxism. Wrote Lenin in 1902:
". . . subservience to the spontaneity of the labour movement,
the belittling of the role of the 'conscious element' of the role
of Social-Democracy, means, whether one likes it or not, growth
of influence of bourgeois ideology among the workers." [19]

Let us observe, in passing, how fixedly, for the moment, the
eyes of this Russian revolutionary are on the West, on England

[19] *Ibid.*, p. 39.

and Germany. The Russian worker in 1902 is far away indeed from the status and feelings of the English or German trade unionist. But looking ahead to further industrialization of Russia, Lenin has no doubt that the great danger to the revolutionary élan, to revolutionary Marxism, is the slow but continuous and inevitable ebbing of the revolutionary impulse of the worker, his acquisition of trade-union mentality, of a savings account, of the feeling of amelioration of his status, which makes the desperate revolutionary reaction at first less urgent and finally unrealistic and unnecessary. "Hence, our task, the task of Social Democracy, is to *combat spontaneity,* to *divert* the labour movement, with its spontaneous trade-unionist striving, from under the wing of the bourgeoisie and to bring it back under the wing of revolutionary Social Democracy." [20]

"To combat spontaneity . . ." The literal statement sounds almost ridiculous, doubly so in the circumstances of its first formulation. Who is to divert the growing working movement in Russia from its natural course? A handful of revolutionaries—some of them in Tsarist jails—operating through a newspaper published abroad. But the statement contains the essence of Leninism, the perception that the *natural* development of material forces and the *natural* response of people to them will, in time, lead far away from Marx's expectations about the effects of industrialization on the worker. You do not jettison Marxism because it failed to predict the psychology of the worker in an advanced industrialized country, says Lenin. You "improve" and advance this psychology in the revolutionary direction by means of a party. A remarkably illogical performance. You reject the major premise of your ideology, yet you claim strict orthodoxy. Your argument is rationalistic and materialistic, and yet you set out, almost in Sorel-like fashion, to propagate the myth of revolution, the necessity of which, you have just asserted, the workers will feel less and less!

[20] *Ibid.,* p. 41.

The aproach in *What Is to Be Done* reveals a very significant factor in the reception of Marxism in Russia. To Lenin and his contemporaries *Marxism means revolution*. Marxism as a re-action against the factory system, as a philosophy of materialism and economic determinism—these are secondary considerations both to Lenin and to his opponents. It is in the meaning of Marxism as a *specific road to political revolution* that they are chiefly interested. To the Russian intellectual, the philosophy of Karl Marx came not as an aesthetic protest against the industrial revolution, not even as a sudden vision of a better and more just society; it came primarily as the culmination of a century's search for a concrete and convincing philosophy and strategy of revolution. It is striking that missing from Lenin's pamphlet is a discussion of the issue that divided the Western Marxists at the time and that really lies at the bottom of the problem of spontaneity versus revolutionary consciousness: Is or is not the worker's standard of living worsening under capitalism? Both Lenin and his opponents are really interested in the "secondary" reflection of the problem: What kind of activity will enable the workers to carry off a revolution? The whole theoretical discussion of "immiseration," which fills up the life of the Western Social Democrats, is almost entirely missing in the Russian debate. Bernstein, Kautsky, Rosa Luxemburg, and Bebel quarrel about the historical trends, Lenin and his opponents about *tactics*.

And this explains how Lenin in 1902 can consider himself a materialist and yet reject spontaneity; how he can plead for a conspiratorial, centrally controlled revolutionary party, and yet feel that he is a democrat. For the conditions of Russia of 1902 make the revolutionary interpretation of Marxism as convincing, for all the logical paradoxes of the doctrine, as it had been in Western Europe of 1848. Industry is growing by leaps and bounds in the Russian Empire, but the necessary political com-ponent of industrialization is lacking even more than it had been in France or England of 1848. The contrast is stressed

again and again by Lenin: "The Western-European Social Democrats find their work in this field facilitated by the calling of
public meetings, to which *all* are free to go, and by the parliament in which they speak to the representatives of *all* classes.
We have neither a parliament, nor the freedom to call meeting. . . ."[21] If the normal rudiments of parliamentary institutions are missing, if political activity is banned, then also missing
is the vital element of the confrontation of the Marxist dogma
with political and social reality which makes a Western socialist
at least visualize the problem, and which by its absence enables
the Russian Marxist to swallow the doctrine as a whole and to
ponder only its tactical implications.

In a sense the Russian intellectual of Lenin's time lived in a
jail. A comfortable jail if he did not choose to revolt, but a jail
nevertheless, which separated him from the normal activity of his
Western counterpart. Reality—the reality of an advancing industrial society, of vigorous artistic and scientific activity, encompassed in a political system which was by definition and in fact
an autocracy—was in itself so fantastic that the paradoxes and
incongruities of a revolutionary theory did not have the jarring
impact they had in the West, but paled into insignificance against
the urgency of revolution. For a century now the Russian intellectuals had sought a theory that would both explain and remove
the humiliating political backwardness and impotence of their
society: a revolutionary analysis, and a prescription of action.
To the small groups that had been assembling illegally, Fourier,
Saint-Simon, and Proudhon all provided material for analysis
and revolutionary theories, but little for an effective political
movement. Scientific and social theories, often politically neutral
when enunciated in the West, were under Russian conditions
transmuted into *philosophies* of revolution. Marxism, when it
appears on the Russian scene in the 1880's, appears as a philosophy of total liberation: it is science, philosophy, and a general

[21] *Ibid.*, p. 79.

guide of action. It inherits much of the impulse that drove people into Saint-Simonian and Fourierist cults. It inherits much of the original political excitement that, after the liberation of the serfs in the 1860's, drove many politically conscious Russians into the ranks of the Populist movement.

The synthetic function of Marxism in gathering into itself various revolutionary and intellectual movements and impulses is nowhere as well documented as in Russia at the beginning of this century. To a socialist, as to a revolutionary disappointed in the fruitless terrorism of the "People's Will" of the 1870's and '80's, Marxism comes as a superior, systematic, and scientific revolutionary creed and method. The other non-Marxist or even nonpolitical sources of modernism, which in the West tempered the appeal of the doctrine, were in Russia almost nonexistent. Political liberalism prior to 1905 was prosecuted as vigorously as Marxism, or even more so, because the Tsarist regime feared esoteric intellectual doctrine less than the claims of "respectable people" for constitutional rights on one hand, and the terroristic activity of the heirs of the People's Will on the other. It was thus the autocracy that was the real barrier to the spontaneity of modern social development, which has in the West encroached upon the Marxist appeal. It is, then, no paradox but a fact—amply explained by the circumstances of the formulation of Leninism at the beginning of this century—that Russian Marxism can proclaim itself democratic and yet demand an elitist party of revolutionaries run in a dictatorial manner; that it is materialistic and rationalistic but wants to *impose* its ideology upon the workers. Again, as in the case of early Marxism, the combination of incompatibles into a single doctrine can be understood only in terms of specific circumstances of a specific society that make the paradox not only possible but convincing.

The struggle against the development of "trade-union consciousness" among the workers was but one aspect of Lenin's struggle against "spontaneity." Three years before his famous pamphlet, he had completed *The Development of Capitalism in Russia*. In his concluding remarks, he observes that the development of capitalism in Russia has been slow and adds astutely: "And it cannot be but slow, because no other capitalist country has preserved to such an extent institutions of the old, incongruous with capitalism, hampering its development, infinitely worsening the conditions of the producers who 'suffer both from capitalism and from the insufficient development of capitalism.' " [22] And he criticizes the Narodniks, the Russian Populists, for not understanding the development of industrialism and capitalism, for moralizing instead of applying Marxist criteria to the problems of politics and economics.

Secondary as the economic side of Marxism was to Lenin *at the time,* it was already important enough to make him reject the populistic side of the Russian revolutionary movement. There is very little in Lenin of the strain that saw revolutionary hope in Russia's happy preservation from the evils of full-fledged Western capitalism. The strain that held the hope of socialism in the *mir* (the Russian peasant commune), which in an obscurantist fashion derided the West for its "materialism," finds in him but little echo, though Marx in his old age had, rather surprisingly, discoursed on this theme. The revolutionary movement, Lenin holds, must acknowledge in a hard-boiled fashion that capitalism is finally coming to Russia, that though it operates there under conditions different from those in the West, it is both illusory and harmful to imagine that Russia can "skip" the stage of capitalism.

More basically, Communism as fashioned by Lenin reflected, in addition to the revolutionary impulse, his and his contemporaries' impatience with the torpor and backwardness of Russian society and their feeling of the need and inevitability of modernization. The elements of difference and local charm that strike the Western reader in the Russian novel of the nineteenth century

[22] V. I. Lenin, *Sochinenya,* Moscow, 1946, III, 527.

were anathema to Lenin and, by and large, became so to his movement. In Marxism he found the ideal of technology and science regulating society. His admiration of things German was not confined to the German Socialist Party before 1914, but included "German" efficiency, science, and talent for organization. In that sense, Germany represented to Lenin what Stalin later meant when he pleaded for a combination of Communism with the "American method": rejection of the whole complex of introspection about Russia's backwardness, rejection of intermittent self-contempt and glorification of Russia's "difference" from Western Europe, of the Russian soul, etc. It is in the same vein that the Bolshevik leaders of today condemn Pasternak's *Doctor Zhivago,* not only because it is apolitical and not written with "socialist realism," but also, they feel, because its tone and concerns are out of keeping with modernized and industrialized Russia forty years after the Revolution. Lenin's impatient Westernism, his longing for an emancipation from the interminable philosophical discourse and for *doing* things, is fully discernible before the Revolution of 1917, and illuminates in what sense Marxism "made a difference" in this revolution.

It follows that the struggle against the danger of trade unionism is to him no more important than the struggle against another type of spontaneity. Almost contemporary with the organization of the Social Democratic Party of 1898 was the birth of another revolutionary organization, the Socialist Revolutionaries. The latter, in effect, though not without an infusion of Marxism in their ideas, picked up the tradition of the People's Will, of revolutionary socialism looking to the small peasant rather than to the worker as the base for a future democratic society. The essential anarchism of the Social Revolutionaries and the practice of terrorism by its left wing represented to Lenin a danger as great as the reformism of the "Economists" (the would-be Russian followers of Bernstein) and the alleged proximity of the Mensheviks to the middle-class spirit. The Socialist

Revolutionaries represented *par excellence* the reaction against industrialization that we have already encountered. The official democratic and socialist terminology of the movement ill concealed the essential anarchistic, anti-industrial reaction of the peasant *both* against the economic process that was disrupting the traditional economy of the countryside and against the political and class system that denied him more land. The Socialist Revolutionaries were, like all Russian parties and movements, led and staffed by intellectuals. But their ideology and political behavior up to the point when, after the revolution of 1917, having clearly become the leading party in terms of popular support, they were first split and then eliminated by the Bolsheviks, show clearly all the characteristics of anarchist, anti-industrially originated movements: organizational instability, inability to integrate the facts of the modern state and economics into ideology, and susceptibility to the extremes of nationalism on the one hand and anarchistic terrorism on the other. A recent study of the party shows well the instability of both its program and organization and its consequent defeat after the theft of its revolutionary appeal by the Bolsheviks.[23] In an industrializing society, with rapid growth of industry projected against the still overwhelmingly peasant character of the country and its backward political system, it fell eventually to the Socialist Revolutionaries to prepare the necessary anarchist and revolutionary background on which Marxism could achieve power.

The other aspect of the struggle against spontaneity was, then, Lenin's struggle against the *uncurbed* and *undisciplined* revolutionary impulse itself. Individual acts of terrorism, to a Marxist, are not only personal indulgence in heroics, which cannot affect the forces of history, but under the Russian conditions they resulted, as Lenin was sensible enough to see, in the alienation of large segments of public opinion rather than in

[23] Oliver Radkey, *The Agrarian Foes of Bolshevism,* New York, 1958.

coercion of the government into concessions. To base your revolutionary activity *merely* on the peasant's aspirations—and again the Marxist instinct of centralization and technological progress supplements the revolutionary's impulse—was to base it upon an essentially disorganized and vacillating element, susceptible both to the most primitive anarchism and to the most reactionary appeals of nationalism and religion.

It is a magnificent analysis of the deficiencies of various kinds of spontaneity that emerges from Lenin's heavy prose. The workers, if left to themselves, will eventually develop trade-union consciousness and will neglect the revolution for higher wages and better working conditions. The middle class will stop their revolution when they have constitutional rights, i.e., when they can play at parliaments and parties and preserve their property. The peasants? God only knows what the limits are to their aspirations! They will want to confiscate the lands of the gentry, but preserve their inefficient cultivation by the individual household and communes. They will press for all sorts of decentralization of political authority, thus making impossible any socialist economy, but will respond to the appeals of Russian chauvinism (or of other nationalisms in the non-Russian areas of the Empire) or religion. The conclusion should have been that there was no social basis in pre-1914 Russia for a *socialist* revolution.

It is here that the instincts bred into Lenin by immersion in Marxism prevent him from reaching the logical conclusion and enable him to come out, really unconsciously, with a fantastic solution. If all the widespread revolutionary pressures within the population still do not add up to socialism, why not create a party that, for all its allegiance to literal Marxism, will be able to appeal and capitalize on the disparate revolutionary aspirations of various classes? A party that at different times and with varying intensity will still be able to associate itself with the claims for better working conditions for the workers, with the basic demands for democracy and a constitution, with the peasant's hunger for more land, and with an oppressed minority's desire for autonomy or independence; a party not limited and confined to these aspirations but using and pushing them as the means of achieving socialism? In *What Is to Be Done,* this idea is still only sketched and somewhat incoherently presented: "To bring political knowledge to the workers the Social Democrats *must go among all classes of the population,* must despatch units of their army *in all directions,*" and again, "We must go among all classes of the people as theoreticians, as propagandists, as agitators, and as organizers." [24]

But the organizational pattern is already clearly implied: to be that flexible and yet ideologically monolithic the party *has* to be elitist and centrally directed. It has to be a party of activists and not of mere sympathizers. The quarrel over a phrase that split the Bolsheviks and the Mensheviks in 1903 expressed not the ridiculous pedantry of contentious dogmatists but the issue of an inherently elitist and dictatorial concept of the party as the assimilator and guide of revolutionary impulses versus the party as their mere reflection. The Mensheviks, in their way as doctrinaire Marxists as Lenin, balked at the former.

It is always tempting to see a great historical figure as a genius developing the victorious formula for revolutions and wars in a flash of intuition. Actually, the concept of the party was only sketched by Lenin in 1902-1903. Its full formulation came through long years of theorizing and activity, not without hesitations and retreats, which led to November 1917. And the concept itself owes as much to the political acumen of Lenin's mind as it does to its narrowness, to his conviction that Marxism must mean revolution above everything else and that only Marxism can be the guide to revolution. A lesser but more sensitive man would have seen the paradoxes inherent in the Leninist solution. The party thus devised proved to be a workable concept under conditions of political suppression, but could

[24] *Op. cit.,* pp. 76, 79.

hardly have survived had the Revolution of 1905 been followed by a really constitutional and free political life in Russia. The Bolsheviks proved to have the ideal organization and the ideal ideology to capitalize on the political and economic anarchy into which Russia was plunged after March 1917. Had the war and defeats not come, or had they come after another decade of vigorous industrialization, expansion of parliamentary customs, and the growth of the rural middle class, again it is most likely that the Bolsheviks would now figure in history as an insignificant fanatical wing of the Russian socialist movement.

The "ifs" and "buts" can be multiplied. What is important in this study is to observe the relationship of Marxism to Lenin's concepts. Lenin instinctively groped for the *uses* of Marxism under Russian conditions and found in it the road to revolution. There is enough democracy in Marxism to have enabled a Russian revolutionary to associate himself with the need for freedom felt by all Russian society before 1914. There is enough of the raw appeal of anti-industrialism and anarchism in Marxism to have enabled the Bolsheviks in 1917 to respond, and not insincerely, to the peasant's aspirations and to seize the leadership of the urban proletariat. What under normal "spontaneous" conditions of economic and political development would have been the fatal shortcoming of the doctrine proved under the anarchic conditions of 1917 to be the key to victory.

Lenin groped for the kind of party that Marx defined in the *Manifesto*:

The Communists, therefore, are on the one hand, practically, the most advanced and resolute section of the working class parties of every country, that section which pushes forward all others; on the other hand, theoretically, they have over the great mass of the proletariat the advantage of clearly understanding the line of march, the conditions, and the ultimate general results of the proletarian movement. (p. 334)

Under democratic or even quasi-democratic conditions the workers will feel that they themselves have the "advantage of clearly understanding the line of march" and that they do not need the kind of party that tells them what they "really" want as distinguished from their immediate and trivial demands. The Leninist party is, then, practicable under conditions peculiar to any society in transition, where the class interest of the workers, in fact, the industrialized working class itself, has not hardened into a definite mold, and where the process of industrialization and modernization has all the confusing and bewildering effects that it had in the West when Marx wrote the *Manifesto*. The Leninist party becomes not only the repository of dialectical wisdom; it becomes the dialectic itself. It is the party that decides whether the "objective factors" make the given society ripe for the bourgeois or socialist revolution, whether capitalism has reached its full potentialities or not, whether the given country, having passed the stage of socialism, has entered the communist stage. It is the party that "decides" that the workers want to join the broad democratic front (though the mass of the workers may be happily unaware of the existence of the problem, not to mention the desire) or whether, contrariwise, they want to strike on their own against the bourgeois parties. The concept, to those who have witnessed the behavior of the Communist parties in the West, is quite fantastic. It is as if one were to get rid of the unpleasant and unforeseen variations in the weather by vesting the power to decide whether it rains or snows in a committee allegedly endowed with the essence of wisdom about meteorology.

The full implications of the pattern became obvious only after the Bolshevik's seizure of power and their attempted imposition on the socialist movement in the West and elsewhere of the formula that had procured them victory. But the framework is set in *What Is to Be Done*. The pamphlet marked an as yet overly intellectual statement of Leninism. The use of ideology as a technique of acquisition of power became clearer to Lenin as successive developments in Russia proceeded to offer both opportunities for and setbacks to revolutionary socialism. Thus the Revolution of 1905 provided a demonstration of the vitality of two issues that became incorporated into the victorious formula of 1917: the soviets and the peasant question. The revolution, in fact, demonstrated the indifference of life to stilted formulas: it was not a "bourgeois-democratic" revolution, nor was it a socialist one. It was a tremor of revolutionary excitement, which seized the Empire: peasant outbreaks, revolts of the sailors, and nationalist outbreaks in the non-Russian parts took place alongside and uncoordinated with the workers' revolutionary activity in the major industrial centers. For the first time, the raw materials of the effective revolutionary appeal were vividly demonstrated: the national aspirations of the non-Russians, the worker's propensity to form committees of action-soviets as the means of struggle, and—the master cause of all unrest, of all anarchism seeping into Russian society—the peasant's incoherent but steady protest against the social and political order, and his demand for more land immediately. Less than two generations after his emancipation, the peasant began to respond with political protest against the half-oppressed, half-emancipated status in which the measure had left him, against his exposure to, but not assimilation by, industrialization.

To Karl Marx, the peasant problem was, of course, one with which socialism would not have to deal at all. With his eye on the British economy of his time he assumed that capitalism would obligingly solve this problem as it would solve the problem of the artisan: by elimination. Large landed estates, run scientifically in accordance with advanced industrial techniques, would fall into the lap of socialism as easily as the great industrial and banking combines. The peasant, that curious figure defying class classification, radical and reactionary at once, attached to his property, enemy of the state and science, would not, in any appreciable quantity, be around by the time the expropriators are expropriated. Already the German Social Democracy had discovered that the German peasant, unlike his English brother, not only refused to die out but viewed with considerable distaste any socialist proposals to turn him into an agricultural worker.

By 1906 in Russia, it was fairly clear that the overwhelming mass of Russian peasants would never opt, either by election or revolution, for a program that would envisage their elimination as individual householders and cultivators, and that for all the alleged communistic propensities of the peasant and his traditional attachment to the mir, his radicalism included anti-property feelings on the subject of landlords, church, and state estates, but stopped short of the logical application of the same principle to his own holding. To the Marxist, the preservation of the peasant's small holdings or of their collective version in the mir was almost inconceivable. The small peasant bars the road to industrialization. The mir, in which some superficial Western observers professed to see a preview of the Soviet collective farm, was, of course, nothing of the sort. It was an obsolete form of communal organization of the peasantry in the Great Russian part of the empire, kept by the Tsarist government after the Emancipation for the purpose of preserving control over the peasant. To liberals and Marxists alike, the worship of the mir by the Slavophiles and the Populists was obscurantist nonsense. The mir was economically inefficient, inhibited better methods of cultivation as well as initiative and social mobility of the peasants. In retrospect, its belated retention helped to preserve in the peasant this peculiar combination of conservatism and radicalism, which under economic or political stress breaks out in anarchism.

It would take us too far to go into all the involved discussions of the peasant question that occupied Lenin and his Bolsheviks, the Mensheviks, and the Socialist Revolutionaries up to the Revolution of 1917. In April 1917, involved formulas and Marxist scruples all disappeared in the flash of intuition that Marxism indeed can come to power on the wave of anarchism; the painful formulas were superseded by Lenin's slogan: "Land to the peasants."

But as early as 1906 Lenin had been groping his way toward a formula with a concrete revolutionary appeal to the peasant. The Bolshevik program was explicit on the confiscation of all church-owned landlords' and state lands, on giving the peasant the right to dispose freely of his plot. In a much more subdued tone, almost in small print, it was stated that *after* the democratic revolution the socialist party should strive to replace private property in land by national ownership.[25] Literal Marxism on the land question was unavailing in view of the Socialist Revolutionaries' and other Populists' hold on the peasant. Thus Lenin in practice appropriated the Socialist Revolutionary program on the peasant question, while he retained, for what seemed the distant future, the Marxist aim of socialization of the land.

How the ideas of *What Is to Be Done* cease after 1905 to be bookish concepts and become endowed with life is equally demonstrated in Lenin's attitude toward soviets. The intellectual enemy of spontaneity could not at first take kindly to the spectacle of *ad hoc* committees of the workers thrown up by a revolutionary situation or a general strike, committees subject to no common ideology, occupied exclusively with the conduct of the struggle at hand, and uniting people of the most diverse political opinions. This practical application of syndicalism, for that was what the soviets in 1905 and initially in 1917 were, must have appeared to Lenin as being quite far from the idea of disciplined revolutionary action by the workers in obedience to the call of the socialist party. To digress, it is impossible to

[25] *The Fourth (Unity) Congress of the Russian Social Democratic Workers' Party in 1906* (in Russian), Moscow, 1934, p. 501.

overestimate how much Lenin revered the German Social Democrats and dreamed of the Russian Marxists' coming to resemble in organization and power their German brothers. This worship, which collapsed when the German Socialists meekly acquiesced in the Kaiser's war, kept Lenin, before 1914, from the complete and conscious repudiation of parliamentarism that was implicit in his theories and activity as early as 1902-1903. Yet the experience of 1905 demonstrated the revolutionary viability of the soviets. It must have become obvious that revolutionary socialism under Russian conditions could operate more successfully through the fluid structure of the soviets, whose very looseness and improvisation favored the kind of disciplined party which the Bolsheviks were, or were to become, than through formal, regularly elected parliamentary bodies, where under the most favorable conditions the Bolsheviks would be in a minority. The full realization of the role of the soviets again belongs to 1917. Lenin's slogan "All power to the soviets" becomes one of the key factors in enhancing the Bolsheviks' popularity and influence. In a volatile, unstable organization, which a soviet of workers or soldiers represents, the decisiveness and unity of the Bolsheviks, their lack of scruples in following the political mood of the moment give them an enormous advantage even over other revolutionary parties.

What is the sum of the effects of the Revolution of 1905 on Lenin? It is not unfair to characterize it as the growing realization, though he does not admit it to himself or to others, that a revolutionary situation in Russia would not follow any neat socialist preconceptions, but would be, in essence, an anarchist revolution. For the Marxist party to succeed, political authority would have to collapse; the instruments of coercion (i.e., the army) would have to become demoralized; the mass of the peasantry would press for their immediate interests; and political power would become parceled out among a variety of local organs—the soviets. The elaborate agrarian programs and parlia-

mentary schemes would be of no avail. What would count would
be the sensitivity and responsiveness to the variety of revolutionary impulses stirring up the society. The task of the socialist
party, in Lenin's view after 1905, becomes not so much to "combat
spontaneity," but to *manage* revolutionary spontaneity without
becoming subservient to it.

Again, the realization is neither full nor decisive until 1914.
The pattern of literal Marxism—industrialization, the bourgeois
democratic revolution, and only then the socialist revolution—
is persuasive enough to make Lenin reject Trotsky's thesis
that in Russia the historical process might be telescoped and that
a socialist revolution might follow the bourgeois one immediately,
rather than after an interval. Until the war and the collapse
of the liberal international order and, in his eyes, the abdication
of the Western socialists, Lenin cannot embrace the thesis of
"permanent revolution," and the fact that he does not do so
is a tribute to his realism. The Revolution of 1905 was followed
by two major reforms, which, if they had had time to work out
for more than a few years, would have made the permanent
revolution of 1917 most unlikely.

The constitutionalism introduced after 1905 was of the lamest
sort; and the parliament, the Duma, was very far from being a
true legislative and representative body. Yet the rudiments of
parliamentary procedure and civil rights existed, and they began
tempering the revolutionary protest and channeling it into concrete political demands. More important, Prime Minister Stolypin
instituted agrarian reforms, which looked forward to the break-up
of the mir and to allowing the capitalist process to take its
course in the countryside. Like his predecessor Witte, Stolypin
believed in bureaucratically inspired industrialization as being
the only solution of Russia's predicament. The break-up of the
commune and a vast program of peasant resettlement would
enable "nature," i.e., capitalism, to take care of the peasant-land
problem. Eventually a class of individual, prosperous peasants

would replace the inefficient, discontent-breeding communes and would become the rural middle class. The financial burdens on the peasantry, dating from the Emancipation, were lifted, and incentive was given to the peasants to become "separators"—to take their land out of the communes. The scheme, in the few years it enjoyed, proved to be a success.

It is unlikely that the sum total of the reforms and the social engineering by the Tsarist bureaucrats would have undercut social discontent or the appeal of socialism. But the reforms were providing this institutional and social framework for industrialization, which, as we have seen, channels the revolutionary protest into reformism and strips the socialism of the worker and peasant of its anarchistic and hence revolutionary character. The Marxist in Lenin had to greet these developments with an ambivalent feeling: from one point of view they were according to the script. Capitalism in Russian society was becoming stronger, less hampered by the pre-capitalist remnants. Yet by the same token the prospects for revolutionary socialism were becoming less hopeful. Trotsky's permanent-revolution theory frankly implied that the socialist revolution would emerge from backward rather than advanced capitalism. But Lenin was never ready to depart from even the *letter* of Marxism unless there were concrete revolutionary dividends to be gathered up. The acceptance of the practice of permanent revolution was thus postponed until there was in fact permanent revolution in Russia.

One is struck again by the fact that a certain narrowness of mind—perhaps one might call it the lack of speculative imagination—was a contributing factor in Lenin's greatness. Before 1914, he could believe that he was a good social-democrat, with equal emphasis on both sides of the hyphen. In 1917, he became, for all purposes, an exponent of anarchism. All this time, his belief in the canon of Marxism remained undisturbed. This quality, which becomes inherent in Communism, cannot be traced exclusively to personal characteristics. It is the product of thorough immersion in Marxism under conditions of society where the logic and the conclusions of the doctrine are *not* shown to be mutually contradictory. In 1917, without the slightest hesitation or introspection, Lenin was to grasp that although the letter of Marxism includes democracy and ordains socialism to proceed from advanced capitalism, the spirit of revolutionary Marxism is the exploitation of the anarchism inherent in backwardness.

The breakdown of the international liberal order illustrated by World War I was the signal that the synthesis of democracy and Marxism implied in the position of the German Social Democracy—especially in that of Karl Kautsky, who had been to Lenin before 1914 a theoretical guide and exemplar almost on the order of Marx and Engels—had equally broken down. In his most unoriginal work, *Imperialism,* written in exile in Switzerland in 1915, Lenin "demonstrated" the necessary tendency of capitalism, in its later stages, toward monopoly and then imperialism. While the argument of the book is borrowed from J. A. Hobson's book of the same title, and the Marxist interpretation from Hilferding and Rosa Luxemburg, the book in conjunction with the war arrives at the most catastrophic and hence, for a Marxist, optimistic view of the evolution of capitalism. The prosperity of capitalism, its ability to raise the worker's standard of living in the West, its democratic features—all these apparent refutations of Marx are but temporary delays of the inevitable doom, purchased by the ruthless exploitation of colonial and backward areas. The postponement of Marx's prognosis is but temporary, for imperialism is bound to end up in vast conflicts among the imperialists: "From all that we have said about the economic essence of Imperialism it follows that it should be characterized as transitory, or to be more exact, dying capitalism." [26]

The apparent contradiction of Marx by the facts is thus

[26] V. I. Lenin, *Imperialism,* Detroit, 1924, p. 128.

explained away. There is no reason to soften the revolutionary rigor of Marxism by reading into it democratic and parliamentary postulates. The war is the dying pangs of capitalism. In their struggle for investment markets, the capitalists have to arm the proletariat. The expropriation of the expropriators will now become an international phenomenon, with the war-weary workers turning their arms against their capitalist masters, transforming the imperialist war into civil wars for socialism. The war enables Lenin to dispel the last doubts about the incompatibility of Marxism with an outright revolutionary position. The undercurrent of doubt, the perhaps subconscious questioning of the prophecies of the master can now be laid aside. Marxism means revolution. Those Western socialists who participate in the war activities of their states or who prattle about pacifism are traitors and opportunists.

It is impossible to explain the concentration, decisiveness, and drive of Lenin and the Bolsheviks in 1917 except by the enthusiasm of believers whose doubts about their canon had collapsed and who saw in their faith an infallible guide to success. In a few days after his arrival in Russia in April 1917, Lenin was able to dissipate the last social democratic notions of his colleagues and to undercut any attempt at a reunion with the Mensheviks. Though the Bolsheviks had existed as a separate party since 1912, no one had previously excluded the aim of a reunion of all the Russian Marxists. But soon after his arrival Lenin wanted the party's name to be changed to "Communist," so as to consecrate the break with the past tradition of doubts, democratic scruples, and reinterpretations. He was to get his way only after the November Revolution, though by that time the whole democratic tradition had already been rejected in fact.

The revolution which in March 1917 overthrew the Tsar and vested power in the provisional government is classified in Marxist semantics as a "bourgeois democratic revolution." In reality, it very soon became much more than that. The whole structure of authority, the rudimentary and growing social and political institutions of industrialization, were swept away. The veneer of authority vested in the provisional government concealed the essential state of anarchy, political as well as social. As Sir John Maynard wrote: "In explanation of what happened in rural Russia, let me again emphasize the virtual disappearance —outside of the *Mir* and the Canton Committee—of all authority. Tolstoy had counselled his countrymen that each should say: 'For me there is no state.' They had taken his advice and the State had vanished into air." [27] The soviets in the cities and soon among the armed units even at the front shared in this anarchic process. In brief, Russia found itself in a state of anarchy with just a shell of parliamentary and modern political institutions imperfectly concealing the chaos. The political party closest to anarchism, the Socialist Revolutionaries, became the most popular movement in the country. Even after the November coup of the Bolsheviks in the election to the ill-fated Constituent Assembly of January 1918, the Socialist Revolutionaries demonstrated that their combination of anarchism and agrarian socialism commanded the sympathy of the majority of the electorate. But anarchism, while it is the mood of revolution, cannot become the organizational principle of it. The Socialist Revolutionaries, with their interminable dissensions, with opinions among the leaders ranging from constitutionalism and the desire to continue the unpopular war to direct revolutionary action and defeatism, demonstrated the historical incapacity of anarchism to provide viable political and economic formulas.

The slogans—All power to the Soviets! Land to the peasants! End to the war!—thrown by Lenin on his return revealed his identification of revolutionary Marxism with anarchism. The party built upon the denial of spontaneity and upon the principle of centralization and military discipline was in the best position to use the spontaneous revolutionary impulse of the people

[27] *Russia in Flux*, New York, 1948, p. 182.

without itself being carried by it. Until the end of the Civil War, the Bolsheviks not only used anarchist slogans and practices; they became in all respects, *save the internal organization of their party,* anarchists. It was by deepening the anarchist character of the revolution, by sabotaging any attempt to erect a temporary shelter for constitutionalism, that the Bolsheviks sought power. The Mensheviks, or most of them, clung to the literal interpretation of Marxism, to the impossibility of erecting socialism in Russia without first going through the democratic phase. No Marxist inhibitions held Lenin back from advocating the complete smashing of the state by parceling out power to the soviets; from assuring the Bolsheviks the support or at least the benevolent neutrality of the peasants by inciting them to seize the landlords' estates and force the "separators" back into the mir; and from encouraging the dismemberment of the empire by a radical advocacy of national self-determination and of defeatism in the face of the German advance. It is customary to attribute all these moves to political acumen rather than to ideology. But the latter provided a wonderful reassurance to the Bolsheviks that in sponsoring anarchism they were in fact promoting socialism. Unbelieving apostles, it has been said, are usually unconvincing. Because of Marxism, Lenin's party could and with conviction did become, in revolution, anarchists, just as with revolution and Civil War barely completed they could turn around and begin to stamp out the anarchy, begin to build modern history's most centralized and absolute state.

An observer as sympathetic to revolutionary Marxism as Rosa Luxemburg could not, in her comments on the Bolshevik revolution, restrain her misgivings about its anarchist character. The Bolsheviks, she observed, in their desire to propitiate the peasant, officially nationalized land, but in fact let the peasants seize and cultivate land in small units. More fundamentally, Lenin erred in instituting revolutionary terror, which denied democracy and the freedom of activity even to other socialist and revolutionary parties. But her criticisms failed to perceive that revolutionary Marxism *has* to be essentially anarchist in character. It has no chance unless the structure of authority and the habits proper to organized industrial society break down, and it forsakes its opportunity if it sticks to the democratic and centralistic parts of the Marxian canon.

The immersion of the Bolsheviks in anarchism is best demonstrated by Lenin's *State and Revolution,* written on the eve of the Bolsheviks' *coup.* For all the self-conscious denials that his theory of the state is anarcho-syndicalist rather than Marxist, Lenin propagates the views for which Communists in 1921 and 1922 were, at his command, to be read out of the party, the views which in 1921 were to inspire Kronstadt sailors to rise against a Bolshevik regime already on the road to centralization and bureaucracy. The state is to be smashed away, the bureaucracy and professional civil servants abolished; egalitarianism is to rule supreme—all this, not in the distant stage of communism, but at once under the dictatorship of the proletariat.

All officials, without exception, elected and subject to recall *at any time,* their salaries reduced to "workingmen's wages"—these simple and "self evident" democratic measures, which completely uniting the interests of the workers and the majority of the peasants, at the same time serve as a bridge leading from capitalism to socialism.[28]

And what, if not anarchism, is this statement:

With such *economic* prerequisites it is perfectly possible immediately, within twenty-four hours after the overthrow of the capitalists and bureaucrats, to replace them, in the control of production and distribution in the business of *control* of labour and products, by the armed workers, by the whole people in arms. . . . *All* citizens become employees and workers of *one* national state "syndicate."

[28] V. I. Lenin, *The State and Revolution* [1917] New York, 1932, p. 38.

All that is required is that they should work equally, should regularly do their share of work, and should receive equal pay.[29]

These words of August 1917 should be read in conjunction with the plea for a centralized (i.e., hierarchical) party of *professional revolutionaries* in *What Is to Be Done*. They should be read in conjunction with what Lenin had to say immediately after the revolution when he confessed unabashedly that it was impossible to replace the capitalists and bureaucrats in "twenty-four hours." Every factory, he was to say in 1919, every industry, represents the concentrated experience of capitalism which we do not have. He was not as yet to say, as Stalin was to explain eleven or twelve years later, that socialism had to acquire the experience and, incidentally, the methods of capitalism. But Lenin was ready to sneer at those who accused the Bolsheviks of inconsistency or hypocrisy, now that the Communists' anarchism and belief in the people were visibly cooling off: "As if one could undertake a major revolution, knowing in advance how to conclude it! As if this knowledge could be drawn from books!"[30] And he went on to talk about the need for military and civilian specialists.

Here, then, is Leninism. Is it an ideology? Or is it a political temperament and an eclectic technique enabling one to respond to power situations, at one point to be a social democrat, at another an anarchist, at another a bureaucratic enforcer of state power and capitalism? The sum of theoretical innovations by Lenin is meager; his views on Marxism are usually applications to Russian conditions of some German Social Democrat's interpretations. Yet it is Lenin's *use* of Marxism that stamps him as a new and, in a way, original synthesizer of the original doctrine and the Russian revolutionary conditions. In 1917,

---

[29] *Ibid.*, p. 83.
[30] *The Protocols of the Eighth Congress of the Russian Communist Party in 1919* (in Russian), Moscow, 1933, p. 21.

Lenin was capable of grasping the revolutionary sense of Marxism, its portrayal of the peasant's and the proletarian's psychology of opposition to the state and the forces of modernism, and applying it to the problem of seizing power.

His socialist opponents, who saw Marxism only as a series of political prescriptions based on economic stages of development, were inhibited from seeing that a Marxist revolution was possible in Russia precisely because capitalism had *not* fully developed in the country, precisely because Russia was *not* ready for socialism. The same instinct after the Revolution and even during the latter stages of the Civil War caused Lenin to begin to discard the anarchism and egalitarianism needed for popular support during the struggle for power. Whence came the realization that real national self-determination, real regional autonomy, and really independent trade unions were against the grain of Communism? It is easy to equate them with unideological attachment to power and the very human unwillingness of rulers to weaken their authority. But the almost immediate, sharp reversal of party policy would have been impossible without the psychological mechanism instilled by Marxism in its devotees, which makes them prone to anarchism in the time of revolution, to centralism and inegalitarianism after power has been won. It was Lenin's achievement to construct a party that could best instill in its members the separateness of the two parts of the task: one, the conquest of power; the other, the use of power. This lack of susceptibility of the Communist party to democracy, to the desires of the people whom it represented, to their own slogans, was not only freely acknowledged but boasted of by the Bolshevik leaders. Said Zinoviev, then the spokesman for Lenin, at the Eighth Congress:

The whole basis of our disputes with the so-called "economists," the Mensheviks . . . was based on [their] confusion of two concepts, the party and the class. Those people did not understand that the party is different from the class and the class from the party;

that the party should be the leading part of the class, that it sets aims which the working class does not understand completely today but will understand tomorrow.[31]

It would have been impossible to make this avowal of what in common-sense language is simply duplicity without the strong sanction of and unbounded belief in the ideology. Otherwise Zinoviev's statement, which in various versions has been the leitmotif of the Communist leaders from 1902 up to our own day, would have been a species of self-destructive cynicism verging on the most extreme naïveté.

Thus on the morrow of the Revolution "the aim which the working class does not understand today" is the exact opposite of the aims it understood and supported in the Revolution: the building of the strong authoritarian state; industrialization, which will require methods more severe than those employed by early capitalism; and the consequent erection of a totalitarian structure. The totalitarianism inherent in building an industrialized society under Marxist auspices was brought on by the very success of the revolutionary slogans. Not only the workers but many of the Party members were carried away by the slogans they had been proclaiming. It took Lenin's party some time to realize that Marxism in power is the exact opposite of Marxism in revolution and that the first task of the victorious Communist party is the extirpation of revolutionary democracy and anarchism in its own ranks.

[31] *Ibid.*, p. 292.

V THE OTHER SIDE OF MARXISM

With the Bolshevik Revolution and the almost miraculous survival by the Communist regime of the attacks by diverse domestic and foreign forces, a new era was opened in the history of the Marxist movement. Prior to November 1917, Marxism had always been in opposition or in revolution; now a party proclaiming itself to be an orthodox Marxist movement achieved power in a great country. Enough has already been said about this feat's being achieved under conditions quite contrary to Marx's expectations and in the spirit that we have classified as anarchist rather than Marxist, if by Marxism is meant a scrupulous adherence to the main strictures of Marx and Engels. But once the Civil War and the danger of the immediate overthrow of their regime was over, the Bolsheviks were faced with an unprecedented task. Even the external characteristics of this task were back-breaking: the economy thoroughly ruined, the promising industrial development prior to 1917 almost totally undone, the ruling party a garrison amidst a hostile or indifferent population, the idea and the reality of the modern state barely visible against the canvas of universal lawlessness and disorganization. And the fundamental issue: How to build socialism? Where to begin and with what? The idea of a universal socialist revolution in the wake of the Russian one, of the help extended to the young socialist state by its more advanced partners was shown by 1921 to have been a mirage. To the Communists fell the historical task of showing what the other side of Marxism was, demonstrating socialism in action, proving that Marxism could not only carry off a revolution but rule and develop a society.

STALINISM

To "practical people" in 1921, socialism was a vague concept associated with street fighting, strikes, and fantastic theories. Communism in its Russian version was identified with a group of wild revolutionaries, whose very appearance and behavior marked their separation from the main stream of European culture and development. Anarchism, atheism, terror, and destruction of private property—these were the things for which the Bolsheviks were known. Could those people organize the state, collect taxes, fit their country with a modern economy and civil service? Where was a guide to enable them to set and develop the intricate mechanism of the modern state and economy? Even sympathetic observers who applauded the revolutionary romanticism of the movement, its aura of struggle, of bold innovations, even of terror, felt pity at its predicament: how would these revolutionary heroes become prosaic legislators, tax gatherers, and managers? How would they stay in power, not to mention the lifting up of their barbarous society to socialism?

A revolutionary optimist in the West would have predicated success upon one thing: the Revolution, having freed the people from the shackles of capitalism and the remnants of feudalism, would have created a new and unprecedented grass-roots democracy and popular participation among the people of Russia, and almost with no direction or compulsion the whole nation would bend its energies to the task of creating a better life. A more moderate supporter of the new Soviet state would "realistically" expect the regime to cool off in its revolutionary fervor and, after an interval, to rule in the usual way, in the immemorial fashion of revolutionary groups who, having seized power under the banner of a utopian creed, after due time revert to the "usual" ways of politics and economics. The beginnings of the New Economic Policy, inaugurated by Lenin in 1921, were greeted by the "realists" as proof of their wisdom: the regime was settling down, forsaking the extremes of Marxism, and allowing a modicum of private property and initiative. The political aspect of the regime? Here historical experts knowingly discoursed on the eternal forces of Russian history: the people's susceptibility to despotism, their instinct for "collectivity," which made them endure the despotism of the Bolsheviks as cheerfully as they had that of Peter the Great. (The comparisons with Ivan the Terrible became more fashionable with the period of Stalin's terror.)

What the realists, the revolutionary sympathizers, the historical experts, and those who saw in the Bolsheviks simply the embodiment of Antichrist all agreed upon was that the thing least important about the Bolshevik state was its alleged connection with the obscure and impractical theories of Karl Marx. Yet, paradoxically, it is Marxism and its importance in the development of the Soviet Union which makes the preceding judgments superficial. Had the foreign observers taken the trouble to study the ideology and the extent to which both the leaders and the rank and file of the Bolsheviks were grounded in it, they would have realized the cohesive function of the doctrine, the extent to which it held the party together, and the degree to which it determined the character of postrevolutionary Leninism as well as the main traits of what we call Stalinism. It is difficult for us in the West to admit and understand how real, live human beings can be affected in their behavior, in their concept of self-interest and duties, by something somebody scribbled a century before; and it is most difficult to conceive of people in power, with a multitude of choices, being directed by the imperatives of an ideology. This is the basic reason why so many have seen the development and policies of the Soviet Union as an enigma inexplicable by anything in historical experience. It is this pragmatic bias, in reality, the unreflecting acceptance of *our own ideological premises* as having universal validity, that must be overcome to assess the development of Communism.

The theory of and habituation to Marxism were all that the Bolsheviks had in the way of economic and state-building experience. To the most unfriendly observer, the magnitude of the task, and the administrative and economic skill displayed by the Bolsheviks in restoring their country's economy and in laying the administrative foundations for the prodigious transformation of the whole society that took place under Stalin are extremely impressive. The Bolsheviks were imbued with administrative and economic instincts without which the later transformation of Russian society would have been inconceivable. One is drawn to think of another group of fanatics who, faced with concrete material tasks, displayed engineering and managerial abilities unsuspected in their original obscurantist creed: the Saint-Simonians. It is as if the selective function of Marxism had been to draw into the Leninist party the people who, under the cover of their revolutionary doctrinarism, possessed in the highest degree the managerial and administrative instincts required to erect the modern industrial state. Projecting into the Stalinist period the picture of the Communist, one sees him in Marx's words:

Fanatically bent on making value expand itself, he ruthlessly forces the human race to produce for production's sake; he thus forces the development of the productive forces of society, and creates those material conditions, which alone can form the real basis of a higher form of society, a society in which the full and free development of every individual forms the ruling principle.[1]

[1] *Capital*, p. 649.

Is this Marx's description of the socialist? No, this description—
and how well it will fit the self-proclaimed task of the Communist party under Stalin—is of the capitalist.

Before the Communists could turn to the task, which can unabashedly be characterized as the construction of Marxist capitalism, they had to dispose of revolutionary Marxism. One may
think of Marxism as a "two-stage" ideology. The revolutionary
stage drops off after the revolution. The democratic undertones
of Marxism are disposed of, revolutionary anarchism is extirpated,
and the task of construction in spirit and by means antithetical
to the revolutionary stage is begun. The process is neither smooth
nor automatic. It comes in a series of realizations, first by Lenin,
then by Stalin, that a faithful application of the principles under
which the party had been carried to power would, in the postrevolutionary era, hamper and make impossible the construction
of socialism. It comes almost as the process of natural selection:
those Bolshevik leaders who had become most imbued with
the democratic and anarchist slogans of the revolution, those who
temperamentally were most averse to the negation of the revolution that now must take place, get broken and then eliminated.
The process becomes associated with the struggle for power,
where the fighters and orators who made the revolution possible
have to yield to the administrators.

And the political transformation has its social and artistic
accompaniment. The revolution and the postrevolutionary era
extending until the late 1920's is characterized by the outburst
of social and artistic exuberance that always follows in the wake
of a great historical transformation. Unrestrained individualism
and nonconformity in personal and artistic behavior, unconven-
tionality and inventiveness in the arts follow November 1917.
As the new order crystallizes and the main task of society becomes to industrialize, the shackles of conformity, orderliness, and
socialist respectability are imposed upon the arts and social
mores. It is as if all the varied forces which had assured that

the bourgeois culture and mores of the nineteenth century became subjugated to the task of industrialization—nonconformist moral precepts, intellectual and artistic fashions of Victorianism, the overwhelming materialism of society—now became concentrated in the interpretation of Marxism that the party was imposing upon Russian society.

In retrospect, then, this is the picture of the interpretation of Marxism imposed upon Russian society by Communism. While it is possible to attribute the terror, violence, and pathological aspects of the process to the tyrannical personality of one man, or a group of men, it is impossible to deny that the essential authoritarianism of the process is implied in the logic of Marxism and in the concept of the party which boasts that it "sets the aims which the working class in their totality does not understand today but will understand tomorrow."

On the morrow of the revolution, the masses—to use this unlovely expression of the Communist vocabulary—want socialism. But they do not "understand" that socialism can come only to an industrialized society. They "understand" even less that industrialization means a strong centralized authority, the strong state. Who does not understand, said Stalin in 1930, when he could afford to be frank, that it is one of the creative paradoxes of Marxism that, although we Communists are for an eventual demise of the state, we are for the present for the dictatorship of the proletariat, "which is the strongest and the most powerful form of government of all that have existed?" [2]

Had the masses understood that, the Bolshevik revolution would in all likelihood not have taken place. The state was to be smashed, popular initiative and participation were to take the place of the professional civil service, the necessary economic and political coordination was to be the result of free and spontaneous coordination of autonomous, democratically elected

[2] *The Sixteenth Congress of the All Union Communist Party, 1930,* in Russian, Moscow, 1930, p. 56.

regional authorities. This promise of revolutionary Bolshevism, one of the main points of its popular appeal in an anarchically minded society, was solemnly embodied in the first Soviet constitutional documents. The letter of the law followed closely the modified anarchism of Lenin's *State and Revolution;* the unwieldy constitutional structure seemed to offer the widest scope to local autonomy; during the very first years of the Soviet regime, no *formal* links connected the Soviet republics of Russia, Ukraine, and Byelorussia. Individual workers' unions and the unions as a whole arrogated to themselves considerable powers over the industries. Short of the temporary requirements of the united effort against counterrevolutionary forces, the constitutional structure promised to offer the widest scope for local and professional autonomy. With the rather considerable exception of members of the former exploiting classes, democratic rights were guaranteed to everybody, again with temporary limitations for the period of the Civil War. If we add the peasants' appropriation of the landlords' and the state's estates and the egalitarian mood and practices of society, we get an official structure just this side of anarchism.

Yet from the very beginning this picture has been a mirage. The *real state* in Soviet Russia—the agency not only for political and economic coordination and legislation but also for the vast schemes of social engineering and of coercion of society—has always existed in the Communist party. The "bourgeois democratic" state has, in effect, been smashed; but, in ironic fulfillment of Karl Marx's dictum of the state's being the executive committee of the exploiting class, the executive organs of the Communist party became the state. The decentralization, national and regional autonomy, and autonomy of various social classes were and have been the façade behind which the real political process in Soviet Russia has been taking place within the Communist party. If the party was to be monolithic and united, then all the constitutional autonomies and separations of power were not to matter one iota. If the party was to be run dictatorially, as turned out to be the case, then all the guarantees and inviolabilities were not worth the paper on which they were inscribed. *The party became the state.*

The struggle for the centralized state was bound to take place within the party. The story has often been told of the attrition and then elimination of the last, lingering democratic instincts within the Bolshevik party. A few weeks after the November 1917 coup, a few Bolshevik leaders could still resign from Lenin's cabinet in protest against his concept and practice of one-party government. Yet these doubts soon disappeared, and the party unanimously supported the suppression of all parties, even of other revolutionary and socialist parties, and the curtailment of freedom of the press and of political life in general. The remnants of any democratic feeling in what used to be the Social Democratic Workers' Party of Russia evaporated with such rapidity that, in 1926 at the Fifteenth Party Conference, Zinoviev, fighting against Stalin for his political life, could yet describe as an "unheard-of libel" the accusation that he and the rest of the anti-Stalin opposition wanted to transform one-party rule into a "democratic republic." Lenin's party was not likely, in any case, to attract as members, people with overly democratic instincts.

Other groups and parties could be eliminated, but the ruling party itself remained, for a time, as the arena of contending principles. The party was—and on this all its members agreed—the vanguard of the working class. But in which direction should the vanguard move? The acceptance of an ideology as the ruling, if not the only, guide of action is always a dangerous inhibition to the freedom of a political organism. Personal conflicts, differing temperaments, must be expressed in the ideological jargon. It is difficult for the contestants to admit that there can be several alternative courses of action. There *must* be only one "correct" line, and the proponents of other views must be in error or, worse, in sin, or, to express it in the Communist parlance, subject to other class interests, viewing problems from the non-Marxist standpoint. What, then, inhibited from the very beginning any democratic life within the party (and it should be remembered that when Lenin formulated his concept of the party in 1902 and 1903 he explained its undemocratic features as imposed by the then impossibility of free political life in Imperial Russia) was the concept that the Bolsheviks were not a *mere* party: they were the carrier of the true ideology and the correct interpretation of history. It is as if the fathers of the American Constitution had not been guided in their deliberations by the problem of devising the most practical and workable constitutional arrangement, but had operated from the assumption that on every issue—even the most minute—there was only one correct solution, which must be found in and justified by recourse to the writings of, say, John Locke.

Whatever the personalities involved, the inherent ideological assumption of the Communist party made it of necessity a totalitarian party. What is referred to as the period of party democracy, until 1925-1926 when Stalin emerged as the undoubted dictator, is really the period of groping *for the organizational expression* of the totalitarian formula; and it is unlikely that the result would have been less totalitarian, even if the application might have been more humane or less efficient, had Lenin lived on or had Zinoviev or Trotsky emerged in ascendance.

It was this inner logic of the development of the party that made it not only the instrument of the centralized authority of all kinds—something which is implied in Marxism—but also an instrument of totalitarianism, i.e., of suppression, and of liquidation of any freedom of discussion, any free development at all—something for which not Marx but Lenin's concept of the party and its application by Stalin must be blamed. It was, then, almost inevitable that Marxism, which, whatever one may say about it, is a rationalist and intellectual technique, would be elevated into a mystique and ritual and that disagreements or varying interpretations would become translated into the problems of orthodoxy and heresy. The product of nineteenth-century liberalism, the technique for modernization and industrialization, became the means of ritualistic incantations accompanying purges and brainwashing.

It is this aspect of Marxism in the Soviet Union, the horrible terminology of "left" and "right" "deviations," the paranoiac expansion of the study of class and personal motivations (if Zinoviev and Kamenev were against Stalin, it "really" meant that they had been against Lenin and that they were "really" ready to sell the Soviet state to the Western imperialists), that makes the importance of ideology in the Soviet context so difficult for a Western observer to discern. We long for a direct rather than a circuitous and ritualistic statement of the relationship of the aims and means. Why could not Lenin after the revolution simply say: "The revolution is over; the logic of the situation, which is also the logic of Marxism, means that we cannot have socialism without industrialization. We cannot have industrialization without a strong centralized authority, without experts, wide disparities of pay, and so on. Hence, we must forget all the nonsense propagated by us during the revolution about smashing the state, equality of pay, status, and so forth. Let us get on with the job." But before this degree of rationality and ideological introspection could be *almost* achieved by the party (and when it is completely achieved Marxism will cease to play any role in the Soviet Union) Communism had to go through debates, splits, purges, and terror.

The most immediate difficulty was that the party itself was thoroughly imbued with democratic and semianarchist ideology. Any drastic attempt to apply the logic of Marxism in defiance of its revolutionary spirit would have met, in the Communist party of 1919 or 1920, with repudiation by a vast majority of its members. It is instructive to study one aspect of the problem centering about the so-called Workers' Opposition. This group, as early as 1919, attacked the tendency to build the state bureaucracy, to employ bourgeois specialists, in brief, the whole attempt to create the machinery of state under Soviet power. The Workers' Opposition and the Democratic Centralists, another group akin in spirit, discerned as early as 1919 and 1920 (the period which from the present perspective or even that of thirty years ago, appears as one of drastic economic egalitarianism in society and of relative democratic procedures in the party) the growth of the oligarchical principle in Communism and the related phenomena of official favoritism and bureaucratic mentality. This, to repeat, took place in the USSR of 1920, which, from today's perspective, looks like an anarchist paradise. Yet a considerable body of Communists was already chafing under inegalitarian conditions and dictatorial and bureaucratic methods in the party and the state!

What did the Workers' Opposition want? Their whole complaint is not so much a definite policy as a reflection of a malaise —the feeling in wide circles of the workers that something is wrong with the revolution, that the reality of Communist life is not in accordance with Communist promises. The specific proposals advanced by the opposition within the party look, in effect, toward syndicalism. It is difficult otherwise to interpret the leader of this opposition, Mme. Kollontay, as she phrases the demands:

To form a body from the workers-producers themselves—for administering the people's economy. . . . All appointments to the administrative economic positions shall be made with the consent of the union. All candidates nominated by the union are non-removable. All officials appointed by the union are responsible to and may be recalled by it.[3]

[3] Alexandra Kollontay, *The Workers' Opposition in Russia*, Chicago, 1921, p. 33. The Russian text was unavailable to me. The English translation is unauthorized and obviously inexact.

The practical effect would be the vesting of the control of the economy—more properly speaking, of government—in the hands of the workers' unions rather than the party. Mme. Kollontay, daughter of a Tsarist general, did not hesitate to recommend that the Communist party should become even more proletarian and that all the nonworking elements who joined the party since the November Revolution should be expelled.

Appointments by the leaders must be done away with, and replaced by the elective principle all along the party line . . . all the cardinal questions of party activity and Soviet policy are to be submitted to the consideration of the rank and file and only after that are to be supervised by the leaders.[4]

It is even possible to feel some sympathy with Lenin, head of a devastated and disorganized country, confronted with this millennial demand to introduce immediately a syndicalist utopia, until we remember that Mme. Kollontay's demands are but more detailed elaborations of what Lenin had said in *State and Revolution*. The Workers' Opposition argued from the premise of the Communist and proletarian dictatorship, with little thought of the rights of the nonproletarian majority of the people.[5] But the fulfillment of its postulates could only have meant the breakdown of the incipient structure of the Soviet state.

Not connected with the Workers' Opposition but another evidence of the anarchist mood and condition of the country was the uprising at the great naval base of Kronstadt. In 1917 the Bolsheviks had no stronger supporters than the sailors of the Baltic Fleet. Then, in 1921, the very same element rose against them. The sailors claimed freedom of activity for all the left socialist and Anarchist parties, full freedom for the peasants to do as they liked with their land, abolition of the special position

[4] *Ibid.*, p. 40.
[5] Leonard Schapiro, *The Origin of the Communist Autocracy*, Cambridge, Mass., 1955, p. 294.

of the Bolshevik party, and equal food rations for all.[6] Both within and without the party, the Bolsheviks were confronted by the danger that the same tide of anarchism that had carried them to power would now engulf them.

Two things became obvious within the context of the Russian situation between 1920 and 1922. The Marxist instinct of the Communist elite and their self-interest in preserving power went hand in hand in keeping Lenin and his group from giving in to the democratic and or syndicalist demands. At the same time, a complete about-face from the slogans of November 1917, frankness about the goals and methods of the Communist state (such as was to be exhibited by Stalin in the 1930's) not only would have been psychologically impossible but would have shocked the majority of their own followers to the extent that the leaders could not have kept power. It took all Lenin's prestige, as well as considerable chicanery, to defeat the Workers' Opposition at the party congresses. The Kronstadt uprising had to be drowned in blood.

What would have been the effect had Lenin said, in 1921, as Stalin was to say in 1930, that egalitarianism in wages was a petty bourgeois superstition and had nothing to do with Marxism and that the unions should not get in the way of industrial management? The man who approached this bluntness about the meaning of Marxism in postrevolutionary Russia was Lev Trotsky. It was he who employed "specialists" in the army and industry and talked with frankness about the economy's requiring complete subordination of the unions to the party. But this very bluntness and forthrightness, Trotsky's ability to see the sense of Marxism in every concrete situation, was probably the cause of his future weakness among the rank and file of the party and among its leaders, of the attribution to Trotsky of the dictatorial designs that Stalin was soon to carry out so successfully. The practical meaning of Marxism under the condi-

[6] *Ibid.*, p. 301.

tions of Russia of 1921—the building of the strong centralized
state, the use of essentially capitalist methods and incentives to
restore and then to industrialize the economy of the country—
could not have been bluntly acknowledged or formulated, in the
face of the anarchist and democratic sentiments intensified by
revolutionary Marxism. An outright about-face would have led
to other Kronstadts and would have magnified beyond control
the turbulence of inner-party struggle.

It is ideological self-deception rather than conscious hypocrisy
that led Communist autocracy to change thus into outright
totalitarianism and made Leninism shade into Stalinism. Neither
Lenin nor his associates could acknowledge to themselves that
Marxism, Communism, now must mean something other than
what it meant during the Revolution. The old terms have to be
preserved. Those who propagate the Bolshevik slogans of the
past "must" be shown to be "really" counterrevolutionaries. The
socialists of other varieties, exponents of popular discontent,
must be demonstrated to be foreign agents, agents of the landlords,
and Tsarist generals. "Objective historical reality" teaches the
party that a Menshevik pleading for democratic rights is a counterrevolutionary and a worker demanding the fulfillment of the
Bolshevik promises of 1917, an agent of the White Guards. The
same element of part self-deception, part political acumen keeps
Lenin from formulating clearly the issues separating him from
the opposition in the party. The workers' unions are not yet
fully subjugated, as Trotsky had desired, but are proclaimed, in
a soothing formula, to be schools of communism for the workers.
At the same time the administration of the party is turned over
to those who appear most capable of subduing its unruly and
syndicalist wings and of turning it into a monolithic organization.
The New Economic Policy of tolerance toward the remaining
elements of capitalism and of relief for the peasant is proclaimed
as a measure to restore the economy rather than a drastic departure from the promises of the revolution.

Inherent in all these measures, or in the way they were presented, was the attrition of the sense of political reality, an attrition characteristic of true totalitarianism. Lenin's party recognized that "the masses" might not share its aims or approve its policies of the moment, but it hoped it would win their support in the future. Stalin's party assumed and required immediate support of the dictator's policies. Lenin admitted that the masses might be swayed by petty bourgeois prejudices, and the workers by their "trade-union consciousness." These stilted formulas still contained an approach to real life that Stalinism was to reject, its simple assumption being that whatever the dictator had ordained was desired by the people.

The full flowering of Stalinism in Soviet society had to await the forging of the party into a monolithic organ of totalitarianism. This process occupied some years after 1922, when Stalin was installed as Secretary-General. Details about the elimination of Trotsky, then of Stalin's original partners, Kamenev and Zinoviev, then of his later allies, Bukharin and others, do not belong in this study. It is important, however, to draw attention to one aspect of Stalin's rise to power that is not often given its due. It is easy to read the whole story in the Secretary-General's talent for intrigue and in his administrative maneuvers. But the initial stages of Stalin's ascendance cannot be divorced from the popularity of the program and ideological tendency he represented, and from the persuasiveness of his position. With the anarchist stirrings suppressed and the country recovering economically under the NEP, the Communist party was increasingly being infiltrated and officered, especially at the lower levels, by young and rather unsophisticated people who joined it after the Revolution. Such people were different in their habits and thinking from the older type of revolutionary worker. To them, the nascent bureaucracy, socialism-Marxism, meant a series of concrete jobs to be done rather than ideological wrangling. Stalin of 1924 and 1925 stood as the symbol of Communist "normalcy" and common sense, as the advocate of the restoration of the economy and administration, rather than of foolhardy social policies and dogmatism. Moderate policies toward the peasant, cautious industrialization, the maintenance of the international revolutionary appeal of Communism, but with the eschewing of dangerous foreign adventures for the young and feeble Soviet state—these were the points of Stalin's "platform." In contrast, his opponents in the crucial years were maneuvered into a position where they could be presented as wild-eyed fanatics: Trotsky as allegedly desiring to postpone the building of socialism in Russia until after Communist revolutions in more advanced countries; Zinoviev and Kamenev as allegedly desiring to oppress and coerce the peasants. It becomes understandable how the Secretary-General and his group could command an overwhelming majority at the Fourteenth Party Congress in 1925 and the Fifteenth Party Conference in 1926, the last occasions on which anything resembling free political discussion took place within the Communist party.

The focus of political power in the Soviet Union was already the Secretariat of the Communist party, which, from its insignificant administrative beginnings in 1919, was to grow under Stalin into the policy-formulating organ for the party, the state, and society, with its departments and divisions paralleling and supervising the major branches of party and state activity. The real state in Russia was thus no longer even the party as a whole but just its administrative machine. It was no longer only the constitutional organs of the state that atrophied in real importance. In the evolution of Stalinism, the same fate awaited party congresses, conferences, even the Central Committee. The "withering away" of all the democratic and anarchistic appurtenances of the revolution was thus a mere matter of a few years. The enthronement of the administrative organs of the party and Stalin's personal dictatorship are an ironic commentary on Lenin's promise of the Communist state where the people will rule themselves and where "accounting and control . . . are the *chief* things necessary for the organizing and correct functioning of the *first phase* of Communist society." [7] With the state, the organ of social coercion, reborn in its most intense form in the Soviet Union, the next phase of Marxism—the development of "those material conditions which alone can form the real basis of a higher form of society"—can now take place. In *State and Revolution,* Lenin credited to Bernstein and other "philistines" the view that centralism means "something from above, to be imposed and maintained solely by means of bureaucracy and militarism." [8] This is not a bad characterization of Stalin's centralism and its superbureaucratic character.

The problem that confronted Stalin and his advisers in 1927-1928, with the country's economy recovered to, roughly, the prewar level, with the state and party firmly in their hands, was the classical problem of Marxism: the transition to socialism and the method of industrialization under Russian conditions. Shortly before his death Stalin summarized the problem confronted by Marxism in Russia:

. . . What should the proletariat and its party do in a country—including our country—where conditions favor seizure of power by the proletariat and the overthrow of capitalism . . . but where agriculture, despite the growth of capitalism, still remains so scattered among numerous small and medium owner producers, that there appears no possibility of raising the question of expropriating these producers? [9]

And the alternatives which confronted him in 1927, though with his typical obfuscation he speaks as if the problem had been confronted and solved by Lenin in 1917, are also sketched:

The answer is not, of course, provided by the opinion of some pseudo-Marxists who say that in such circumstances seizure of

[7] V. I. Lenin, *State and Revolution* [1917], New York, 1932, p. 83.
[8] *Ibid.,* p. 46.
[9] J. V. Stalin, *Economic Problems of Socialism in the U.S.S.R.,* in *Current Digest of the Soviet Press: Current Soviet Policies,* ed. Leo Gruliow, New York, 1953, I, 3.

power should be rejected. They propose to wait until capitalism has contrived to ruin the millions of small and medium producers, turning them into farm laborers, and has concentrated the agricultural means of production. . . . Likewise unacceptable is the view of other pseudo-Marxists who would, if you please, seize power and set about expropriating the small and middle producers in the countryside and socializing the means of production. Marxists cannot agree to take this senseless and criminal course. . . .[9]

The whole passage is typical of Stalin's rewriting of actual history. The implication is that the whole problem was solved by Lenin's formula of voluntary collectivization and that this solution was, after 1928, put into effect by his faithful pupil Stalin. The fact is, of course, that the actual policy adopted by Stalin after 1928-1929 was that of the "pseudo-Marxists" who "set about expropriating the small and middle producers in the countryside." Collectivization was not voluntary; it was a euphemism for the subjection of the peasant to the most stringent control, and as such it was resisted by the mass of the peasantry and accomplished under conditions of extreme violence, necessary to break down passive and active resistance of "small" as well as "middle" peasants.

The peasant collectivization illustrates the meaning of Marxism under Russian conditions. The decisions to collectivize and the parallel course of rapid industrialization initiated after the Fifteenth Congress of the Communist Party in 1927 denote the second and decisive phase of applying Marxism structures to Russia. Marxism-Communism became equated with rapid and drastic industrialization. At its altar were sacrificed all the previous revolutionary, anarchistic, and democratic elements of the doctrine and practice of Communism. For a generation the imperative to produce, to expand the industry, to make Russia into a modern industrial state not only takes precedence over any other objective, but subordinates and absorbs everything else in society. The power motivation of the rulers and the urge to industrialize become practically identical.

The actual decision may be related to several practical necessities and features of the Soviet regime around 1927 and 1928. It reflects the fact that the NEP had restored the Russian economy to the point at which further economic expansion required thorough industrialization. It was not unconnected with the difficulty of obtaining grain from the peasants, pampered, from the Communist point of view, during the NEP. It was a reflection of the international situation: an industrially backward Russia would be at the mercy of the capitalist aggressors. It can be seen as the natural consequence of the dynamics of totalitarianism: the dictator and his group have consolidated their grip on the party and the country. Now comes the moment to build up their power externally.

All the preceding considerations, taken separately or together, do not begin to explain the drastic and violent character of the process. In view of the weak position of agriculture and the lack of capital, the decision to industrialize rapidly and to telescope into ten years what, in the West, took generations represented a vast gamble, which a regime thinking *solely* in power considerations and about clinging to its dictatorial position might have hesitated to undertake. When in 1929 Stalin decided that the planned tempo of collectivization was too slow and that the major part of the task must be accomplished before 1933, he was entering upon the most hazardous period of his rule. Famines, deportation of hundreds of thousands of peasants, lowering of the already pitifully low (from the Western point of view) standard of living—all those measures and effects strained the coercive powers of the regime to the utmost, and confronted not only the dictator but the Communist state with mortal danger. Years later, Stalin confessed to Churchill that even the most depressing moments of the Russo-German war did not approach in devastation or in danger to the country the years of the first

Five-Year Plan and the crucial period of collectivization. Power considerations are insufficient to explain why the regime at the height of its strength should plunge into a vast socio-economic reform, the character of which, as well as the methods by which it was executed, would bring the regime to the brink of disaster. Ideological as well as power considerations, or more properly power considerations seen through an ideological prism provide the explanation.

To Marxism, industrialization means not only the creation of heavy industries and their appurtenances—economic independence and military security—it means the creation of a new national psychology. Just as the liberal in the nineteenth century had believed that industrialization would create an enlightened population fit for democracy and impervious to the irrational and emotional appeal of class hatred or religious and national fanaticism, so the Communist leader wanted the assimilationist potential of industrialization to create the new Soviet man—materialistic and pragmatic in his psychology, automatically responsive to the command and propaganda of his party. The elimination of the individual peasant household was not only a function of the desire to make agricultural methods more efficient through large-scale cultivation and thus to release millions of peasants for work in the new factories. The millions of peasant households, each tilling its small plot, were not only a bar to rapid industrialization, but the breeder of anti-industrial, hence anti-socialist, attitudes. The peasant, with his psychology of the small property owner and ingrained traits of conservatism and radicalism, had to be transformed into the agricultural worker, as materialistically and pragmatically minded as his industrial counterpart. Old Russia, with its backwardness, mysticism, torpor, and inherent anarchy, emanating not from any "Russian soul" but from the anachronism of peasant society, would be replaced by a modern, scientifically and materialistically minded state and society.

Here, then, is the sense of Marxism in Russia, the meaning of what has been called the third Russian Revolution of 1928-1933. The Marxist state, through compulsion and planning, was striving to achieve what an unplanned and undirected conglomeration of social and economic forces had achieved in the England of the first half of the nineteenth century. The ideology of Marxism was revealed as being much more self-consciously the technique of industrialization and science, than its ancestor liberalism had been. Both had to ride roughshod over the sensitivities and feelings of the bulk of the population, which was forced into occupations and ways of life strange to it. The edicts of the dictator replaced, as the mechanism of change, the allegedly impersonal forces of the market and acts of parliament. This time, it was not the casual indoctrination of the middle class with industrial values but the forced imposition of these values upon the whole society in the name of socialism that provided the dynamics of the process. It is as if in some perverse fashion Karl Marx's oversimplified description of the state as the executive committee of the exploiting class, designed to give political and social sanction to the extraction of surplus value from the worker, has finally found its mark in the Communist state. But there is nothing perverse in this relationship: it is the meaning of industrial fanaticism that Marxism had inherited from early liberalism, which, now that the revolutionary and anarchist ballast of the doctrine had dropped off, was displayed in its full power.

The nexus *ideology-power* is best demonstrated in the attempted solution of the peasant problem. During the NEP, Stalin was displayed as, and gathered political credit for being, an advocate of moderate measures toward the peasant. In 1924 and 1925, the party under his leadership had granted the peasants the right to lease land and hire labor—strange doings, his opponents observed, for the regime committed to the ending of "exploitation of man by man." He was in those days an apparent follower of

Bukharin, whose alleged injunction to the peasants to "get rich" was later quoted as evidence of a disgusting right-wing deviation. From the Marxist viewpoint, Bukharin's policies were far indeed from being a crime. Industrialization, then socialism, can come, Marx teaches, only after agriculture, like industry, has become concentrated in large units. Why should the Communist state not imitate, within limits, Stolypin's formula? Why not let nature take its course? The more enterprising, more capitalistically minded peasants, the kulaks, would absorb more and more land. Their less enterprising brothers would be forced off the land and supply the industrial proletariat. The average unit in agriculture would become larger and more efficient, industrial labor would be forthcoming, and the future socialization of land would deal with a relatively small class and not with millions of individual households. But this course, acceptable from the viewpoint of academic Marxism, cannot be accepted by a Marxist party that wants to industrialize in a hurry and does not want to lose any part of its power in the process. As any class gains in economic well-being and becomes more materialistically minded, it comes to desire more than just economic rights. The prospect of the growth of the rural middle class had always filled the Bolsheviks with alarm. As Lenin said: "Small scale production gives birth to capitalism and the bourgeoisie, daily, hourly, with elemental force and in vast proportions." [10] In 1927 and 1928 the peasants were reluctant to sell grain to the state. Since they were not getting enough money for it, they preferred to consume it or to feed it to their animals. To let "nature to take its course" in the countryside meant structuring prices and producing enough consumers' goods for the peasants. If you appease the peasant economically today, won't he demand political rights tomorrow?

Hence the adoption, as we have seen, of what Stalin was later on to characterize piously as a "senseless and criminal course"—

[10] Quoted in Merle Fainsod, *How Russia is Ruled,* Cambridge, Mass., 1953, p. 443.

driving the peasant by compulsion into the collective and state farm. The slogan of extermination of the kulaks as a class was a hypocritical cover-up for the coercion of all the peasants; the party fell with a fury upon the countryside, upon the vast social element that had baffled Marxism for generations, had stood as the massive barrier to the industrialization of society, as the embodiment of what Marx so pungently described as "the idiocy of rural life." The immediate objectives of collectivization—release of millions for industrial work, and the government's control over agricultural production—were attained, though at a terrible human cost. But a solution to the peasant problem in complete accordance with the desires of the regime eluded the despot and is still on the agenda of his successors.

The definition of the struggle repeated by Stalin during the first years of industrialization was one taken from Lenin: "Who will get whom." In Stalin's phrasing, it not only became the formulation of the Communist demonology—the forces of light (the Communist) fighting against all the real and imaginary enemies of Soviet power and industrialization (foreign capitalists, kulaks, saboteurs, all of them somehow connected, their malevolent and "wrecking" activity explaining the suffering and temporary reverses of the great industrialization). It also became the slogan of the historical task of Marxism in Russia, of socialism fighting against the immemorial forces of lethargy, popular apathy, and superstition to create a scientifically and industrially minded modern society. The aim was often obscured by the means employed: terror, propagation of the myth of wreckers and saboteurs, portrayal of the peasant clinging to his miserable plot as the class enemy. A strange way to achieve modernism and progress, and one that has caused believers in the "continuity" of Russian history to draw parallels with Ivan the Terrible, with his "Oprichnina," and with Peter the Great's brutal efforts to Westernize his country. But while it is shallow to forget, slight, or excuse by the magnitude of the task *that* aspect of

Stalinism, it is equally unhistorical to ignore the other side of the coin: the realization of Marxian strictures about industrialism.

Here again a complete and drastic break had to be made with the egalitarian and anarchist part of Russian Marxism. In the twenties, Stalin courted popularity as the exponent of pragmatic, living socialism as against the stilted exegeses of his opponents. Were Engels alive today, said Stalin at the Fifteenth Conference of the party, he would undoubtedly say: "May the devil take the old formulas; long live the victorious revolution in the U.S.S.R." [11] With all power in his hand, no such frivolous approach toward the ideology was tolerated. At the Seventeenth Party Congress in 1934 Stalin "explained" that Marxism is an enemy of the equalization of wages, that the latter has nothing to do with socialism but is in fact a petty bourgeois superstitution! In the frank adoption of vast inequality of wages and salaries, in the adoption of capitalist incentives to production, there is not even a trace of the embarrassment with which Lenin was explaining the slight departures from equality in 1921 and 1922. Stalin said: "And so our task is to put an end to the instability of labor power, to abolish equalitarianism, to organize wages properly and to improve the living condition of the workers." [12] In the same speech in 1931, Stalin called for full authority of the industrial managers in the factory and for no union interference with management. In 1923, the then Commissar of Trade, Leonid Krassin, had called for similar attitudes toward industrial management. Krassin, an engineer by profession, was ridiculed and attacked as an "inclinator" toward capitalism and was soon removed from his position. Now Stalin proclaimed unblushingly the necessity of the most stringent capitalist methods of organization of industry. The trade unions by 1930 had been subordinated to the party to an extent surpassing Trotsky's most drastic ideas

[11] *The Fifteenth Conference of the All Union Communist Party* (in Russian), Moscow, 1927, p. 721.

[12] J. V. Stalin, *Leninism*, New York, 1933, II, 431.

in 1921. And the subjugation of the worker to industrialism was demonstrated not only by the abandonment of egalitarian pretenses and of the worker's right to interfere with management, but by an industrial code meting out punishments undreamed of under the most extreme laissez-faire capitalism for absence from work, repeated lateness, or unauthorized abandonment of one's employment. Strikes become unthinkable, and wages are fixed by fiat from the planners.

It is easy to lose sight of the human elements of the transition. Forced industrialization meant heavy investments in the means of industrial production. These investments could be financed only by lowering the already low standard of living and by pushing into insignificance the production of consumer goods. The general lowering of living standards, the widespread famine in the Ukraine in 1930, and the general dislocation of the countryside throw into insignificance the turbulent effects of the unplanned industrialization of the West early in the nineteenth century. It is inconceivable that any regime, even one endowed with absolute power, would have survived this accumulation of human misery without some element of popular support. All accounts of the period stress the enthusiastic response of the Communists, especially the younger strata of the party, to the task of industrialization. The explanation of this response cannot be found only in "propaganda" or in young people's susceptibility to indoctrination. The enthusiasm of an elite group, amidst the sea of human misery that surrounded it in the crucial years from 1929 to 1933, can be explained only by the essential agreement between the ideology in which they had been bred and the industrial fanaticism which they were now exhibiting. The worship of the machine, lyricism over production figures, which later on became artificial and officially propagated myths of "socialist realism," are for the early 1930's a not inaccurate representation of the mentality of the Communist activist, who well might have felt that he was creating "those material conditions, which alone can form the real basis of a higher form of society, a society in which the full and free development of every individual forms the ruling principle." And like an early capitalist entrepreneur defending the employment of children in factories, a Communist official forcing peasants into a collective could feel that he was an agent of progress and an executor of benevolent laws of historical development.

In step with the introduction of capitalist incentives in economic life and the harnessing of the whole society to the task of industrialization, the regime felt constrained to enforce social and artistic mores consonant with the change. The revolution, like all revolutions, brought a breakdown in social conventions. The ideology then sanctioned the rejection of bourgeois "philistinism" in the spheres of family life and sexual relations. Essentially, Marxism has never condoned libertinism or bohemian attitudes toward morals. But legal restraints were always associated with the hypocritical standards of bourgeois society; and in the twenties divorce was made easy to obtain, abortion was legalized, and the whole sphere of personal relations and behavior was considerably freed from law-enforced conformity. The change is very pronounced in the decade of Great Industrialization. Abortion for other than health reasons is declared illegal. Divorce is discouraged by the courts and expensive to obtain. The penal code invokes heavy penalties for homosexual acts. The sanctity of the family tie is invoked both in official pronouncements and in Soviet literature. The Communist party has always required of its members dedication of their personal lives to the cause and a consequent high standard of personal behavior. But now the whole sphere of social behavior of every citizen is officially prescribed to be in accordance with the most conventional, most bourgeois pattern. Bourgeois respectability becomes the expected pattern of socialist behavior.

As in the case of morals, the arts, literature, and even science become increasingly subjected to the authority of the party. The depiction of the unusual or the morbid, stress on individual problems unconnected with the building of socialism, is in effect prohibited. It is not even convention, as in the case of Victorian England, but the state with its police powers that enforces the desirable pattern on arts and literature and commands the proper approach to science. "Socialist realism" depicts the Soviet man striving victoriously against nature and the class enemy for the attainment of collectivization and industrialization, in the process, submitting his personal interests and feelings to those of society and the party.

The Bolshevik revolution meant, and proclaimed, the rejection of Russia's past. Her history was sketched by the Marxist historians as a long story of obscurantism, oppression of the people by successive governments, a story only illuminated from time to time by "progressive" figures and movements. In this respect also, the thirties mark a sharp turn. The inculcation of Russian nationalism, both as a unifying political force and as an added incentive to the prodigious national endeavor, prohibits the presentation of the past as a story of unmitigated darkness. Russia's past is officially rehabilitated, and an excessively Marxist reading of the motives of such figures as Peter the Great and Ivan the Terrible is prohibited. In *Russian* nationalism the regime now sees one of its strongest supports. Political centralization is enhanced by the imposition of national domination, as Soviet chauvinism is by Russian.

The sum of the changes that can be found in the most diverse and minute aspects of society makes the USSR of the 1930's a thoroughly totalitarian and xenophobic society. It is, seemingly, worlds apart from what is meant by "Western" culture and from the traditional atmosphere of Marxism, which, though authoritarian in its conception, breathes some of the rationalistic and cosmopolitan spirit of liberalism. And yet the effect of the great changes is to inculcate in a large part of society the good bourgeois values of the nineteenth-century West: the importance of hard work, of saving, of measuring one's station in life by one's income and the quantity of material goods, etc. The alleged aim is socialism, and while one may become rich in the Soviet Union, one may not own a bank or a factory. But the end and the total effect of the reforms, made in the name of socialism and by means of compulsion that have no parallel in modern history, is to instill the attitudes and aspirations of a middle-class society. Even the external characteristics of the plutocratic West are revived: old titles in the army, decorations and uniforms even for civil servants. The constitution of 1936, adopted to celebrate the completion of the socialist phase of the development of Soviet society, gives the USSR a paper constitution which in its parliamentary structure and political terminology is an unabashed copy of the Western documents of the same type and abandons the populistic phraseology of the earlier Soviet constitutions.

The meaning of Stalinism is the triumph of the logic of Marxism over its revolutionary spirit: the creation of a powerful state and an industrial and scientifically minded society. Missing from the picture entirely is what Karl Marx imagined would be the result of that development: democracy. Marxism in Russia has shown its aptitude first as a technique of revolution, then as a technique of industrialization and modernization. It has not brought socialism or democracy, in the sense in which a nineteenth-century socialist defined these terms. It falls to another chapter to analyze the predicament of Stalin's last years and that of his successors: the dilemma of preserving totalitarian methods in a society that this very totalitarianism has made modern and materialistically minded to the point at which it chafes under the shackles of the police state and a now unreal ideology.

Historical "forces" and "developments" cannot obviate the fact that Stalinism has also meant terror, purges, and infinite abasement, on a national scale, of human personality. It is possible to view various types of relationships between this trio:

Marxism, totalitarianism, industrialization. An apologist for Stalin as well as a detractor of Marxism will see a clear and logical connection between Marxism and totalitarianism. If the former ordains industrialization, then a whole nation has to be coerced into new ways. "It is too bad," says the apologist, "but see how much has been achieved." And to the detractor, Marxism, by its inhuman insistence on historical laws, and Communism, by its presuming to tell people what is good for them, already premise terror, purge trials, and confessions—in brief, Stalinism. Then there are a handful of non-Communist Marxist idealists for whom the tie-up is unnatural: Russia could have been transformed without totalitarianism: it is the essentially un-Marxist character of Stalinism, not Marxism, that explains Soviet totalitarianism.

The truth, as usual, is more complicated than any of these simple views would have it. It was sound historical instinct, but bad history, when Khrushchev in his "secret" speech in 1956 tried to divide Stalin into two persons: a faithful pupil of Lenin and a great socialist statesman in his earlier years (until 1934), and an increasingly paranoiac tyrant after that. It was sound historical instinct because Communism, in its conception, involves social compulsion that Khrushchev does not want to disclaim, the kind of compulsion that led, in 1929 and 1930 and afterward, to the death or expulsion of hundreds of thousands, if not millions, of peasants. It was also sound to realize that the terror of 1934, the decimation of the party, the filling of the labor camps with millions of prisoners, and the weird rituals of the purges were in no sense connected or justified by Marxian social engineering (as pro-Communist apologists had claimed before 1956), but represented the then unrestrained sadism of the dictator and the Byzantine atmosphere of his entourage and secret police. By 1934, the great breakthrough had been accomplished, the opposition in the party had been cowed, and no real or imaginary plots justified the blood bath into which the whole society was plunged.

But the analysis falls short of the truth insofar as it ignores the fact that the methods adopted after 1934 were inherent in the Bolshevik policies dating back to the earliest postrevolutionary period. One can grant that the task before Russian Marxism could not have been accomplished according to the precepts of Western constitutionalism or democracy. Of the alternative methods available for political consolidation and economic reconstruction, the policy chosen at every step was one that would vest the most additional power in the dictator and his entourage. It was not so much the attrition of the democratic instincts (of which they never had had an abundance) that led the Bolshevik party to the full excesses of Stalinism and the "cult of personality." It was, in addition to the much more fundamental attrition of the humanitarian instinct, the urge to present every decision, even the most unpopular, as coming from the "masses." The Communist party—or, in actuality, the dictator and the small group around him—acted as a kind of prompter on the historical stage, "reminding" the masses how they should act. Thus the campaign for collectivization was accompanied in the official language by the "sharpening of the class struggle in the countryside," i.e., by party-sponsored violence of the poorer peasants against the kulaks. The very pretense of democracy by the essentially undemocratic system was thus the major reason for the manipulation and exploitation of popular prejudices, passions, and fears, which made the Soviet state even more totalitarian than warranted by the premises of Communism in Russia.

THE INTERNATIONAL ASPECT

The idea of creating a new international Marxist organization to replace the Second International had been with Lenin since 1914. In 1919 this idea received organizational expression, and the

Third International, the Comintern, was created. The Second
International had been a loose conglomeration of socialist and
labor parties, not all of them of Marxist or revolutionary character. Thus, the British Labour Party was a member, and the
Russian Socialist Revolutionaries were for a time represented,
as were the Bolsheviks and the Mensheviks. The Comintern, on
the contrary, was to be a highly centralized, definitely Marxist,
and revolutionary body. The participating parties from the beginning had to pledge conformity with Leninism insofar as their
ideology and organizational pattern were concerned. The Second
Congress of the Comintern, in 1920, laid down twenty-one qualify-
ing conditions for membership, which included the need of
"democratic centralism," i.e., the organizational structure evolved
by the Bolsheviks, of a clandestine organization to be set up even
where a Communist party was legally permitted, and of periodic
purges to rid the parties of "opportunists" and "reformists."
Formation of the Comintern marked the repudiation on an international scale of the social democratic tradition that the Bolsheviks had definitely repudiated internally by 1917.

The result was the general split of the international labor and
socialist movement. The Second International, recreated after
the war, continued the older tradition; and European socialism,
as distinguished from Communism, became more and more
pragmatic, more responsive to the circumstances of each given
country's political and economic conditions than to the injunc-
tions of Marxism. By contrast, the socialism of the Communist
International was to become more responsive to the dictates of
the policy of the only existing Communist state. It was inevitable
in the nature of things that the Soviet Communist leaders would,
from the beginning, play a dominant role in the Third International. It was almost equally inevitable (anything else would have
taken an inhuman degree of self-restraint in the Russians) that,
for all the assumed equality of all member parties of the Third
International, the Soviet party would exercise dictatorial direc-

tion and that in due time the international Communist movement would be used as an instrument of Soviet policy. The history of the Comintern reflects the shifts in the internal politics
of the Soviet Union, with the splits, purges, and other internal
developments of the Communist party therein. What is of primary
interest to us is how the Soviet Communists assessed the role
and possibilities of Communism on the international scale and
how their policies illuminate the nature and opportunities of
Marxism in the interwar world.

World War I had marked the definite death of the liberal
utopia. The demise of the earlier type of liberalism was nowhere
else more evident at the end of the war than in its international
premises. To the man who was to formulate the economics of new
liberalism, the collapse of the older type was obvious and vivid
on the morrow of the Western powers' victory:

What an extraordinary episode in the economic progress of man,
that age which came to an end in August, 1914! The greater part of
the population, it is true, worked hard and lived at a low standard
of comfort, yet were to all appearances reasonably contented with
this lot. But escape was possible, for any man of capacity or
character at all exceeding the average, into the middle and upper
classes, for whom life offered, at a low cost and with the least
trouble, conveniences, comforts and amenities beyond the compass
of the richest and most powerful monarchs of other ages.[13]

And the most characteristic aspect of the liberal ethos before
1914 is evoked by Keynes:

But, most important of all, he regarded this state of affairs as
normal, certain, and permanent, except in the direction of further
improvement, and any deviation from it as aberrant and scandalous.
The projects and policies of militarism and imperialism, of social
and cultural rivalries, of monopolies, restrictions, and exclusion,
which were to play the serpent to this paradise, were little more

[13] John Maynard Keynes, *The Economic Consequences of the Peace*, New
York, 1920, pp. 11-12.

than the amusements of his daily newspaper and appeared to exercise almost no influence at all on the ordinary course of social and economic life, the internationalization of which was nearly complete in practice.

The economic side of the old system is recalled by Keynes in terms suggesting mid-nineteenth-century "fundamentalist" liberalism:

Europe was so organized socially and economically as to secure the maximum accumulation of capital. . . . Herein lay, in fact, the main justification of the Capitalist System. If the rich had spent their new wealth on their own enjoyments, the world would long ago have found such a regime intolerable. But like bees they saved and accumulated, not less to the advantage of the whole community because they themselves held narrower ends in prospect. . . . Thus, this remarkable system depended for its growth on a double bluff or deception. On the one hand the labouring classes accepted from ignorance or powerlessness, or were compelled, persuaded or cajoled by custom, convention, authority, and the well established order of Society into accepting, a situation in which they could call their own very little of the cake that they and Nature and the capitalists were cooperating to produce. And on the other hand the capitalist classes were allowed to call the best part of the cake theirs and were theoretically free to consume it, on the tacit underlying condition that they consumed very little of it in practice. The duty of "saving" became nine-tenths of virtue and the growth of the cake the object of true religion.[14]

How close to the early capitalist, or to Marx's view of the function of capitalism, is this picture. Like all evocations of the allegedly golden past, Keynes' description is perhaps too one-sided and overlooks the fact that the change was not simply the result of one dramatic event, the war, but also the product of forces and tendencies already visible and growing prior to 1914. But this lyricism over the past, the conviction that old-

[14] *Ibid.*, p. 20.

fashioned capitalism was gone forever, was typical of the immediate postwar psychology; and the conviction was not limited to the revolutionaries. To a stout believer in the virtues of the old system, which Keynes was in 1919, the future was foreboding and revolutionary: "The bluff is discovered; the laboring classes may be no longer willing to forego so largely, and the capitalist classes, no longer confident of the future, may seek to enjoy more fully their liberties of consumption so long as they last and thus precipitate the hour of their confiscation." [15] And when we read this we are reminded, and the reader will forgive the insufferable repetition of this point, how much of Marxian apprehension there was underneath the liberal's economic optimism, and how much of the liberal's obsession with production and capital formation there is in Marxism.

The general feeling of the collapse of the old order and of the imminence of world revolution was most acute among the Bolsheviks following their own victory. In the beginning there was no idea of a possible conflict of interests between the Soviet state and foreign Communist or revolutionary movements. The very first instinct of the Bolsheviks tells them that their own revolution cannot survive short of revolutions and seizures of power in the more advanced states. To the radical socialists in the West, in the wake of World War I, the intricacies of Bolshevism are unknown and unimportant: Soviet Russia is a "workers' state." In 1918-1919, even some trade-union leaders in Great Britain and socialists in France and Germany, later on very unrevolutionary indeed, talk about forming their own soviets. All Europe between 1918 and 1920 appears to the majority of Bolshevik leaders as Russia did between March and November 1917: the dissolution of the old order releases the revolutionary potential of society. Germany is several times on the brink of a Communist take-over. Soviet regimes spring up in Bavaria and Hungary. Never again was the idea of Com-

[15] *Ibid.*, p. 22.

munism to have so much popular appeal and revolutionary potentiality in Europe as in the very infancy of the then devastated and almost impotent Soviet state. And then the revolutionary wave passes and Western capitalism becomes stabilized.

The coexistence with capitalism, which history has imposed upon the Communists and which they have had to accept as at least temporary reality, created certain problems for both domestic and international Communism. These problems are not of the kind usually conceived of in the West as the dilemma of Communism. The usual phrasing erects a neat antithesis, as in the question: "Are the Soviet leaders sincere in talking about a world revolution and the triumph of Communism, or do they cynically exploit foreign Communists for the sake of the power of the Soviet Union and with no scruples about what happens in the process to the foreign Communists and the revolution?" As usual when we ask this question, we demand and expect in other people a degree of introspection into their motives and a logical clarity about them of which we concede ourselves to be quite incapable in our own actions. It is simple common sense to assume that from the very beginning the Soviet leaders had thought, and quite "sincerely," that what was good for the Soviet Union was good for world Communism. By natural selection, the foreign Communist parties eventually came to be led by people who also (though the psychological mechanism here is more complicated) became convinced, and "sincerely," of the truth of the same proposition. Doubts and conflicts, in the latter case, were bound to occur on a large scale only when some Communist parties achieved power in their own countries. The problem is not the world revolution versus the selfish state interest, or Communist idealism versus power cynicism. A more sophisticated and useful way of attacking the problem is to study the changing appraisal of foreign revolutionary possibilities by the Soviet leaders.

The earliest and most millennial period of expectations was, as pointed out, closely connected with the very weakness, vulnerability, and isolation of the Soviet state. It is psychologically quite understandable how to the average Communist, in the period of famines and the Civil War in Russia, a Communist uprising in Hamburg or Budapest seemed as urgently important as what was happening in his own country. A few years later a good Communist still might think of himself as being equally solicitous about the welfare of foreign Communists, but there was now a concrete and promising job of socialist construction at hand in Russia, and somehow the foreign Communists loomed less important.

This inevitable "pragmatization" of life paralleled certain domestic developments: in 1920, amidst appalling devastation and backwardness, the party could be terribly agitated by the question whether it was or was not according to the canon for a commissar to be paid more than a skilled worker. A few years later, whether one was for or against Stalin, for or against collectivization, no heat could be generated over the old problem, which now seemed simply irrelevant. Within a few years after the revolution, the earlier emotionalism over world revolution or any particular foreign revolution became unthinkable. It was characteristic of the political acumen of Stalin that he capitalized on this very natural evolution of feeling and, professing scrupulous regard for the international aims of Communism, suited his policies to the prevailing mood.

It was typical of the reaction of the opposition to Stalin in the early twenties, the reaction of a drowning man grasping at what is at hand, that they tried to make a point of the alleged sacrifice of world Communism by the leadership of the party. Some of them were asinine enough to complain to the Executive Committee of the Comintern about the behavior of their leaders. It is almost incredible that a man with Trotsky's intelligence, the earliest advocate among the Bolsheviks of rapid industrialization and modernization of Russia, could let himself be maneu-

vered into appearing as the enemy of "socialism in one country."
In 1926 Stalin could ask what Trotsky's alternative was; he was
able to upbraid Trotsky as an adventurer whose policies would
plunge the unindustrialized Soviet state into a war with all
Europe.[16] Trotsky's retort that one could build socialism in one
country but could not finish building it while capitalism survived
elsewhere would have been, at one time, regarded as a fine
example of Marxist sophistication and subtlety. But to the as-
sembled party and state bureaucrats, it was now just double talk.

The inevitable, complete subordination of the world Communist movement, like the crystallization of personal dictatorship in Russia, was a matter of several stages. The initial divisions
and wrangling among the Soviet leaders found their echoes
abroad. Thus Trotsky's disgrace had considerable repercussions:
to foreign Communists his name approached that of Lenin's in
glamor; more cosmopolitan in his outlook than his opponents,
his disgrace was followed by the defection of the most individualistic among the foreign Communists. On a smaller scale, the
same thing was to happen in the wake of the descents of Zinoviev and Bukharin, the successive leaders of the Comintern.
By 1930, the Stalinist pattern was firmly impressed, as it was
in Russia, on the most foreign Communist parties, their leaders
for the most part were miniature Stalins: rough-hewn party
bureaucrats with little of the intellectual *éclat* and individualism
of the generation of Trotsky, Radek, and Bukharin. The parties
became "bolshevized," as the official phrase went in the 1920's,
i.e., not only did they become obedient to Moscow but they
became small copies, ideologically and structurally, of the Communist party of the USSR. Like Pavlovian dogs, they are now
not only obedient but conditioned to obedience: a bell would be
rung in Moscow and soon an identical response would be coming

[16] *The Fifteenth Conference of the All Union Communist Party, 1926,* in
Russian, Moscow, 1927, p. 456.

from *Humanité* in Paris, *Die Rote Fahne* in Berlin, and the *Daily Worker* in London and New York.

The development in Russia was, in a sense, a natural if perverse product of the Russian conditions of Marxism. To impose the same pattern, the same mentality, upon the Bulgarian or British Communist as upon the Soviet one was, by definition, to impose a considerable artificiality upon foreign Communist movements, to isolate them from the main trends of their national life, to the point where even the revolutionary aspirations of their societies could not accommodate themselves freely in bodies that to all purposes appeared as agencies of the Soviet government rather than native expressions of revolutionary Marxism. The foreign Communist lived in a world much more artificial and ideologically crippling than even his Soviet brother did. In the case of a foreign and especially a Western Communist, the denial of spontaneity, on which Leninism was originally based, was carried to the extent of the suppression of one's political and social instinct, to an *unnatural* alienation from one's society. The natural impulses of Marxism—the sense of social injustice, materialist iconoclasm, and revolutionary impatience —had themselves to be restrained and doled out in accordance with orders from Moscow. The violent verbal behavior of Western Communism and its almost voluptuous self-abasement before the Soviet Union and Stalin are the reverse psychological effects of the constricted political lives that Western Communists had to lead. It is equally remarkable how at the times when they were allowed to act "naturally," to exhibit, within limits, "spontaneity" (as during the period of the Popular Front or during the Second World War and the Resistance), the sense of release made of the automatons and repeaters of stilted formulas brave revolutionary leaders and resourceful politicians, capable of seizing a popular following and strategic social and political positions. But the leash on which international Communism was held during the interwar period usually gave it but little opportunity to exploit the chances for revolutionary Marxism in any Western country.

The basic trouble lay in the heavy-handed application to very different societies of the same formula that had provided the victory of Communism in Russia. Lenin's party was assumed to be the microcosm of revolutionary forces in society, its leaders, because of their Marxist sophistication, always one step ahead of the actual revolutionary movement in their society. Marxism and "objective facts" teach that the peasants are likely to become stirred up; lo and behold, the party forges ahead in proclaiming and exploiting the peasants' grievances. In power, the Bolsheviks served themselves with the same formula. The Soviet leaders assumed the role of prompters in the historical drama unfolding to a script by Karl Marx.

But what gave the spectacle an *appearance* of reality in the Soviet Union was lacking in the world at large; namely, the prompter also being the producer and having complete control over the actors. A Soviet textbook that blithely proclaims that the class struggle became sharper in the countryside in 1929 and 1930 expresses partial truth: the kulaks were being persecuted and expropriated. Never mind the fact that the "peasant masses" fell upon the kulaks because they were being egged on and coerced by the party and the police, and not because of their heightened class consciousness. In Western Europe in the late twenties, the Communist parties had been told to intensify their revolutionary propaganda and attacks on the "socialist traitors." The "objective facts" and Marxism told the Soviet masters of the Comintern that the "masses" in Germany and elsewhere should become convinced of the bankruptcy of the system and turn to Communism as a result of the Great Depression. But the play did not adhere to the script. The German "masses," for instance, turned to fascism. The script was patched up: National Socialism was to be a brief interlude, not to be seriously resisted, for it was the last stage of bankrupt capitalism, to be followed by a spontaneous turn to Communism. But even the revised script failed to be acted out.

The question remains why, even in the West, in the face of the inherent awkwardness of the Communist formula and the inhuman subordination of the Communist parties to a foreign country, Communism still made considerable inroads in the interwar period; and why, after the war, during which the antithesis between Communism and patriotism had disappeared with the attack on the Soviet Union by the Germans, it became, for a while, the most popular movement in Italy and France.

It is best to confine our brief analysis to the interwar era, because the USSR was then not yet a super power. Still, the success of Western Communism during the period, with all the handicaps it labored under and the legal persecutions it was often subjected to, was not inconsiderable. In England, although the Communist party judged itself in luck to secure a seat or two in Parliament, it exerted a disproportionate influence in some of the unions. The French and German Communist parties commanded a considerable following among the working class. In Italy, under Mussolini, Communism gathered dividends from its talent for illegal organization. Indeed, small but well-organized Communist parties existed in all European countries. Even the slaughter of foreign Communists in Russia during the 1930's and the terrible spectacle of the purges did not seriously disrupt the organizational continuity or the blind allegiance of foreign Communist parties to "the Fatherland of socialism."

The answer must be sought in a whole complex of causes. Here we might pause on one that relates the historical role of Marxism to the qualified success of Communism in Western Europe. The breakdown of liberalism as the ascendant philosophy of the Western world led to the disruption or arrest of the process that in all its economic, social, and political effects we

have called industrialization. Keynes's vivid words demonstrate
the shock the system received from World War I. Though the
economy of Europe appears stabilized, and largely by the old
methods, by the 1920's the psychological appurtenances of the
old order are decisively disrupted. Nothing will again instill or
restore the belief that the liberal order of things—political democracy and capitalism—is the *inevitable* product of social evolution. Nothing will restore the illusion of the beneficent laws of
the economy working out their designs with the least interference by governments. The whole network of political rationalism, always fragile and artificial, has been shaken.

We see in Western Europe in the postwar period, developments
reminiscent of the turbulent period of industrialization in the
1830's and '40's, the era which, by the seeming logic of its developments, gave Karl Marx the illusion of the prompt and inevitable
breakdown of capitalism and the revolutionary arousal of the
proletariat. The onset of the Great Depression of 1929 seems the
very fulfillment of all that Karl Marx had prophesied, the veritable *Gotterdämmerung* of capitalism and liberalism, no longer to
be delayed or avoided by the now exposed panacea of parliamentarism and other political illusions. The breakdown of the habits
imposed by the long period of domination of liberal ideology was
thus followed by the breakdown of the liberal economic mechanism. First the international economic system, before World War
I already strained by the development of economic nationalisms,
and then the whole intricate economic machinery of the major
capitalist powers broke down in a way that apparently con-
formed to the blueprint laid down by Karl Marx. All the remedies
developed during more than three generations of the flourishing
of Western capitalism were tried and found wanting.

What is it that Marx wrote in 1848?

Society suddenly finds itself put back into a state of momentary
barbarism; it appears as if a famine, a universal war of devastation, had cut off the supply of every means of subsistence; industry

and commerce seem to be destroyed. And why? Because there is too much civilization, too much means of subsistence, too much industry, too much commerce. The productive forces at the disposal of society no longer tend to further the development of the conditions of bourgeois property; on the contrary, they have become too powerful for these conditions by which they are fettered, and as soon as they overcome these fetters they bring disorder into the whole of bourgeois society, endanger the existence of bourgeois property.[17]

In the 1930's, for the first time, Marx's prophecies appeared to be justified. The higher the extent of industrialization of the given country and the more complex and advanced its capitalist structure, the deeper appeared the character of the economic crisis, the more profound the shock to the established mores of the older liberal creed.

It is not surprising, therefore, that the party that proclaimed itself the inheritor of revolutionary Marxism should have been in a position to capitalize on the developments consequent upon the great crisis. In retrospect, even the Great Depression does not vindicate Marx the prophet. The Depression was the breakdown of the social psychology as well as the mechanics of the older type of liberalism. The revolutionary situation created over much of Europe had, as we observed, many elements in common with the very revolution that brought liberalism into ascendance and capitalism as the ruling economic system. But, as we also saw, the popular radicalism generated by the Industrial Revolution was by no means of the prevailingly socialist variety. We noted in England from 1820 to 1850 the presence of movements and strains of thought of the proto-fascist as well as the proto-Marxist variety. The optimistic assumption of Marxism—the breakdown of capitalism leads to a socialist revolution—which was inherited by Communism, paradoxically proved to be in itself a remnant of nineteenth-century liberal optimism.

Now in the century of mass communication media, mass

[17] *Manifesto*, p. 327.

political movements, the anarchist feelings contained but not erased for generations by the discipline of industrialization and the ethos of liberalism erupted under the spur of depression, but by no means exclusively in the direction of socialism or Communism. The breakdown of middle-class values, the hostility toward banks and industry, the feeling of unreality about a constitutional and democratic system in a time of profound economic crisis, all these quasi-anarchist feelings can flow into revolutionary fascism as well as into revolutionary socialism. National Socialism, for all of its links with big business, which foolishly saw in it a defense against "radicalism" and its identification with extreme nationalism, actually had its roots in anti-industrial and anti-state feelings. The philosophy of "blood and soil," the obscurantist worship of race and of the peasant as its ideal representative, the echoes of syndicalism, virulent anti-Semitism—the Jew again, as to many radicals of the Industrial Revolution, the embodiment of materialist and "rootless cosmopolitan" viewpoints—this whole irrationalist complex of its popular appeal springs up from the undoing of the large part of the institutional and psychological appurtenances of industrialization. The same in a lesser degree can be said of Italian fascism. The social focus of earlier radicalism, including socialism during the Industrial Revolution, i.e., the lower-middle class threatened by the new economic forces, is now recreated in the spheres most susceptible to the appeal of fascist radicalism: the same strata, now including parts of the working class and the peasants, whom the depression has ejected from the seeming security and status by which a century of material progress had stilled their inherent anti-industrialism. Thus even the most catastrophic event in the history of Western capitalism justifies only Marx the sociologist of revolution, not Marx the prophet of socialism as the receiver of bankrupt capitalism and liberalism.

The fact that the decline and then the catastrophe of the old economic order did not give the Communists in Europe a more substantial success can be attributed, in the main, to two reasons. The first is the type of direction provided by Moscow. To capitalize on diverse sources of revolutionary feeling in diverse societies would have required of the local Communists the kind of sensitivity to local conditions and feelings that would have precluded in the first place their blind dependence on Moscow. The British Communists would have had to be, and *convincingly,* attuned to the now firm traditions of political democracy in England, the French Party *genuinely* responsive to the syndicalist and anarchist trends in the French revolutionary makeup, the Germans mindful of both German nationalism and the German working-class feeling of solidarity. But the logic of *spontaneous* response to the revolutionary possibilities in their societies, the logic that is ordained by revolutionary Marxism, would have made the foreign Communists unable to obey almost instinctively what the comrades in Moscow saw as the urgent tasks of the given Communist party.

Even when the Soviet masters of the Comintern appraised correctly (especially when it coincided with the interests of the Soviet state) the most promising line of activity and propaganda of the given Communist party, the consequent behavior of the German, French, or Spanish Communists was usually too artificial, too transparently managed, to enable them to swim with the tide of revolutionary spontaneity in the way that the Russian Communists had done so successfully in 1917. Putting aside all moral considerations, such as the suppression of the instinctive feeling of national pride and the psychologically and intellectually crippling mechanism by which people have to rationalize the transmuting of their humanitarian and revolutionary motives into the service of a despotic foreign state, the dilemma of European Communism was and is (though as we shall see a major change was attempted after Stalin's death) a paralyzing one. To illustrate this dilemma: how far would the

Bolsheviks have got in 1917 if, instead of responding readily to the rapidly shifting revolutionary moods, they had had to check their policies with a foreign center of Communism, if some organization or dictator sitting, say, in Vienna had to decide whether the slogan "All power to the soviets" was a "correct" or "incorrect" one, and if they had to arbitrate between Lenin and Zinoviev about whether to undertake the November uprising? The predicament of the European Communists was often a tragicomic one: a new policy would be sanctioned of, let us say, wooing the nationalist element in Germany. The greater the enthusiasm and devotion with which the given leaders pursued this aim, the greater the danger of their inability to shift at the next change of the party line, and their consequent purge. In fact, instead of the management of revolutionary spontaneity, the premises and operations of the Comintern, often led, insofar as European Communism was concerned, to the drying up of its spontaneous revolutionary response.

The other reason for the failure of Communism is perhaps more basic. As much as the Great Depression reopened the social wounds inflicted by the Industrial Revolution, it was unable to create in the most thoroughly industrialized societies of the West a "Marxian situation." The discipline of industrialism, the habits of democratic politics remained too strong in Great Britain, the Low Countries, and Scandinavia to allow a social dissolution reminiscent of Russia of 1905 and 1917, or Germany in the early 1930's. The ultimate defeat of early liberalism was followed there not by a reversal to an earlier, basically anti-industrial type of radicalism but by the development of a new type of liberalism, state- and welfare-oriented, perhaps sliding easily into what has been called laborism, but worlds apart from revolutionary Marxism. The development of Keynesian economics provided a new economic "science" to bolster the instinctive turn toward the state and the democratically dictated tendency toward economic equality. Communism in the most thoroughly industrialized societies of the West (and again, "industrialized" referring not only to the existence of an industrial economy but also to the existence of appropriate social mores and institutions) had no function to perform and no overwhelming appeal to exploit.

It is interesting to digress on some exceptions to the rule. Admittedly in the thirties and during and immediately after World War II, Communism had its pockets of influence and attraction in Great Britain and the United States. The nature of this appeal was related more—the distinction is difficult but important—to the real or imaginary accomplishments of the Soviet Union than to the relevance of revolutionary Marxism in the given society. The French or German worker "fell" for Communism largely because its exposition of revolutionary Marxism appealed to some of his basic instincts and needs. The British worker was more likely to opt for Communism because of the mistaken notion that the Soviet Union was a "workers' state" founded upon social and economic equality. The attraction of a Western intellectual was more often than not grounded on distaste for the "bourgeois philistinism" which surrounded him and the vision of a socialist society where—how fantastic in view of what was going on in Russia in the 1930's—bold experimentation and nonconformity were encouraged. There was more substance in the views of those who, struck by the collapse of the premises of liberal economy and the resultant economic chaos, looked enviously at the planning and the scientific and technological development of Soviet Russia. But despite some views to the contrary, frustrated bohemianism and dissatisfied intellectuals do not add up to the foundation of a revolutionary movement.

At the other side of the scale from the failure of Communism in the West lies its very considerable success in the colonial and semicolonial areas. The extent of this success became apparent only after World War II, with Communism engulfing large parts of Asia and becoming a powerful contender for many other underdeveloped countries. But the seeds of this success, then undoubtedly enhanced by the tremendous emergent power of the USSR, lie in the policies and principles adopted in the inter-war period. As in other areas, the successes or failures of Communism reflect the peculiar circumstances of each country and each Communist party. But there are also basic differences between the appeal of revolutionary Marxism in the West and in Asia. And here there is no doubt that Marxism has provided a master revolutionary formula for the underdeveloped areas and that Communism had applied this formula, as it did not apply Marxism in Europe, with instinctive skill.

Proof of this lies not only in the Communist postwar conquests which resulted more from concrete Soviet help than from any inner "necessity." A more objective proof is the general use of Marxist categories, even in their vulgarized Communist form, by many typical, even anti-Communist, intellectuals from the colonial and semicolonial areas. It is found in the general revolutionary volatility of political movements in Asia and their affinity with Communism. There is something natural, and it would be foolish to disregard it, in the appeal of Marxism as a system of thought for an Asian revolutionary; there is something natural in the technique of the Marxist party for the political movements of the underdeveloped countries. In both cases, the Marxist phase may never coincide with the Communist one, or it may eventually be left behind, but it is almost inevitable. Marxism in such a society promises, even before the first modern factory is built, the road to modernization, the technique of emancipation from traditionalism, a rationalization of the disturbing forces of modern life as well as a protest against them.

The recognition that an economically backward country offers a more fruitful field for revolution than does an industrialized one is implicit in Lenin's interpretation of Marxism. This "discovery" of Lenin was anticipated in Marx's writings on Ireland, India, China, etc. While held back by his own theory from postulating *socialist* revolutions in these countries, Marx had the essential insight that societies in the process of transition have a considerable revolutionary potential and that the effect of colonial rule is in many ways equivalent to the beginning phases of industrialization. Although primarily preoccupied with the industrialized West, Marx had seen, long before Lenin's *Imperialism*, that colonial areas were the vulnerable areas of the capitalist world and that the road to socialism in Asia, just as in the oppressed European countries (Poland, Ireland) led through *national* revolution. From these rather marginal elements of Marx's revolutionary sociology, the Comintern, as early as a few years after the Bolshevik revolution, forged its scheme of Communist expansion in Asia. Two factors explain this strategy: the prospects of revolution in the West vanished for the time being, but at the same time it became clear that World War I had destroyed most of the appeal of liberalism as a proselytizing creed of modernization and that in Asia, at least, Marxism could in a fair way become its successor.

In conditions of underdevelopment *and* foreign domination, the inherent paradox of Marxism—the cult of modernization and technology, and the exploitation of the unsettling effects of industrialization—does not provide an obstacle to the spread of the doctrine. It is the foreign rulers who in the popular mind become associated with all the evils of the transformation: the destruction of old customs and ways of life, the ruin of the handicrafts, and agrarian poverty. Even the most primitive rudiments of industrialization, i.e., a slight improvement in sanitary and medical conditions, bring with them pressures of population upon land that, under conditions of primitive economy, create insufferable conditions of rural overcrowding, inefficient cultivation, and all the consequent economic evils. The leitmotif of nationalist propaganda against imperialism almost always has this twofold refrain which fits in with Marxism: like the capitalist in the nineteenth century, the colonial power is blamed for the economically destructive effects of the modernization at the same time that it is accused of keeping the colonial territories in backwardness and of denying them the benefits of modernity. The counterpoint of Marxism has, under Asiatic or African conditions, a natural affinity with nationalism. The keynote of Marxian propaganda can be presented with double effectiveness, because the "exploiter" is, or certainly was in the interwar period, a foreigner or a Westernized entrepreneur or landlord.

Into this naturally Marxist situation the Comintern injected the most effective revolutionary policy: the muting of other elements of Marxism, or their de-emphasis, in favor of revolutionary policy based on the encouragement of nationalism. The nationality policy inside the Soviet Union during the first decade after the revolution gave this policy a high degree of external plausibility. The opening of educational opportunities on a wide scale to the non-Russian elements of the population, the encouragement of cultural autonomy within the Soviet Union, the nationally heterogeneous composition of the Bolshevik leadership, all these developments obscured the already existing link between Soviet imperialism and international Communism. The incongruity between the revolutionary aspirations in the given society and the dictatorial sway over the given Communist party by Moscow, which was so jarring in the case of European Communism, did not exist on the same scale in Asia. Rather than fighting against the nationalism in the given party, the Soviet leaders more often than not had to restrain the Marxist fundamentalism of their Asiatic followers and try to teach them to appear as good nationalists. Radek said to the Chinese Communists in 1922:

You must understand, comrades, that neither the question of socialism nor of the Soviet republic are now the order of the day

. . . the immediate task is: 1) to organize the young working class, 2) to regulate its relations with the revolutionary bourgeois elements in order to organize the struggle against the European and Asiatic imperialism.[18]

An *oppressed* nationalism easily becomes an ally of revolutionary Marxism. In Asia, foreign domination or foreign economic exploitation created revolutionary possibilities and situations analogous in many ways to the conditions in Europe in the nineteenth century that gave rise to Marxism. The national revolution in Asia, after World War I and up to our own day, has taken the place of and often been synonymous with the Industrial Revolution. But the symbiotic relationship between Communism and nationalism was bound to be of a different order than the same relationship between Marxism and anarchism. In exploiting the latter, Marxism gave a revolutionary organization and theory to varied and largely formless forces of social protest. In their selfish collaboration with colonial and semicolonial nationalisms, the local Communist parties have allied themselves with and attempted to exploit specific parties or movements, each with its own organization and ideology.

After an interval, the nationalist movement, especially if it had a social basis in the middle class, would often perceive the incompatibility of its aims with those of Communism and would refuse to serve as an interlude in the unfolding of the Marxist scheme of history staged by Moscow. The local Communist parties found themselves partners of movements which, instead of being eventually absorbed or destroyed by the Communists in the manner of the Left Socialist Revolutionaries in the Russian Revolution, aspired to and were often capable of turning the tables on the Communists. Militant nationalism sometimes appeared capable of superseding the Marxist formula, of exploiting the traditionalist reaction and social disturbances

[18] Quoted in Benjamin Schwartz, *Chinese Communism and the Rise of Mao*, Cambridge, Mass., 1951, p. 37.

due to modernization, and, contrariwise, of satisfying the craving for modernization and the breaking down of old customs and traditions.

The limitations of any overly deterministic pattern of linking the social development with prospects for Marxism are well illustrated by Japan. Here is a classical case, in many ways parallel to prerevolutionary Russia, of a rapid industrialization taking place in a society still pre-industrial in its social structure, with the land-peasant problem persisting in all its acuteness. Yet, for all the existence of strong Marxist movements, the economic tensions of the transition found their release not in a socialist revolution but in militant nationalism, which utilized the traditional symbols for economic and imperial expansion.

Elsewhere in Asia, between the two world wars, Communism appears to have unwittingly helped precipitate nationalist revolutions without eventually turning them to its own uses. The picture in China after the Communist-Kuomintang break and in the countries where national consolidations and modernization took place under nationalist and dictatorial auspices (as in Turkey, Persia, and, in a way, India) would have led to the conclusion that for all its greater sophistication in Asia, Communism failed there in its expansion as badly as it did in Europe. Just as the literal reading of Marxism—mature capitalism leads to a socialist revolution—proved false, so the sociological insight contained in the Communist exploitation of backwardness proved almost equally futile. One might have supplemented Lenin's dictum by saying that if in an industrialized society the spontaneous development of the workers leads them to acquire trade-union rather than revolutionary consciousness, so in an "underdeveloped" country the social development will lead the elite, perhaps after a Marxist phase, into nationalism rather than Communism.

This view had a degree of plausibility, but it should not be carried to the point at which we make every specific political situation the outcome of personalities involved, military and diplomatic factors, and plain accident. The interwar period was used for this analysis of international Communism because Soviet Russia was as yet not capable of installing Communism in a given country by sheer might, whatever the "underlying social forces" and "the stage of economic development." But even a superficial comparison of the role of revolutionary Marxism in the most industrialized segment of the world with its role in societies in the process of transition points out differences that cannot be completely explained by personalities, by the efficiency or inefficiency of the given police system, or even by the correct or incorrect "line" imposed by the Comintern.

Industrialization, if supplemented by appropriate political and social development, instills a network of habits and institutions that make the appeal of Communism, even under optimum conditions, as during the Great Depression, limited and temporary insofar as the mass of the industrial workers and society as a whole are concerned. In a country beginning the process of modernization, or at a point where modern industry coexists with peasant or colonial problems, the necessary barrier of industrial and middle-class habits and values has not been erected to replace the traditional ones and ward off the revolutionary forces engendered by the process of new economics and new ideas moving in. In underdeveloped societies, Marxism as the promise of rapid industrialization and escape from humiliating backwardness, as the beneficiary of the tensions and tribulations of modernity, is always a strong contender for power, even though the actual Communist party may be small or uninfluential.

The Russian Communists have tried with varying success to apply the formulas learned in their history to promote revolution abroad, first, as protection for their own vulnerable state, and then for imperialist reasons. In their domestic evolution, "life" has taught them that the practical meaning of Marxism in power is state capitalism and the instilling of essentially bourgeois values in the whole nation. To foreign Communists, they expound revolutionary Marxism not as an inflexible set of ideas but as tactics for exploitation of whatever there is in the way of revolutionary, anti-industrial potential in the given society. In societies where the lesson is relevant, the Communists are spared the ideological scruples and contentions of pre-1914 Marxism. In the quarrels and purges of international Communism, the motivating factor is no longer a disagreement on principles or about "what Marx really meant." The seemingly ideological arguments are but the invocation of scriptural authority for the disgrace of this or that leader and his group because of the failure of their "line" or their loss of favor in Moscow. If the average person feels the sanctions of religion more strongly after a moral transgression has involved him in misfortune, so a Communist feels that he has sinned against Marxism only if his anarchist or nationalist "act" has led his party to a defeat. The old ideological dilemmas and scriptural subtleties of the Plekhanovs, Trotskys, and Martovs, seeking the *one* right and legitimate formula for Marxism in Russia before 1917, are replaced by the recognition of the variety of the means to revolution.

Thus the man who was to be the most successful of Soviet Communism's pupils was at pains to point out that Marxism should freely use and associate itself with peasant anarchism, but it should not become lost in anarchism, which is but a *stage* in its revolutionary tactics. Speaking in 1927 about the peasant riots in Hunan, Mao Tse-tung must have had in mind the Lenin of 1921 confronting the anarchist slogans of the Lenin of 1917. In a didactic fashion, Mao asked: "Are we to get in front of them and lead them, or criticize them behind their backs, or fight them from the opposite camp?" And he continued:

An agrarian revolution is a revolution by the peasantry to overthrow the power of the feudal landlord class. If the peasants do not apply great force, the power of the landlords consolidated over thousands of years can never be uprooted. There must be a revolutionary tidal wave in the countryside in order to mobilize tens of thousands of peasants and weld them into this great force. The excesses described above result from the tremendous revolutionary enthusiasm of the peasants. In the *second revolutionary stage* of the peasant movement, such acts are very necessary. In this *second stage,* an absolute peasant power must be established, no criticism of the Peasant Associations should be allowed; the gentry's power must be totally liquidated, the gentry knocked down, even trodden upon.[19]

What Lenin had stumbled upon as the proper revolutionary tactics for Marxism, i.e., the exploitation of peasant anarchism, was for Mao already only a "stage," and in 1927 one could see that if Chinese Communism should come to power it would not take as long as it took the Bolsheviks to liquidate the anarchists and to move to further "stages." The history of Asiatic and especially Chinese Communism is long and involved and cannot be considered here. But even this one quotation shows that if Chinese Communism is "different," as sometimes believed in the West, it is different in having learned well the uses of Marxism as demonstrated by the history of the Communist party of the USSR, and in attempting to go consciously and rapidly through the phases that the Russian Communists traversed painfully and by improvisation.

The story of international Communism is varied and complex. An attempted generalization will always evoke a protesting echo about exceptions and qualifications. No single strain can be found: it is an automatic result neither of social and economic forces nor of a conspiratorial design laid down in Moscow. But the story confirms the impression of extraordinary vitality of two elements of Marxism: its sensitivity to the revolutionary

[19] *A Documentary History of Chinese Communism,* cit. Conrad Brandt, Benjamin Schwartz, and John K. Fairbank, Cambridge, Mass., 1952, pp. 80, 82.

stirrings of a society where the traditional culture and traditional economy have broken down and have not yet been replaced by firm new structures; and its ability to inspire political fanaticism in the service of industrialization. The achievement of the Communists—and it is not of primary importance whether in so doing they have been faithful to Marxism as a whole—has been to harness both elements to their struggle for world domination.

VI

THE CRISIS
OF MARXISM

At the Eighteenth Congress of the Communist party of the USSR in 1939, Andrei Zhdanov told a story which, despite its inherent humor, could not have appeared very funny to his listeners. At the height of the purges in the 1930's, some resourceful Communists in a certain locality provided themselves with medical certificates, each certifying that because of the poor state of his health Comrade X could not conceivably become a "tool of the class enemy." Stalin's then right-hand man used the story to illustrate the excesses to which the Great Purge—known later on as "Yezhovshchina" from the name of its main figure, liquidated in his turn—had been carried. The "genius-like" leader of socialism was himself drawn to admit that errors had been made. This was the last Congress of the party held for thirteen years (its statutes then called for one at least every three years). Terror never again reached the heights of the 1934-1939 period, but from what we know from the scant revelations after Stalin's death, the Communist party as a deliberative, policy-forming organization, even though in a totalitarian setting, practically ceased to exist. Only one meeting of the Central Committee is reported to have taken place between 1945 and 1952. Even the Politburo met irregularly. The government of Russia lapsed into the hands of the despot and whoever happened to be his favorite of the moment. Day-to-day functioning of the machinery became the preserve of the party and state bureaucracy. In the expectation of the aged tyrant's demise, his closest collaborators were attempting to carve out strategic preserves within this bureaucracy. The secret police apparently became a state within a state. The burden of fear imposed upon the average citizen in those years was as great, if not so often punctuated by widespread violence, as during the Great Purge. His isolation from the outside world became more extreme than ever. The life and death struggle of the war was succeeded not by any relaxation, any reward to the people, but by new repression and the straining not only to rebuild the economy, but to "catch up and overcome" the West in technological development. This is one side of the picture.

The other side is better known: the USSR passing the examination as a great military and industrial superpower in World War II; Russia rebuilding her industry at a tremendous pace after the war and forging to the very front rank in technology and science; Communism acquiring satellite states in Eastern Europe; the party contending for power in France and Italy; and the great victory of Chinese Communism, which makes Communist power in Asia no longer a threat but an overwhelming reality, the favored contender for ascendancy in the whole continent. Over large areas of the world, the combination of Soviet power and the attraction of revolutionary Marxism made it more than possible that the modernization and industrialization of the underdeveloped countries would take place under the auspices of Communism, and this, in the circumstance, would redound to the increased power of the Soviet Union and to the further weakening of the democratic powers and the ideologies they represent.

The two sides of the picture taken together do not add up to the usual Sunday-school view of politics. Terror and deception rewarded by the erection of a powerful industrial state; lack of democracy and the most basic freedoms leading not to the overturning of the tyranny but to the consolidation of the Soviet Leviathan and to its world-wide influence—such must be the gloomy conclusions of anyone who would believe that the democratic virtues of the West should bring tangible rewards instead of the attrition of the political and ideological influence of the democratic powers.

However, if we try conscientiously to separate the facts from our desires and preconceptions, the picture is far more complex. After Stalin's death the official communiqué of the Soviet regime spoke of the steps taken to prevent "disorder and panic." The despot's death was followed by a series of steps relaxing some of the most oppressive features of totalitarianism in the USSR. In other words, the recipe for tyranny was not perfect. Only the masochistic imagination of a writer could conjure up a perfect totalitarian system, a *1984,* in which propaganda and oppression erode the last traces of human individuality and economic and social pressures disappear before an omnipotent state. The general principles of social and political development do not lose their validity even under the most oppressive totalitarian system. They do not operate as "laws," automatically enforcing the commonplaces of the simplified democratic catechism, but neither can they be eliminated by the most stringent police and propaganda apparatus.

It is not presumptuous nor is it wishful thinking to characterize the developments in the Soviet Union since 1945 as being profoundly affected by the crisis of the ideological basis of the state and society. This crisis certainly does not mean an "overthrow" of the regime, certainly not a "democritization" of Soviet life in our meaning of the word. It means, in the first instance, that the ideology—Marxism—which has served the regime and its logic, which went with the logic of the development of the Soviet state, have increasingly, since the end of the war, become less relevant to the problems of the state and society. Less obscurely, both in the Revolution and during the industrialization, Communism, for all of its departures from *literal* Marxism, could generate enthusiasm and popular support, because what it was doing was the dictate of one part of the Marxist doctrine and could evoke the almost religious enthusiasm of its devotees. Even at the height of the purges, an average Communist could find a rationalization for his submission in the idea that for all its aberrations, the regime, through industrialization, was laying down the road to the promised land of socialism.

With Russia essentially industrialized, the sense of the historical mission of Communism in the USSR becomes less and less clear. Where is Marxism to lead the USSR next? To the "withering away" of the state, to perfect equality? With large parts of the population having imbibed the ethos of industrialism, having become middle-class in their values and views, these slogans now sound unreal and distant. The dynamics of the industrial development itself, Marxism or no Marxism, can now assure the further growth of the economy. If the ideological element becomes less important and relevant, what is to take its place as the necessary rationale of the totalitarian system? For a time the very fact of relaxation of the most oppressive features of the regime, and the growth of material well-being will assure acquiescence, or even enthusiastic popular support. But to people with Marxist historical sophistication, the leaders of the Soviet Union, the very achievement of a higher standard of living by the people brings with it further economic and, eventually, political aspirations. The Soviet leaders may genuinely believe in their oft-repeated slogan that "in our century all the roads lead to socialism." But where does socialism as it presently exists in the Soviet Union lead?

The outlines of the crisis became legible during the last years of Stalin's rule. The crisis and the attempted remedies for it were undoubtedly connected—though the details we do not know —with the personal struggles in Stalin's entourage, with the purges that actually took place in the Soviet high command and with the preparation, in process when the despot died, for another greater purge, perhaps to rival the "Yezhovshchina." As to the personal intrigues and counterintrigues, we know little. It is risky in discussing Soviet politics (more so than any other) to assume that the relationship between political issues and personalities is a straightforward one, or that we can identify leader X with a "right wing" or Y with a "left wing" policy because of a speech, an accusation, or even a confession. As we saw during the much better documented period of the twenties, the maneuverings of totalitarian politics would trap people in ideological postures, which the winning group, having denounced them as the height of heresy, would then itself adopt. Hence the needed caution in analyzing, e.g., the conflict between Malenkov and Khrushchev as between the policy of more consumers' goods versus the stress on heavy industry. What are the major dilemmas that have confronted the regime since the period before Stalin's death? We might borrow a term from the Marxist vocabulary and talk about *the inherent contradictions* in the Soviet system as they have appeared to Stalin and his successors.

The Party and the State

Toward the end of his life, Stalin must have realized that the imposition of totalitarian controls on the party had reached dimensions threatening the very totalitarian system itself. The party grew in membership during the war, and the losses of the purge had more than been made up. The almost complete attrition of the older generation of Bolsheviks, through natural and unnatural death and the forced labor camps, led to a new character of the party. Membership became a reward, a mark of success in Soviet society. It became a body composed of managers, officers, "leading" workers, collective farm officials, and intellectuals, with little of the proletarian character that had dominated it until the early thirties. The deliberative bodies of the party, its congresses, conferences, even the Central Committee, had atrophied. In a bureaucratically run body of this kind, the ideology must of necessity become something of a "Sunday" thing, an external veneer for people engrossed in their careers and material pursuits.

The danger inherent in this situation, if not immediate, still loomed very great. If the party loses its *esprit de corps* and its sense of mission, will not the average party member think of himself more and more in professional rather than party terms— the army officer more of his community of interests with the army circles; the state bureaucrat of the viewpoint of the officialdom; and the trade-union leader in terms of the union postulates—rather than in relation to the all-transcending feeling of membership in the party of Lenin and Stalin? If so, what would prevent at some future crisis, say, the dictator's death, a clash between leaders, each representing a professional or bureaucratic interest, and the eventual emergence of the army or the secret police as the dominant power, with the party ruling in name but slated for impotence? This problem might have been in Stalin's mind when he asked the question:

The point is that we, as the leading core, are joined each year by thousands of new, young cadres fired with the desire to help us, eager to prove themselves, but lacking an adequate Marxist education, uninformed of many truths well known to us, and thus obliged to wander in the dark. . . . What is to be done with these comrades? How are they to be brought up in the spirit of Marxism-Leninism? [1]

Russian Nationalism and the Nationality Problem of the USSR

World War II was won not under the banner of Marxism-Leninism, but mostly on the impulse of *Russian* nationalism. In one of his rare outbursts of sentimentality, Stalin, at the

---

[1] J. V. Stalin, *Economic Problems of Socialism in the U.S.S.R.*, in *Current Digest of the Soviet Press: Current Soviet Policies*, ed. Leo Gruliow, New York, 1953, I, 2.

Victory Banquet in the Kremlin, thanked the Great Russian people for the support rendered to the regime, which he modestly admitted, another phenomenon rare in the dictator, had made mistakes! Notwithstanding the dictator's being Georgian, Russian chauvinism was officially sponsored and propagated after the war. Anything smacking of a suspicious idealization of a non-Russian nationality's independent past or existence, whether an ardent ode by a Ukrainian poet, a historian's denunciation of *Tsarist* imperialism in central Asia, or an excessive glorification of a nineteenth-century Caucasian fighter against the Russian conquest, became condemned. "Cosmopolitanism"—how ironic for a regime tracing its descent from Karl Marx and Friedrich Engels—became a transgression next to treason. Anti-Semitism, often an undertone in earlier Soviet politics, as when Stalin had been fighting Trotsky and Zinoviev, now reached the status of an almost official policy. The Jews, once so frequently in higher party and state positions in the Soviet Union, were now, with the exception of a privileged handful, removed, and some of them were slated for a worse fate.

It is impossible to determine what motivated the extent of the officially sponsored xenophobia. Russification and Russian nationalism had been the order of the day since the 1930's, but never until the postwar period was the policy so explicit and, as in the case of anti-semitism, so openly designed to arouse popular passions. "Rootless cosmopolitanism" was denounced as violently as any suggestion that even before the Revolution the Russians were not in the forefront of civilization, inventors and initiators of scientific and technological achievements universally acknowledged as having been done elsewhere first. There are two possible, not mutually exclusive, explanations. Russian chauvinism was a belated reaction to the revealed wartime hostility to the Soviet regime and separatism, especially in the Ukraine and among the national groups in the approaches to the Caucasus, which had become obvious even in the face of the brutality and political stupidity of the German occupying forces.

More essential is the recognition that the postwar period demanded tremendous economic sacrifices in view of the government's determination not only to rebuild but to enhance the tempo of the industrial expansion. That, and the impression of another standard of living gathered by millions of Soviet soldiers even in the ruined countries of Eastern Europe and in Germany, required the counteracting effect of widespread propaganda. In an atmosphere reminiscent of the officially sponsored hysteria about the activities of the "wreckers," "saboteurs," and the agents of foreign imperialism of the first Five-Year Plan, the new industrial effort and sacrifices were given the emotional spur of Russian chauvinism and of the search for the agents of "international Zionism" and imperialism.

The inherent contradiction and danger of this policy lay in the dimensions of the nationality problem of the USSR. The early policies following the Revolution raised the specter of this Frankenstein monster, because the Soviets then were genuinely trying to promote non-Russian national cultures. Those policies and industrialization have created and developed the Ukrainian, Uzbek, Tartar, and other intelligentsias, whom now even the most repressive policies could not turn into Russians. Open anti-Semitism represented such a very fundamental repudiation of the basic postulates of socialism that its uncontrolled spread in itself would have eventually hurt what remained of the morale of the Communist party.

Industrialized Society and the Peasant

More than twenty years of collectivized farming has not sufficed to turn peasant into worker, with the same mentality and responses as the city worker. The resistance of the peasant masses had not arrested collectivization but had forced the government to change its character. Less reliance than had been expected could be placed on the state farm, the *sovkhoz,* which was ideologically the ideal form of rural economy, because in the sovkhoz the peasant becomes simply the agrarian worker. The structure of the kolkhoz itself had to be modified, with its prevailing form, the *artel,* representing a concession to the peasant's instinct for property in land by allowing him to keep for his own use a small garden plot, fowl, perhaps a cow. Thus the element of private property was not completely eliminated. By 1936, more than 90 percent of arable land was in collective and state farms. The collective farm was not regulated and run by its own members, but was subject to the most centralized direction. Peasants worked in teams and brigades, the manager of the kolkhoz usually being appointed from outside the peasant community. The remuneration was according to one's job and performance. In addition to the strict direction of the collective farm, the added element of control was provided by the state-owned machine tractor stations, each supervising the plans and performances of several kolkhozes.

For all the great success in imposing collectivization, its final shape as it crystallized by the late thirties was never considered by the Soviet leadership as being the final answer to the problem. For one, the "idiocy of rural life" lingered on in the private plot, which drew the peasant away from collective work and psychologically constituted the link with the mentality of the small producer and the spur to the resentment of the whole collective system. For another, the prodigious growth of Soviet industry was never paralleled by anything close to a corresponding growth of agricultural production. For all its mechanization, Soviet agricultural output by the 1950's was approaching or barely surpassing the precollectivization figures, while industrial production showed manifold growth. Here then was the major socio-economic problem of the Soviet society: the peasant had not been allowed to turn into a farmer, all the compulsion and violence had not quite transformed him into a worker.

The regime pursued a zigzag course on the peasant problem. At times a squeeze would be put on the private plot, its size severely delimited, its products more heavily taxed. At other times a greater latitude would be shown: the peasant's income less heavily taxed, the structure of the collective farm relaxed in the direction of giving its members more latitude. The late forties witnessed a crisis. Contradictory policies were enunciated and then tried, reflecting the uncertainty about the needed remedies for the twin problem of increasing agricultural output and integrating the peasant into (socialist) capitalist society. In 1949 Andrei Andreyev, chairman of the Collective Farm Committee, came out publicly for the loosening of the kolkhoz structure in a direction that might transform it into a genuine cooperative farm instead of its being merely another term for a government-run grain factory. But Andreyev was publicly denounced, and the opposite policy was adopted. Several collective farms would be combined into one large kolkhoz; the peasants, working in brigades, sometimes miles away from their homestead, would find it impossible to devote much time to their individual plots. Nikita Khrushchev, in 1950, formulated an even more drastic proposal. He advocated *agrogorods,* or agro-cities, where the collectives would be combined into still larger units in which peasants would live in apartment houses and be transported to cultivate the outlying fields. The garden plot would presumably disappear; the peasant would be assimilated, in his habits and psychology, to the city dweller. But the plan proved impractical, and in turn Khrushchev's proposal was repudiated.

Industrialized Society and the New Class Mentality

The economic transformation was accompanied and enhanced by

a social one. The inculcation of the mores and habits proper to an industrialized society, the creation of way of thought and action characteristic of the middle class, ceased in the 1940's to be a revolution and became a fact. A society in which wide disparities of income and status were no longer merely tolerated but encouraged and accepted as a matter of fact, where proletarian romanticism gave way to the Communist version of the Horatio Alger stories—a poor working or peasant boy becomes, through hard work, an engineer, factory manager, or doctor, and then a deputy to the Supreme Soviet and winner of the order of Lenin—such a society needed very little by way of additional lessons in bourgeois values or "proofs" that egalitarianism is a petty bourgeois prejudice and has nothing to do with Marxism. It is a commonplace that material progress and values bring with them political aspirations. The concept of democracy or of the rule of laws was almost unimaginable to the average Russian after thirty years of Communist dictatorship. But the much more modest desires for a modicum of legality and of personal security, for the enjoyment of life and some minimal contact with the outside world were the logical consequences of the industrial and social development. Terror, compulsion, labor passports, the settling of artistic and scientific disputes by Party decree, could have had some, even if perverse, logic during the period of the most intense industrialization and during the war; but the same logic was lacking, even to the most indoctrinated Communist, in the continuation of the same unabated severity into the more advanced industrial period. A totalitarian system, operating in a society in which organized political opposition was not only impractical but unimaginable, did not confront an immediate danger. But the continued application of extravagant and obsolete aspects of totalitarianism threatened to undermine the morale, and in the long run the economic and scientific efficiency, of society.

Soviet Domination and the New Communist States

Soviet victories, geography, and the deplorable policies of the
Western powers combined to give Eastern Europe to the USSR.
In addition to its European satellites, each of them weak actually
and potentially when compared with the USSR, a tangled course
of events brought China into the "camp of socialism." The
problem of Moscow's dealing with Communist parties in power
was soon shown to be essentially different from the usual pattern
of Moscow's domination of foreign Communists, in which complete obedience was expected and usually received. Too much
water had flowed under the bridge since the first days of the
Third International to expect, in the 1940's, Stalin and his
group, accustomed to unabashed despotism, to exercise diplomacy
and tact when dealing with the men who a few years before
had been their obedient agents, or to show understanding of
the national susceptibilities and economic peculiarities of the
countries that had fallen under their sway. Without going into
the wider aspects of the Soviet position in Eastern Europe, it
is important to look at the problem of the relationship of the
Communist party of the USSR to those in the satellites and in
China.

The Comintern had been dissolved in 1943 to reassure the
Western allies. The gesture was quite meaningless: the foreign
Communists' habit of obedience and the Soviet ability to command them were so well ingrained that a formal organization
meant merely a waste of scarce housing space in Moscow. The
Communist regimes in Eastern Europe, whether they came
mainly or partly with the support of the Soviet bayonets, were
led by people who, though some of them had been in Soviet
jails or camps, were neither in a position nor in a mood to offer
the slightest resistance to the Kremlin and were only too glad
to avail themselves of the help, advice, and command of the
Russians. But in the nature of things, granting the premises of

both sides, an eventual conflict was inevitable. Communism is power- and industry-oriented. A former humble servant of the Comintern, when in power, would soon plot fantastic plans of rapid industrialization and expansion, sometimes territorial, of *his* country's power. Soviet economic exploitation, the denial of even internal authority to the local leaders, was bound to jar. Thus men who before had been more fanatical Communists and even more fervent worshipers of Stalin than their Russian comrades tended to fall into "nationalism." The brutality and heavy-handedness of Stalin's policy, seemingly oblivious to the possibility that the slightest whim of the Soviets might be defied by a *Communist,* thus brought to rebellion its initially and still potentially most faithful group of foreign supporters, the Yugoslav Communists. With Tito's defection in 1948, purges and social and economic policies originated directly from Moscow, or from its new international extension, the Cominform, descended upon the satellites.

The satellite policies were from the perspective of the 1950's as obsolescently brutal and, ultimately, dangerous to the dictatorship as some of the internal policies. A more perspicacious policy would certainly have brought better results. The disproportion in power between the European satellites and the USSR, the fact that their Communist leaders had nowhere else to look for support against the West or their own peoples, would have undoubtedly secured their general following of the Russian wishes, provided they had been given some leeway and opportunity to dictate themselves the tempo of economic and social transformation of their countries.[2] But Stalinism by 1948 meant a boundless belief in the power of coercion. The idea of negotiating with or appeasing the satellite Communists would have been unthinkable to the tyrant.

[2] It has to be remembered, however, that some of them, the Yugoslav Communists, for instance, were at first more drastic in their social policies than the Russians would have had them and adopted a completely unrealistic plan of industrialization and collectivization.

The danger was obvious: Soviet Communism survived its most dangerous moments by invoking Russian patriotism. The support of nationalism could not very well be invoked to maintain Communism in the satellites. The overwhelming power of the USSR could and did, with one exception, prevent the defection of the satellites and dispose of the unreliable or potentially unreliable satellite leaders. But the satellites could become liabilities instead of assets to Soviet imperialism: their economy damaged by Soviet exactions and inappropriate policies, their Communist parties demoralized and terrorized, they would present an additional danger in case of an emergency, instead of being reliable allies. The general tenor of Soviet policies toward Tito was having a discouraging effect, especially on pro-Soviet radical movements in Asia. And in the long run, the policy of complete control of subversion of internal Communist leadership by Moscow would almost inevitably lead to a vaster case of Titoism in China, where, in the eventuality of clash, even the qualified success of Stalinist methods (as in Poland or Bulgaria) was unimaginable.

THE RESULTS OF CRISIS

Party and state, nationalism, industrialization, the peasant, and the new class mentality, other Communist states—these are only some of the factors that contributed to the crucial dilemmas of the Soviet state and party on the eve of Stalin's death. To the more perspicacious in the dictator's entourage they must have suggested that the logic of Marxism and the logic of Stalinism had begun to diverge to the point at which the totalitarian system itself, and, incidentally, their own jobs, if not lives, would be endangered by the continuation of the obsolescently severe methods. And more than once the danger of a new world war (as after the Korean conflict) must have appeared real, with the Soviet Union still behind in the development of atomic weapons and Chinese Communism far from having consolidated its hold upon the vast country.

The aging despot could not, understandably, conceive of a basic conflict between the extreme of totalitarianism associated with his name and the interests of the country and the party and of Marxism. If earlier, the greatest crisis of the Soviet state in 1929-1933 had been overcome by industrialization plus a vast scheme of compulsion, the same twofold technique could be applied now. Extravagant and grandiose plans for technological transformation, as well as plots of still vaster purges, occupied Stalin toward the end of his life. *The Economic Problems of Socialism in the U.S.S.R.*, published in his last year, is a largely incoherent restatement of Marxism as the despot understood it, with the reiteration of the technological mania: "What would happen if not individual groups of workers, but the majority of workers were to raise their cultural and technical standards to the level of the technical and engineering personnel? Our industry would be raised to the heights unattainable by the industry of other countries."[3]

Along with this and the more concrete plans for canals, reforestation belts, and industrial expansion, Stalin evidently contemplated a new purge—a pardonable self-indulgence in an old man having few pleasures left in life—that was to begin with some of his closest collaborators. The Nineteenth Congress of the party, in 1952 (the first in thirteen years), laid the framework for the changes in leadership. The new Politburo of twenty-five members included a group of newcomers who were presumably to be given training on the job for the day when Beria, Molotov, Khrushchev, and others would be gathered to their reward. The "Affair of the Jewish Doctors," a group of eminent medical men, some of them on the staff of the Kremlin, "unmasked" as having, at the orders of foreign imperialists, caused or plotted to cause

[3] *Current Soviet Policies*, I, 7.

the death of some notables, was in the best traditions of 1936 and 1937.

The twin recipe—a vast purge and a vast industrial and social advance—were to be the answer to the mounting problems of the dictatorship. In the international field, no major change of policy was contemplated, no relaxation of the stringent policies toward the satellites. The dictator's persistence in operating in the old, by now hardly relevant, categories is visible in his appraisal of the international situation. The eventual conflict between the "imperialist" powers remained for him a cardinal tenet in 1952, as it had been for Lenin thirty years before. World War II had shown that ". . . the capitalist countries struggle for markets and the desire to crush competitors turned out in actuality to be stronger than the contradictions between the camp of capitalism and the camp of socialism," and the lesson is "that the inevitability of wars among the capitalist countries remains." [4]

The actual direction of Soviet policies, had Stalin lived on, is of necessity uncertain as is the question whether the old methods would have sufficed to deal with new problems. As it was, his death in March 1953 interrupted the attempted purge and changed the direction of the reforms which had been forecast in the *Economic Problems*.

The dictator's successors inherited the problems bequeathed by both the successes and the failures of his policies. None of them has inherited the full prestige and power of the deceased. It is natural that, in any discussion of the struggle for power that has gone on since Stalin's death, the Western reader's attention is riveted on personalities and the "Kreminologists" expertise directed at the discerning of the plots and counterplots. But the stuff of politics does not consist solely of the intriguing coups and dramatic intervention by the "secret police," the "army," or the "party apparatus." The actuality of Soviet

[4] *Ibid.*, p. 8.

politics is reduced—not entirely, as strict materialist determinists would have us believe, but to a considerable degree—to social and economic forces which the various contestants try to utilize in their struggle for power. The problems have remained; what has changed has been the approach toward them, and the regime's ability to resolve some of them *merely* by compulsion.

In pre-1953 days, the dictator's word immediately became the official policy. Such a policy might not succeed. Say the dictator ordered the abolition of the collective-farm markets, where the peasants could dispose of part of the surplus of the collectives rather than turn it all over to the state (this was forecast in *The Economic Problems*). Such a policy might not (and probably would not) increase the output of agriculture. But there would not be any trouble or delay at the decision-making stage, despite the manifest unfeasibility of the proposal. And the failure of the policy would not shake the dictator's position in the slightest. The successors could not impose policies simply because of whim, and the failure of a policy associated with leader Z might prove fatal to *his* position, the quarreling satraps being on the lookout for each other's vulnerable spots.

It seems clear that the successors realized the need for popularity, if not in the nation at large, than among the now enlarged group of party and state officials with political influence. The rhythm of Soviet politics since Stalin's death has consisted of competing leaders' attempts to gain credit for liberalizing policies while trying to saddle their opponents with the reputation of being die-hard defenders of the old and bad order. Stalin was hardly in his grave when this "political campaign" for succession began. Each of the contenders tried to secure strategic positions in the party, state, or police apparatus. At the same time, he attempted to associate himself in the popular mind with the repudiation of some particularly obnoxious policy of the old regime. The game was exhilarating if dangerous. If leader X became known as an advocate of a more lenient policy toward

the peasants, this policy would gain him popularity with the
party officials for whom life would be made easier as a consequence of those policies and who would thus tend to support
X in the now resuscitated Central Committee. If, however, X
showed himself too clearly as being too enterprising in the search
for popularity and corresponding administrative intrigues, he
would unite against himself other leaders dreading another
Stalin.

The latter was the fate of Beria. His fellow Georgian's death
had probably saved him from an unpleasant fate, and he regained
the leadership of the mainfold agencies of state security. Along
with installing "his" men in crucial positions, the head of the
police soon identified himself with the policy of "socialist
legality" (i.e., a repudiation of terror) and with a nonchauvinist
nationality policy, an obvious bid for the support by the non-
Great-Russian elements of the party and state hierarchy. His
liquidation at the hands of the other oligarchs was swift and
dramatic, a tribute no doubt to the effectiveness of the appeal
of his "platform." The fall of Malenkov in 1955 was undoubtedly
connected with his too insistent self-identification with the policy
of more consumers' goods, i.e., better life for the Soviet citizen.
Soviet politics still takes place in an atmosphere of personal
intrigue, deception, and violence. But in playing their political
game the leaders must take a much greater account of social
aspirations and premises than at the time when one man stood
so far above everything and everybody.

The insistent nature of the problems confronting Marxism in
Russia is evident in the policies pursued by the current leadership headed by Khrushchev. Under every heading, the policies
have in some way responded to popular aspirations, but they
have stopped at the point where further concessions would injure
the essential totalitarianism of the system. Much effort has gone
into the revival of the party. Two party congresses have met
within the last four years. The deliberative organs, the Central

Committee and the Politburo, meet frequently; and the former, because of the new focus of party politics, has regained *some* of its original importance. The regime has tried to pour new vigor and *esprit de corps* into the party. Excessive Russian chauvinism has been eschewed; and, in an almost demonstrative fashion, the leadership of the local party bodies in most non-Russian areas has been vested in the natives. In many ways, the regime has appealed to the *amour propre* of the non-Russian nationalities. An Uzbek sits in the Politburo; among its alternate members are heads of the Communist parties of Georgia, Ukraine, Latvia, and Byelorussia. The Ukrainians—the most numerous non-Russian nation—have had particular attention paid to them, attention ranging from a large number of Ukrainians in the highest party, state, and army posts (the fact, perhaps, also connected with Khrushchev's long-time association with the Ukraine) to the not very important but demonstrative turning over of the Crimea to the Ukrainian SSR. The domination by the Russian element is clear, but the excesses of Russian chauvinism, as well as demonstrative anti-Semitism, have been stilled.

A general policy of raising the standard of living and greater attention to the production and quality of consumer goods, while not negating the still asserted priority of the development of heavy industry, has softened the edge of the immediate economic grievances. The regime has talked about, and taken some steps toward, shortening the hours of work and increasing pensions and old-age benefits. Radical transformations in agriculture have been eschewed. The Soviets hope for the solution of the greatest socio-economic problem of Communism by raising the standard of living, giving more consumer goods to the peasant as well as by opening up vast new areas for cultivation.

The extent of repression of the individual and the fantastic and senseless controls over every sphere of social and cultural activity under Stalin have given the new leadership a wide scope for "liberalism" without damaging in the slightest the essence of the police state. Secret administrative trials by a collegium of the MVD (the political police) have been abolished, the forced-labor camps largely disbanded. Labor passports, a remnant of the most draconic period of the industrialization, have disappeared. The extent of intellectual freedom, the possibility of contact with foreigners and with the external world in general, while modest in Russia today even in comparison with an average authoritarian state, appears as the extreme of freedom by the standard of Stalin's last years.

The balance of the reforms, while impressive by that standard, can hardly be summarized as being even the first faltering step toward the rule of law, not to mention democracy or liberalism— terms that anybody writing about the Soviet Union for the next generation or so would be wise to avoid. They add up to the conviction of the leaders that they can afford and must practice "sane" totalitarianism as distinguished from the morbid one of Stalin's era; they reflect not only a response to the social pressures but also a sense of confidence that the new Soviet state is strong enough to withstand a citizen's conversation with a foreigner or the news about the number of automobiles in the United States.

Are we then justified in talking about a crisis of Marxism in the USSR, when what we see is a common-sense attempt to abolish the now needless severity? The process has not been without interruptions and regressions, whenever it was deemed that effects had gone too far. Beria and his accomplices—and there must have been others—were certainly not tried in accordance with "socialist legality." After the initial "thaw," the intellectuals have been reminded, not too gently, of the boundaries they must not overstep. The zigzag course of repression-relaxation was, after all, an "invention" of Stalin himself. After the great suffering of the initial industrialization and collectivization drive, the great man had said what Khrushchev and his group have tried to suggest by their behavior: "Life has become better, Comrades, life has become gayer." And then began the Great Purge! Where today is the "collective leadership" so piously asserted in 1955 and 1956?

The reason that we must not see in the current developments in Russia just another temporary device of totalitarianism is demonstrated by a fragment of Suslov's speech at the Twentieth Party Congress in 1956. While talking about the ideological education of party members, Suslov, long in charge of the agitation and propaganda division of the party, quoted approvingly a complaint by a rank-and-file member:

I have been in a Party history study circle for 13 years. For the thirteenth time our propagandists are explaining the Bund to us. Have we nothing more important to do than to criticize the Bund? We are interested in the affairs of our M.T.S. (Machine tractor station), of our district, of our province. We want to live in the present and the future, but our propagandists have got so bogged down in Narodnik and Bundist affairs that they cannot get beyond them.[5]

"We want to live in the present and the future. . . ." Had the party boss pondered the full meaning of those words, he might not have quoted them so approvingly. It is not only the heroic period of the party's history that now holds little meaning to its members, but the whole ideology, the meaning of socialism itself, as compared with everyday concrete problems of life. *Up to a point* this ideological secularization of the party membership is a factor of stability of the Soviet system and a source of comfort to the regime. Abstract questions of democracy, equality, or "real" socialism do not excite the average party member, interested mainly in his career and the amenities of everyday life, grateful, no doubt, to the new leaders for enabling him to breathe more freely and to live better than he did a few

[5] *Ibid.*, II, 79.

years ago. But a *complete* ideological secularization, the relaxation of Marxism-Leninism to the level at which the average citizen of the industrialized West keeps his religion, is something that the regime dreads and a totalitarian system can ill afford. The separation of ideology from the problems of everyday life, or ideological agnosticism, must mean, after a while, one thing: the individual, even if he is externally a good Communist and thinks of himself as such, will find the expression of his interests and social aspirations through the medium of his trade union, his level of officialdom, or his economic class rather than through his party. We encounter our old friend and the intermittent enemy of Communism: "spontaneity." Spontaneous social development, granted the present level of Soviet society, leads to growing absorption in prosaic, material things and to the attrition of that passionate enthusiasm by which the ideology of a totalitarian party buttresses the totalitarian system.

It thus becomes clearer why the regime has tried so desperately to revive the élan of the party, to infuse Communism with meaning and further historical tasks. It becomes clear why the present leadership has decided upon a step fraught for them with considerable danger—baring the worst abuses and excesses of the Stalinist era and giving the party a comprehensive view of some of the horrors perpetuated by Stalin and in his name. A more cautious policy would have followed the pattern of the first two years after Stalin's death: an implied rather than an outright criticism of the late dictator and his methods. In delivering his detailed attack upon the despot, at the closed session of the Twentieth Party Congress, Khrushchev must have been aware of the inference his hearers would make: the denouncers had been Stalin's closest subordinates, Khrushchev himself the executor of Stalin's policies in the Ukraine during the Great Purge. But the psychological risk involved must have been deemed less significant than the potential advantage: it would be demonstrated to millions of party members that Communism is a living and vigorous creed, that transgressions and terror flow not from the ideology but from its perversion by individuals, and that, instead of demanding self-abasement and bureaucratic routine, Marxism and Leninism have creative and regenerating powers. And so the moral: ". . . to return to and actually practice in all our ideological work the very important Marxist-Leninist theses about the people as the maker of history and the creator of all mankind's material and spiritual benefits, *about the decisive role of the Marxist party in the revolutionary struggle to change society,* about the victory of Communism." [6]

The listing of the tyrant's misdeeds, the admission of the blood bath into which he plunged the party and the country, was done with a certain cleverness which underlines its purpose. Stalin the dictator, the architect of great industrialization and the ruthless executor of collectivization, has remained on the pedestal. It is the morbidly suspicious tyrant *after* 1934, who *needlessly* sent people to their death or jail and who persecuted his closest collaborators, who was denounced. The same principle and moral are employed in distinguishing among Stalin's victims. It was "correct" to impose the policy of industrialization and to destroy politically its opponents—

. . . because the political line of both the Trotskyite-Zinovievite bloc and of the Bukarinites led actually toward the restoration of capitalism and capitulation to the world bourgeoisie. Let us consider for a moment what would have happened if in 1928-1929 the political line of right deviation had prevailed among us, or orientation toward "cotton-dress industrialization," or toward the kulak, etc. We would not now have a powerful industry, we would not have the collective farms. . . .[7]

But it was "incorrect" to initiate terror "when socialism in our country had been fundamentally established" and especially "incorrect" to kill off people just because of actual or alleged

---

[6] From Khrushchev's speech, *Current Soviet Policies,* II, 188. (Italics mine)
[7] *Ibid.,* II, 173.

disagreement with the tyrant. Social repression and even terror in the service of a great Marxist aim, like industrialization, says Khrushchev, is all right; whimsical terrorism unhealthy. What other regime could have produced the phenomenon of the dictator confessing that his predecessor had been a murderer, the speaker his obedient tool, and using the occasion for the ideological edification of his hearers?

The effort to revivify the ideology and the party has proved to be a qualified success. But the essential premise of Khrushchev's speech exhibits this basic naïveté: the eternal tendency of the Communist leaders to have their cake and eat it; to have all the advantages of spontaneous support and ideological enthusiasm of the party, at the same time that the main features of totalitarianism remain unimpaired. The ghost of Stalin, even the post-1934 Stalin, has proved too strong to be laid aside. And the reason is that the Communist party cannot quite be the ideologically charged and vital organization it had been during the Revolution and during the crucial stages of industrialization. Thus, terror as a potential weapon of totalitarianism can never be laid aside, and, at periods, as in Khrushchev's disposal of the Malenkov-Molotov group in 1957, its threat, at least, has to be invoked. It is a pleasant dream in which the Communist leaders indulge: a democratic totalitarianism where the free activity of the people moves them in the direction desired by the dictatorship, where not only power but popularity are the rewards of the dictatorship's magnanimous resolve to use terror and illegality only when it is necessary. But their own historical sophistication, the product of Marxism, must tell them that politics is more complex.

Hence the attempt to breathe life into the old formulas. At the Twenty-first Party Congress, Khrushchev discoursed about the perennial problem: the passage from socialism to communism. But the vision of a society of perfect equality, of the absence of coercion, of the withering away of the state, is quite meaningless to the average party member, not to mention the average citizen. The illusion has to be maintained that, by being a Communist, a worker, engineer, or scientist will work better and with a "difference."

To illustrate both the predicament of Marxism in Russia and the necessary qualification of any hasty optimism about the demise of Soviet totalitarianism because of its disappearing ideological *raison d'être,* it is well to keep in mind Marx's story about capitalism. At one time, the story goes, capitalism was a truly revolutionary creed, able to inspire its exponents with the fanaticism and energy capable of destroying the older and obsolete economic system. But then it was capitalism's fate to become reactionary, a "fetter" on the forces of production. But the capitalists refused to recognize their social and economic obsolescence and attempted to continue the system through their command of the instrument of coercion—the state. The story is much more appropriate when applied to the role of Communism and its ideology in Russia. Communism had a revolutionary meaning and function both in the Revolution and in the period of industrialization and collectivization. The ideology, or its different parts, could then go hand in hand with the rationale of the Communist dictatorship and totalitarianism.

But where can Marxism lead the Soviet Union now? Toward democracy? Does anyone seriously believe that the Communist party is desirous or capable of instituting even the rudimentary elements of the rule of law or of the democratic process? To "Communism"? Will this industrialized society move toward the equality of incomes and status away from which it has been moving practically from the first days after the Revolution? Toward the "withering away of the state"? One must not joke!

It is tempting in prognosticating the future evolution of the Soviet system to discern hopeful signs in the undoubted erosion of the ideology and the undoubted secularization of Soviet life.

A latter-day Marxist view sees the Soviet system orienting itself toward the yet distant but discernible goal of Marxism—democracy:

. . . within the Communist Party there already exist various potential trends which will become actual and will crystallize in the processes of inner party discussion. Diverse shades of internationalism and nationalism will come to life. Divergent attitudes toward the peasantry will be expressed. Conflicting views will arise about the tempo of further industrialization, consumer interests. . . . Once the ruling party begins to discuss its affairs it cannot monopolize freedom of discussion for long.[8]

A somewhat less deterministic view would link the quieting down of Soviet expansion to the failure of the ideological prophecy of the collapse of capitalism: "For no mystical Messianic movement—and particularly not that of the Kremlin, can face frustration indefinitely without eventually adjusting itself in one way or another to the logic of the state of affairs."[9]

How easily all of us become historical determinists, believers in "inevitabilities," if by doing so we can assuage our fears and prognosticate developments confirming our wishes! But it is quite possible that the inherent contradictions of Soviet *Communism* may not lead to the erosion of Soviet *totalitarianism,* any more than the inherent contradictions of capitalism, which Marx saw so clearly in 1850 and 1860, did not lead to the transformation of old-fashioned capitalism for another fifty or sixty years. And political power, to which Marx attributed the ability of the capitalists to hang on beyond the clear signs of obsolescence, was not nearly so much concentrated in the hands of the nineteenth-century middle class, nor exercised so ruthlessly and skillfully, as it is by this executive committee of the exploiters—

[8] Isaac Deutscher, *Russia: What Next?* New York, 1953, p. 228.
[9] George Kennan, "The Sources of Soviet Conduct," reprinted in *American Diplomacy 1900-1950,* Chicago, 1951, p. 124.

Soviet totalitarianism. All that a historical study can achieve is to point out the areas of tension and the probability of crises in a system that has outlived its main historical mission. It dare not predict their outcomes. We have pointed out, in discussing the original Marxist argument, the fallacy of its major intellectual premise: history must work itself out tidily, creating no problems it cannot solve; no nooks and crannies in the historical scene can for long shelter an anachronism or the illogicality of an accident. The illogicality of Soviet totalitarianism, of Marxist ideology in a society that has no further need or use for it, may yet for a long time be with us.

In looking for areas where an ideological advance would bolster the totalitarian system, the Soviet leaders can find very little at home in the way of possible directions. The peasant problem remains, it is true, one great, unfinished subject on the agenda of Marxism in Russia. But the regime has evidently decided that, instead of major political pressures designed to transform the peasant into the worker, a fuller integration of the peasant masses into the mores of industrialism and a better economic performance from agriculture can be expected by raising the standard of living in the countryside and by giving the collective farms more autonomy in managing their affairs. The regime has not hesitated to initiate the program of selling the machine tractor stations, traditionally the main lever of economic and political centralized control over the peasants, to the collectives. In 1952, Stalin, considering proposals for exactly this step, characterized it as an inadmissible retreat from the socialist direction:

What would be the result . . . ? How could one justify this exceptional position of the collective farms, by what considerations of progress or advance? Could one say that such a situation would be conducive to raising collective farm property to the level of public property, that it would speed the transition of our society from socialism to Communism? Would it not be more accurate to say that such a situation could only further separate collective farm ownership from public ownership and lead us not closer to Communism but on the contrary further from it.[10]

It remains to be seen whether the basic peasant problem, the inborn hostility to the collective system, can be completely assuaged by economic remedies and more freedom of initiative. But the practical scope of socialist reforms in agriculture, for the time being, remains small. The main source for ideological enthusiasm (one recalls the synthetically produced ideological fervor with which the party in 1955 and 1956 recruited city Communists for the development of the "virgin lands" in Kazakhstan and Siberia) must be sought elsewhere.

And here there is one logical direction. Capitalism, the Communists have held, has been postponing its doom through imperialism. Foreign expansion, both of the Soviet Union and of Communist ideas, remains one major source of "proving" Marxism on the home front. Marxism-Leninism and, one must be fair even if the present Soviet leaders are ungrateful, Stalinism, with their technological orientations have brought the Soviet Union to the position of pioneering the exploration of outer space. But a proud Soviet citizen may begin to suspect that further technological achievements are not dependent upon continued reading of *Capital* or *What Is to Be Done*, much as the regime is trying to establish a connection. On the other hand, the growth of Communism over large parts of the world, the appeal of the doctrine to the nations in Asia, Africa, and soon, perhaps, Latin America are tangible "proofs" of the ideology, sources of inspiration for the party members, and, incidentally, justifications, or so it appears, of the policies and methods of the leaders of Soviet totalitarianism. The international aspect of Communism, its continued expansion, thus becomes a crucial point in the preservation of the ideological motivation of the Russian Communists.

Unabashed Stalinism in relation to foreign Communists was

[10] J. V. Stalin, *Economic Problems of Socialism in the U.S.S.R.*, in *Current Soviet Policies*, I, 19.

found as awkward and obsolescent as the Stalinist methods in domestic politics. The embroilment with Tito had to be liquidated, the terroristic methods undermining the morale of the Communist parties in the satellites ended, and the permissibility of "several roads to socialism," rather than one decided upon in Moscow, had to be proclaimed to obviate future conflicts, unavoidable with China, for example, if the old formula had been adhered to. With their instinctive propensity for eating their cake and having it, too, the Soviet leaders expected solid dividends for their enlightenment and liberalism. Their control over the satellites would remain almost as great as before, but instead of terrorized and dispirited satellite parties, they would now have willing partners and subordinates. The Chinese Communists would fit more easily into the new pattern. The disturbing effects, especially in Asia, of the Tito affair would be dispersed with the return of Yugoslavia to the camp of socialism. Communism, in the world at large as in the USSR, would show its regenerative powers and stand, unencumbered by the ballast of Stalinism, as the road to national liberation and emancipation. In 1955 the Soviet leaders traced their steps to Belgrade (the home of "American agents carrying out espionage and sabotage assignments from their American 'chiefs' against the U.S.S.R. and the people's democracies," as Tito and his group had been characterized at the Nineteenth Party Congress, in language rather restrained for those days) and asked that bygones be bygones. Even earlier, the satellite parties had been told to restrain their local Stalins, liquidate the more obnoxious security chiefs, and rehabilitate the good Communists erroneously shot during the bad old days. Who could accuse the post-Stalin leaders of lack of resolution or of false embarrassment about past "mistakes"?

The new policy probably arrived at not without serious dissensions at the Kremlin, about the tempo if not the character of measures, represented, like the denigration of Stalin at home, a calculated risk. But insofar as the satellites were concerned, it contained one gross psychological error. The satellites had not been through forty years of totalitarianism. Nationalism there, instead of being the natural ally of the regime and in contrast to the USSR, was the natural enemy of Communism. By recognizing its "errors," Communism in Russia gained, at least temporarily, in strength and vitality. But with the extreme of terror discouraged in the satellites, there was little left to preserve their Communist regimes against the long-suppressed wrath of their peoples. With Tito appeased, a premium was being put on a nationalist stance by local Communist leaders. Even some of the most "Stalinist" leaders, as in Poland, switched to a frantic nationalist posture, justly afraid that they would be offered as sacrificial goats in the explanation and expiation of past mistakes. And Tito wanted Yugoslavia not only to be *treated* as an independent Communist state, but to be actually independent. Thus October 1956 in Poland, with Gomulka carried to power in the face of Soviet threats. Thus Hungary, with national Communism spilling into a national revolution *against* Communism. Thus the story of Russo-Yugoslav relations—like an unhappy marriage—of quarrels, denunciations, reconciliations, and cajoleries, but always of essential incompatibility. In foreign Communism, as in domestic, the ghost of Stalin refuses to disappear.

It would be fatuous to describe the satellite policy as a complete failure. Its near catastrophe in the fall of 1956 undoubtedly shook, for a time, the position of the leading group in the Kremlin. The social and intellectual side effects of the liberalization of satellite Communism, which spilled over the borders of the USSR, had some unsettling results in Russia. But a balance between the old and new policies toward the satellites was established in 1957-1958, just as a similar synthesis was being established within the Soviet Union. In both cases, recourse to pure Stalinism is almost unthinkable. But outright compulsion and terror are always there to supplement, if needed, the flexible tactics of partial concession to popular aspirations, economic improvement, and attempted ideological revival.

The appeals and the state of Marxism in the areas not controlled by the Soviet bayonets, the relevance of Communist China's effort to skip the historical stages of industrialization even faster then had the Soviet Union, are described in the final chapter. Here we have dealt with some internal and external aspects of the crisis of Marxism in the USSR. It is obvious that this crisis does not translate itself into an immediate weakness of the USSR, or an immediate danger to Soviet totalitarianism. Yet it is this crisis that is largely responsible for the improvisations, the rapid shifts and reversals, in the domestic and foreign policies of the Soviet rulers. *Somehow* the ideology has to be shown to be important, dynamic, and capable of expansion and conquest. If it is not shown to be so, then even the most rapid growth in the material welfare of the citizens of the USSR will not enhance, but most likely will decrease, the ideological appeal of Communism, with which is bound up the preservation of the leading role of the party and of totalitarianism itself. It is this restlessness in the search for a justification of the ideology, a rationale for continued totalitarianism, which opens up incalculable dangers for world peace. Being intelligent men, desirous of learning about the outside world, genuinely interested in improving the lot of their people, the Soviet leaders cannot desire a world conflict. But at the same time, they are driven by an ideological compulsion much more complex than the now obsolete dream of world revolution, to adventurous and aggressive foreign policies.

VII THE UNFINISHED REVOLUTION

The citizen of the United States lives in an apparently pragmatic and "unideological" environment. If he views his society at all, he probably sees there no irreconcilable conflicts, no "inherent contradictions," only concrete problems always susceptible to concrete solutions. Economic ills will respond to material progress, which is taken for granted; political and administrative shortcomings can always be remedied by legislation and administrative measures; even the major social problems, such as the racial one, will be solved by education, wise legislation, and time. There are no ineluctable laws of history standing in the way of common-sense solutions which will eventually be accepted by a majority of reasonable men. Conflicts of political viewpoints can be reduced to different views on specific policies or, at most, to clashing interests, but certainly not to any historical or economic "forces" or "laws," standing over and above human volition. Why cannot the rest of the world be the same?

National egocentrism likewise pervades the attitude toward Communism. Where *does* Communism lead in relation to world peace? The sources, component parts, and dogmatic vagaries of the doctrine all pale into insignificance when compared with certain questions: Is or is not Communism bound to lead to another world conflict? Is this ideology, which has already conquered one third of mankind, likely to continue its triumphant march?

Answers to the first question vary according to one's estimate of what constitutes the most important operative element of Communism. Is it belief in force? John Foster Dulles phrased one representative approach to the problem when, stressing the peaceful nature of the democratic creed, he wrote: "Unhappily it is otherwise with the creed of Communism, or at least that variety of Communism which is espoused by the Soviet Communist party." [1] Marx, Lenin, and Stalin have all taught the use of force and violence, and Mr. Dulles sees the relationship between ideology and action as a fairly direct one, for he concludes: "These teachings of Marx, Lenin, and Stalin have never been disavowed by the Soviet Communist Party of which Mr. Khrushchev is now the First Secretary. . . . Therefore, I believe that it is necessary that at least that part of the Soviet Communist creed should be abandoned." [1]

At the other extreme is the view that the Communists' ideology should encourage rather than depress us about the prospects for world peace:

They will, while they retain their present philosophy, understand neither our society nor their own. . . . We cannot rely on their good will, but we can, if we act wisely, rely on their patience. Their false philosophy teaches them that time is their ally; and the more they can be persuaded to let time pass quietly the better for us and for them. Let us at least thank God that Hitler is dead and that the dictators we have to deal with are sane. [2]

Both attitudes, it is not unfair to say, suggest a degree of incredulity that other people can be so different from us, or that the difference can be ascribed to something separate from ill will or stubborn ignorance. If the Communists would only

[1] In a letter to *The New Statesman and Nation,* London, February 8, 1958.
[2] John Plamenatz, *German Marxism and Russian Communism,* London, 1954, pp. 350-351.

learn that it is wrong to use violence, says Mr. Dulles. If they could only see how wrong it is to expect the collapse of our system or to accuse it of inhuman iniquities, echoes the other view. The problem, unfortunately, is more complex; and it is impossible, before seeing its full complexity, to realize the predicament of the Western democracies in the face of the Communist threat.

We have asserted here that Marxism is primarily based on two things. One is the insight into the psychology of large masses of the population in a society that undergoes the process of transition from a traditional, pre-industrial phase to industrialization. Without having read a word of Marx or Lenin, an illiterate peasant who is being squeezed economically or forced to give up his land and work in a factory experiences almost instinctively the feelings that Marxism formulates in a theoretical language: a sense of alienation springing from his loss of property and status, and an antagonism toward the people and authority personifying the mysterious forces that have made his previous social existence impossible or increasingly hazardous economically and that have destroyed the whole basis of his beliefs and values without giving him anything in return. To such people, Communism may come not as an esoteric intellectual creed, but as a systematic expression of their own feelings and reactions, something which again makes sense out of an apparently senseless world. What to us, in a society which has left that stage of development long, long ago, looks like an unreasonably complicated and unduly violent doctrine, one almost impossible to believe in except through propaganda or under coercion, appears to a reflecting Asian or African as a sensible and natural description of the world and history. Our own ideology, the product of a long industrial development and a *consequent* democratic habituation appears to them, in contrast, as something infinitely more complicated and unnatural.

But Marxism is more than just a convincing demonology of the forces of the modern world; it gives more, in addition to being a systematic rationalization of instinctive anarchism of a society torn from its traditional moorings. The evils of modernization are conveniently ascribed to a class and a system of authority called *capitalism*. But the promise of full emancipation from the evils of the present and the promise of harmony and welfare far beyond the dreams of a pre-industrial past are also provided. The ideology embodies a passion for material improvement and fanaticism in the service of industrialization. Just as it exploits the nostalgia for a past ruined forever by the capitalists, it appeals to the impatience for the future, which cannot be appeased by democratic and liberal phraseology, by the cautions and procedures natural in a society that has achieved industrialization, but empty-sounding in one in a hurry to find the key to a better future—industry and technology.

For international politics, the first practical consequence of this view of Marxism—to recognize it frankly—is that it is the *natural* ideology of underdeveloped societies in today's world and that, in contrast to it, liberalism as practiced and preached in the West can appeal to a much narrower range of interests and sentiments and is at a disadvantage in competition. But this recognition, hurtful as it is to our *amour propre,* should give rise not to pessimism but to a more realistic appreciation of the policies and techniques needed to obviate the danger that the natural appeal of Marxism will be translated into Communist domination of the new states. Communism in our time has boasted of its ability to skip stages of historical development and rapidly propel a country barely emergent from a pre-industrial stage, toward an advanced modern society. It is this capacity which must be learned by Western liberalism in its dealings with the "underdeveloped" areas, the capacity to help them move through the "Marxist stage" of their development before the shackles of Communist totalitarianism are fastened on them—the shackles that will not drop off of themselves once this stage is left behind.

Paradoxically, therefore, one aspect of the struggle between Communism and liberalism consists not in a competition of ideas, the "struggle for men's minds" as it is often grandiloquently called; it is rather a struggle of techniques of development, of social and economic statesmanship on a world scale. It is, from the Western point of view, the struggle to bring the new countries to the social and economic level and pace of development at which democratic ideas and aspirations can begin to be meaningful concepts in their people's minds as well as constitutional formulas and declarations. From this point of view, it is of secondary importance for an eventful achievement of the rudiments of real democracy whether freedom of the press is or is not observed in Ghana, whether Nasser sulks at the United States or not, or even whether Indian public opinion is indignant about Tibet. A more important harbinger of the future is the pace of economic development and social adjustment to industrialism.

The problem is not simply "economic help" or—what would be hopeless—bringing, within a foreseeable time, the backward areas of the world to the present material level of the West. We have seen how, after the middle of the nineteenth century, in an English society economically "underdeveloped" (from today's perspective), the full strength of the radicalism born out of the transformation began to die out, and English socialism, when it was finally reborn, arrived with a mentality and a language quite different from the Marxist doctrine of class war and violence.

It is not fantastic to draw potential lessons for societies with entirely different political and cultural pasts. As a matter of fact, our quite common puzzlement about why countries at all levels of social and economic development cannot enjoy the rule of law and democracy is often, and paradoxically, accompanied by an unstated premise that these blessings, by the nature of things, are reserved to a charmed circle of Western states. The failure of Marxism in England was occasioned not only by factors specific to English political culture, but also and mainly by the rise in the standard of living of the working classes and the economic dynamisms that inoculated English society with the values of industrialism, which in turn made possible and imperative the growth of democracy. Social protest from an anti-industrial, anti-state form of anarchism, susceptible of being utilized by radicalism of either the left or the right, turned into the more constructive form of the working-class struggle for political rights and a greater share of the benefits of industrialism. Institutions of self-defense or attempted escape from the industrial state, like the cooperatives and trade unions, grew into schools of industrialism and democracy. The English example suggests that to overcome the Marxist phase of the effects of industrialization, economic dynamism must be supplemented by proper institutional appurtenances. Trade unionism rather than universal suffrage, an efficient civil service rather than elaborate constitutional guarantees are the most likely assurances that democratic habits will grow along with economic development.

In other words, social as well as economic planning must flow from a realistic recognition that, in large areas of the world, Communism has proselytizing powers superior to liberalism. Western diplomacy has for a long time persisted in the belief (reasonable in the classical day of European diplomacy but a dangerous illusion in a revolutionary world) that there is a special magic and effectiveness in formal treaties and engagements. The same excessive concern over the externals of politics has characterized our attitude toward the paraphernalia of constitutionalism and parliamentarism in the countries going through the birth pains of the modern economic system. Perhaps we should become Marxists to the point at which we recognize that there is more than mumbo jumbo in the hackneyed phrase about "the underlying social and economic forces." If our policies will recognize this, we shall be making the first step in denying to Communism a monopoly of the formulas of rapid modernization and industrialization.

The second consequence of a realistic recognition of what Marxism means is to see more sharply the relationship between the dynamics of Soviet society and the prospects of world peace. Marxism, we have postulated, has concluded its main work in Russia. From now on, its further aims and formulas are likely to appear increasingly artificial to the majority of Soviet citizens and even to party members. It remains as the official rationale of the totalitarian regime, and, as such, it will continue to be used in official incantations and declamations. But its two points of historical significance—the ability to catalyze human energies for revolution and for industrialization—are no longer relevant under Russian conditions.

But Soviet Russia is not only under a Marxist ideology; it is also under a totalitarian system. We all remember a classical case of ideological disillusionment: an eight-year-old girl who inquired of a newspaperman whether there was really a Santa Claus and received an answer which, though eloquent and moving, would hardly have been convincing. It would not do for a Russian citizen to inquire of Nikita Khrushchev whether there really was socialism rather than state capitalism in the Soviet Union, and whether his society was in effect moving toward the state of affairs where "from everybody according to his ability, to everybody according to his needs" will be an accurate description of reality. The common habits of industrialism and materialism may prompt a Soviet citizen to think and behave the way a man of the corresponding social and economic status does, say, in the United States, but Soviet totalitarianism will not let him do so. It is a reassuring picture of the future of Soviet society that some Western commentators have tried to suggest:

the Marxist ideology teaches the Soviets to be patient, and at the same time this ideology—and its militant aims with it—is eroding as it confronts the reality of world affairs. Much as we wish such an outcome, the view is even more wishfully and perversely deterministic than was the corresponding Communist belief in the imminent collapse of capitalism in the West.[3]

It is indeed possible, if not probable, that the erosion of ideology under the impact of industrialization may lead Soviet totalitarianism to a more aggressive foreign behavior than would otherwise be the case. There is no better method for ideology to preserve its internal function of solidifying and justifying popular support of the regime than by demonstrating Communism capable of success and expansion abroad. No previous leadership, again except for the immediate postrevolutionary days, has spoken so often and so insistently about the coming expansion of Communism, about moving from the stage of socialism to that of Communism, as has that of Khrushchev. As for outright aggressive policies, it is again within the last few years, the era of generally relaxed relations with the West, that the Soviet Communists and their Chinese allies have practiced "brinkmanship," a near-precipitation of a war crisis, as, for example, over the islands off the China coast or over Berlin. There is not the slightest evidence of a desire to precipitate an actual world conflict; the Marxist leaders, with their ingrained appreciation of technology, are too well aware of the abysmal potentialities of a nuclear war. There is every evidence of a continuing pattern of forcing the Western powers into retreats, demonstrating to the world and to their own people their ability to frustrate "imperialist designs."

The increased awareness of the Soviet leaders about the tie-up

[3] Observe this difference: even at the height of the Communist millennial expectations after the Bolshevik Revolution, the hopes for Communist revolution in the West were never accompanied by an assumption that the Soviets should not practice militant policies, or that their strategy should be one of "containment."

of world politics with the internal situation is also vividly demonstrated by some secondary characteristics. The leaders now travel widely inside and outside the "camp of socialism." That they do so reflects not only a natural tendency to see the world, curtailed of necessity when they were merely the most privileged inmates of Stalin's prison, but also a realization that foreign policy is now intimately connected with the problem of the preservation of Marxism and totalitarianism in the Soviet Union. When, some time ago, the announcement of the belated execution of the leaders of the Hungarian uprising stirred up demonstrations against the Soviet embassies in the West, "popular demonstrations" were ordered—unprecedented in recent Soviet history—against the Western legations in Moscow. This was a forcible propaganda lesson for the Soviet people of the relationship between their dignity and the interests of world Communism.

Most studies of Soviet foreign policy ask or imply this question: What can the West do about it? And it is unavoidable that in the process of answering we should often distort the problem according to our hopes or fears. It would be foolish to try to find a deterministic pattern. We live in a world where a dictator's miscalculation, a sudden sharp conflict, or simply an accident may provoke a nuclear war, the result of which is unimaginable, the "underlying forces" and the "decisive trends" be what they may. But what the hypothesis sketched here implies is that no simple mechanistic interpretation of Soviet foreign policy (such as seeing in it a systematic execution of a detailed plan of world conquest or "the Russians always respect force") will do. The Russian leaders act under an ideological compulsion, which, while they shrink from an all-out war, will not allow them to leave the world in peace and let the social forces at home encroach upon their totalitarianism. It is infantile to ask whether the leaders themselves are ideologically motivated or whether they believe that the world will eventually be inherited by the Marxist doctrine. There is no reason not to assume that, say, in Khrushchev's mind, the interests of Marxism, of the Soviet Union, and of his own power do not blend into a harmonious whole.

The Western powers enjoyed for a few years after the World War a thing unprecedented in recent history: a complete monopoly of the absolute weapon. It may be something to regret, in retrospect, that the thorough industrialization of American society, the natural and laudable tendency of a democratic society to return to its materialistic cares and problems at the end of an emergency, made impossible an interest in or an assertion of a nationalism that would have barred Soviet expansion. The question is not, needless to say, of the use or even the threat of use of nuclear weapons against the Soviet Union. But their possession could have made feasible a resourceful and resolute policy, which would have barred Eastern Europe to outright Soviet imperialism and might have made it possible for the modernization and industrialization of China to take place under other than Communist auspices. Would Soviet totalitarianism, then faced, as we now know, with a major ideological crisis and the backbreaking job of restoring and pushing Soviet economy, have been able to remain unaffected by being cut off from territorial and ideological expansion? As it was, the Western powers practiced "containment" when "liberation" was a possibility; then, for a short time, "liberation" was proclaimed the official slogan when "containment" was the only practical policy. The successive incantations of "massive retaliation" and "limited nuclear war," like Wellington's troops in the story of his reaction to them at first sight, may not have frightened our opponents but they have certainly terrified people on our side.

The idea that there is one magic formula, which if found would solve the problem of our relations with the Soviet Union and Communism, is the most common cause of confusion in our thinking about foreign relations. The average person, when discussing his neighbor, displays a considerable dialectical sophistication, an insight into the interplay of human psychology, ideology, and the economic factor. Why, then, in dealing with a group of men or with a foreign society should we assume that the explanation of *their* behavior is so much simpler and can be accounted for in a sentence? Thus, the Communist leaders are either "power-oriented" or "they want peace because they want to develop their countries." A consequence of an over-simplified and static analysis in a complex and dynamic world is the lack of flexibility and the repetitious anachronisms of successive formulas for foreign policies. The same penchant for externals that made so many Americans and Englishmen believe during World War II that Russia was moving toward democracy now makes them deny the reality of any change in Soviet society. The same intellectual indolence that assumed that the Soviet Union, because of her diplomatic engagements, would not communize Eastern Europe now accounts for the erection of, say, the problem of independence for Algeria or diplomatic recognition of Communist China into a moral dilemma rather than one of concrete political and social consequences.

One must repeat that the internal necessities of the Soviet regime dictate to it *at the present* a twofold direction of foreign policy. One is a common-sense desire to avoid a major war; the other, an assertive policy designed to illustrate the viability and missionary significance of Communism. The Western response must establish unambiguously in the Soviet leaders' mind (and it is here that the significance of long and apparently fruitless East-West negotiations becomes clear) the area where an aggressive Soviet policy does involve the danger they want to avoid. In other areas, the democracies' counteracting policies must rely not only on mechanistic devices of treaties and alliances, but also on social and economic measures that weaken the appeal of Marxism to underdeveloped societies and make it less likely for this appeal to become translated into Communist domination.

The reaction of ideological systems to their internal difficulties is, in a way, as trite as that of individuals. A degree of internal trouble often impairs outside expansiveness and aggression, while a major and sharp crisis will often lead to an irrational and violent hostility to the outside world. There is little doubt that an outright threat to the basis of Soviet totalitarianism could make it engage in aggressive policies with catastrophic implications. A real threat of national separatism within the Soviet Union would be viewed by the leaders as a matter of life and death. We have seen, on the contrary, that the weakening of the extent of Soviet control over other Communist states, while obviously disliked by the Soviets and in one case followed by armed intervention, may be acquiesced in by the Russians. Of all the external factors which, short of war, are likely to affect the nature of both Marxism and totalitarianism in the Soviet Union, the predominant one is the future development of other Communist states.

What are the prospects for the satellites? We have seen the reasons that had made the Russians, after Stalin's death, try to adopt more enlightened methods of control and the grief to which those policies *almost* brought them in Hungary and Poland in the fall of 1956. It is symptomatic that the Soviet leaders' foreign miscalculations evidently had internal repercussions within the USSR. Khrushchev's position was threatened in the winter and spring of 1957. (His plan of economic decentralization and reform, announced in the spring, may have been one means of recouping his position within the Central Committee in the expectation of a showdown, which came in July.) It is not that his opponents, Malenkov, Molotov, and the others, were necessarily for "Stalinist" methods; they simply attempted to capitalize on the leader's failure. The intellectual thaw in Poland, which had assumed flood proportions after October 1956, also had some unsettling effects on the Soviet intelligentsia and students.

A new, uneasy balance in Soviet policies toward the satellites was established by 1958: neither old Stalinism, with its unreasonable terror, nor the naïve optimism of 1955-1956 that a considerable leeway for the satellites would automatically produce love of the Soviet Union and of Communism. No vilification of the Yugoslav Communists, but also no more hearty receptions in the camp of socialism for Tito, irretrievably and almost despite himself the carrier of the germ of "Titoism" and of "revisionism." A reasonable amount of Soviet control, a perpetual quarantine for Tito, but also a continued attempt at forging unifying links through common ideological and economic interests.

The whole episode should be most instructive to the Western policymakers; its continued development, of great significance to Soviet foreign policies and internal developments. For there is almost no doubt that Soviet hopes as to the future of the satellites are bound to be disappointed. There may be no further revolts; in Eastern Europe, the last illusions of Western help collapsed in the wake of the Hungarian experience. The tempo of the imposition of the Soviet pattern may be enhanced, as, e.g., forced collectivization, it already has been. But the results —industrialized modern societies in Poland or Bulgaria—are even less likely to conform to the Communist dream and Soviet expectations than society in Russia. From slaves, they are not likely to evolve into grateful junior partners; more probably, they will be troublesome dependents, ungrateful, demanding, always in the need of being watched. The example of their greater flexibility, their wider range of intellectual and professional freedoms, may have a demoralizing effect, from the totalitarian point of view, on the younger Soviet generations. In the Soviet Union, the contradictions between an industrialized modern society and totalitarianism are largely encompassed by *Russian* nationalism. But nationalism in the satellites is unlikely to help Soviet domination or to make them assets to Soviet totalitarianism. And it may be that it will eventually dawn on the Russians that a Communist regime in a foreign country does not reinforce the logic of

Marxism or of totalitarianism in Russia and that any imperialism eventually brings its Algerias and Cypruses.

Communist China is in a different category. Following their break with Stalin, the Yugoslav Communists developed a wonderfully wishful theory according to which Communism in any large country is bound, sooner rather than later, to clash with Soviet domination. From the anti-Soviet point of view, it is a matter of regret, the theory held, that Communism has not seized France or Italy, but in China the clash with Soviet imperialism *was* forthcoming. Democracies have no monopoly on wishful thinking in foreign affairs! The ten years since the prognosis was enunciated have not provided any real substance to the Yugoslav and Western hopes. Even for Stalin, the Chinese problem was of a kind different from that of Soviet relations with the Communists in Poland or Bulgaria. His successors found themselves constrained to give up the last of the Soviet preserves in Manchuria. The Soviets have put the best face on their economic and technical help to the Chinese, and they profess ideological rejoicing at the spectacle of the 600-million-headed colossus being modernized and industrialized. They cannot afford to do otherwise.

The Chinese experiment represents the extreme in the equation: Communism = rapid industrialization. If the Bolsheviks decided to compress the decades of the Western economic development into ten or fifteen years, then the Chinese have evidently determined, in their infinitely more backward country, to compress the Soviet pattern of industrialization into a few years. Only two years separated the stage of distribution of land to the peasants and forcible collectivization. No NEP intervened before a *higher* form of collectivization, the communes, were being imposed on a vast majority of the Chinese peasants—something the Soviet Communists have not yet attempted on a large scale. From the revolutionary stage, likewise, the Chinese jumped immediately into Stalinism, with all its features of compulsion and centralization, something that it took their teachers a decade to accomplish.

An outright conflict between the two great Communist powers would be a drastic refutation of their common ideology, something neither of them will face short of dire necessity. "Before us lies the extremely hard task of transforming the backward agrarian China into a leading industrial country and our experience is insufficient. . . . We have to learn from the leading Soviet Union," [4] said Mao, probably in all sincerity. That two expanding totalitarian systems, one of them led by people who profess their ideology with all the fanaticism of neophytes, can avoid clashes and quarrels is unlikely. It becomes clearer why the Soviets try to strengthen the meaning and the unifying function of ideology. It is not improbable that the Korean adventure was aimed not at the conquest of insignificant territory, but rather at forcing the United States out of east Asia. Between Communist China and a Communist Japan, the Soviet Union could have played longer and more decisively the role of dominant arbiter. But, for the time being, whatever the internal quarrels, whatever the steps that the more experienced Soviet leaders have to take to appease the hunger of the Chinese for technical and economic help and probably to restrain them from aggressive policies, the two sides clearly have too much to gain and almost everything to lose from a public and irreconcilable conflict.

This sketch of the dilemmas of "coexistence" among Communist states suggests forcibly the probable decisive character of their relations in the future of militant Communism and even in the internal development of Soviet totalitarianism. Nothing would be more injurious to the attempt to revive ideology in the Soviet Union, and hence the continued rationale of totalitarianism, than a convincing demonstration of the inability of Commu-

---

[4] *Materials of the VIII All-China Congress of the Communist Party of China,* September 15-27, 1956 (in Russian), Moscow, 1956, p. 5.

nism to provide a lasting link between states, short of domination by one of them. Communism may catalyze the people's energies for revolution, it may provide a short cut to industrialization and modernity, but it has not been able to provide the kind of society for which the revolution was fought or the sufferings of industrialization endured. The last illusion that provides the material for ideological enthusiasm in a society where other points of Marxism have lost their relevance is the claim of the ideology to provide the only basis for a peaceful world order. Many characterizations of the capitalist world by Marx and Lenin have come to be, and as we have seen not without reason, pathetically apt descriptions of *Communist* reality. And so we should not be surprised to see the development of "inherent contradictions" in the Communist camp, and we should not rule out the possibility of clashing imperialisms being the destiny and the "highest stage" not of "capitalism" but of Communist totalitarianism.

The preceding pages offer a general background for the policies of the Communist world. They offer, by the same token, some perspective on the policies of the Western countries. Over and above the clichés of "firmness and patience" and the talk of treaties and weapons which pass for the essence of realism in foreign relations, the most exacting and realistic task is the study of the revolution in which we have lived and will continue to live, the revolution which in certain of its phases and manifestations creates opportunities for our opponents, in others, for us. This study will not provide infallible, long-lasting formulas which inevitably guarantee success or preserve peace, but it will give a more meaningful setting for concrete political decisions. If we believe, for instance, that the forces of industrialism within the Communist bloc must eventually impinge on totalitarianism and Soviet domination, we will not refrain from giving economic help to a satellite country merely because its leaders speak unkindly about us or feel constrained to spout Communist platitudes. If

concrete benefits rather than paper guarantees can be shown
as likely to result from a different Chinese policy by the United
States, then the fact that mainland China is Communist would
not necessarily bar that policy.

Our discussion of ideologies and their manifestations in politics has been throughout in terms of the main doctrine discussed,
i.e., in terms of materialism centering on one major phenomenon:
industrialization. It might be objected that such a discussion is
narrow and constraining, that the ideas of freedom, democracy,
religious ideals have their validity and appeal to men regardless
of the "stages of development," regardless of whether the given
society is agrarian, in the process of transition, or industrialized.
It seems to negate the whole sense of the development of Western
civilization to qualify the attractiveness of freedom and democracy by whether men have or have not acquired the habit of
saving, paying taxes, and working in factories and offices between
nine and five.

It is not proposed here to quarrel with the validity of such
ideas. But the commonplace must be reiterated: specific economic and social conditions are required for democratic ideals to
become operative in the form of democratic institutions. In every
generation, an increase in the productive forces and the engross-
ment of a society in materialistic pursuits has brought with
it dire predictions of the consequent destruction of spiritual and
aesthetic values and warnings of national catastrophe. It was the
historical discovery of early liberalism that *conscious* materialism, not as a philosophical creed but as a way of life, is not
only an innocent but a necessary prerequisite for a *political*
realization of those spiritual and humanitarian instincts that
have been with mankind since civilization began. Marxism
inherited the most rigid expression of early liberal materialism,
but supplanted it with a Hegelian methodology that weakened
the earlier bias toward individualism and, paradoxically, with
an anarchist protest against materialism and industrialism.

Hence Marxism has been able to appeal to both the grievances and the aspirations of a society in the process of transition, whereas liberalism appeals to the society that has forgotten both nostalgia for the past and excessively utopian visions of the industrial future.

Among all the truisms that attempt to put into a formula the nature of the competition between the United States and the USSR, the one that comes closest to the mark sees it as a race between the social and economic dynamisms of the two societies. The continued emphasis on production and technology —although once again considered inelegant and unenlightened— may enable the West to help other societies pass through the dangerous period of transition without succumbing to Communism. And the competition may continue to have beneficent effects on internal institutions in the democratic states. Is the continuing industrialization of the United States and the increasing saturation of all parts of the country with the inelegant values of materialism and industrialism entirely unconnected with the fact that civil rights for minorities are now growing into more than constitutional formulas? On the other hand, it is not impossible that the Soviet Union, in its professed attempt to "catch up with and overcome" the West in material culture, will discover that in the process it has left Marxism behind.

INDEX

ABOUT THE AUTHOR

ADAM B. ULAM received his B.A. from Brown University and his Ph.D. from Harvard University, where he is now a full professor of government. He is also a member of the Executive Committee of the Russian Research Center and Chairman of the Center's Russian Regional Program.

He spent the academic year 1953-54 at the Massachusetts Institute of Technology as a research associate of the Center for International Studies. In 1956-57 he was granted both a Rockefeller Fellowship in Political Science and a Guggenheim Fellowship.

A co-editor of *Patterns of Government*, Dr. Ulam also authored Part V of that book, on "The Russian Political System." Earlier, he published two other books, on the *Philosophical Foundations of English Socialism* and on *Titoism and the Cominform*. In addition, he has collaborated on other books and has contributed numerous articles to professional journals.